standard catalog of®
MERCEDES-BENZ

MW00804856

Jim Luikens
with Mary M. Hedberg

©2008 Krause Publications
Published by

krause publications
An Imprint of F+W Media, Inc.

700 East State Street • Iola, WI 54990-0001
715-445-2214 • 888-457-2873
www.krausebooks.com

Our toll-free number to place an order or obtain
a free catalog is (800) 258-0929.

Library of Congress Control Number: 2008928410

ISBN-13: 978-0-89689-703-8
ISBN-10: 89689-703-6

Designed by Kara Grundman
Edited by Brian Earnest

Printed in Singapore

standard catalog of®
MERCEDES-BENZ

Other Fine Titles in our Automotive Line

American Cars of the 1960s

Anatomy of the Hot Rod

Cars of the Fantastic '50s

Cars of the Fantastic '60s

Chrysler Muscle Cars: The Ultimate Guide

Chrysler Muscle: Detroit's Mightiest Machines

Collector Car Restoration Bible

Corvette Masterpieces

Eddie Paul's Custom Bodywork Handbook

Eddie Paul's Paint & Bodywork Handbook

Extreme Muscle Cars

Great American Hot Rods

Herb Martinez's Guide to Pinstriping

Muscle Car: Mighty Machines That Ruled the Road

Muscle Cars Field Guide

Mustang Field Guide

Old School Hot Rods

Standard Catalog of 1950s Chevrolet

Standard Catalog of 1950s Chrysler

Standard Catalog of American Muscle Cars, 1960-1972

Standard Catalog of American Muscle Cars, 1973-Present

Standard Catalog of Camaro, 1967-2002

Standard Catalog of Chevelle, 1964-1987

Standard Catalog of Corvette, 1953-2005

Standard Catalog of Firebird, 1967-2002

Standard Catalog of Ford, 4th edition

Standard Catalog of Jaguar

Standard Guide to American Muscle Cars, 1960-2005, 4th edition

The Legendary Model T Ford

The Story of Camaro

Dedication

This book is dedicated to our mother, Mary Louise, whose love and support for both of us never waivers.

Acknowledgments

The *Standard Catalog of Mercedes-Benz* was made possible thanks to the experienced team at Krause Publications, part of the F+W Publications family of companies. Special thanks to Mercedes-Benz USA and Daimler AG for the generous use of their photos to illustrate this book. Additional photos were provided from the archives of Krause Publications. All of the historical advertisements are courtesy of the Jim Luikens Collection. A very special thanks to Cyndi Vander Horn for her assistance on this project.

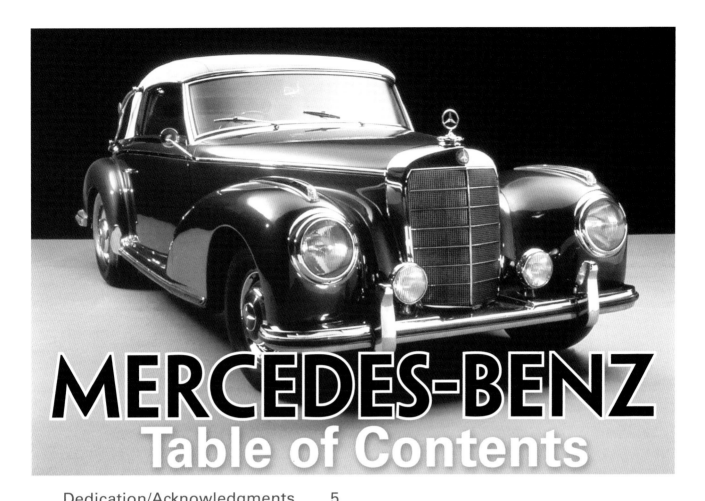

MERCEDES-BENZ
Table of Contents

1990s

2000s

Joint Production poster

The Standard Catalog of Mercedes-Benz 1946-2008

By Jim Luikens and Mary M. Hedberg

HISTORY

Not until 1926 did two early auto manufacturers—both of whom laid claim to creating the first automobile—merge into the German marque that would later produce some of the most dramatic four-wheelers of them all. In that year, the Daimler and Benz firms joined to form Daimler-Benz AG. By that time, however, both companies had 40 years of experience with motorcar production.

Thus, Mercedes-Benz had good cause to celebrate in 1986, a year that marked the 100th anniversary of the German automaker's origin. Precisely a century earlier, in 1886, Karl Benz obtained a patent for a three-wheeled vehicle with a 984 cc single-cylinder engine. In that same year, Benz invented the spark plug, while Gottlieb Daimler built a four-wheeled carriage with a 46 cc, single-cylinder gas engine that he'd patented three years earlier. Amazingly, considering that the two men would turn out their motorcars in the same region of Germany, they were never destined to meet.

Daimler, who'd apprenticed as a gunsmith before turning to engineering, became technical director of the Deutz Gas Engine Works in 1872, working under Gustav Otto, who would gain fame for his own engine creation. The head designer at Deutz was Wilhelm Maybach (yet another famous person in early automotive and aviation history, whose name would be attached to the Zeppelin created at the turn of the century). By 1881, Daimler and Maybach had departed from Deutz and moved into their own shop. The Daimler gasoline engine provided power for a motorcycle and motorboat, even before it went into the four-wheeled vehicle of late 1886. That one was essentially a horseless carriage with an engine rather than a purpose-built motorized vehicle.

Three years later, however, Daimler and Maybach turned out a full-fledged automobile, powered by a V-type two-cylinder engine. Displayed at the 1889 World's Fair in Paris, their creation was called the Stahlradwagen (steel-wheeled car). The engine soon went into Panhard et Levassor motorcars, built in France; and even entered production in America, courtesy of William Steinway (of piano-manufacturing fame). In 1894, a Peugeot, with a Daimler engine, won the Paris-Rouen race. Late in the 1890s, Daimler and Maybach developed a Phoenix automobile with a front engine and chain drive, along with a four-cylinder model.

Over at the Benz camp, what some consider to be the world's first "production" automobile, the Benz Velo, arrived in 1894. Nine years later, in 1903, Karl Benz built a four-cylinder engine that remained in production up to the 1914 outbreak of World War I. In that year came the first six-cylinder (6.5-liter) Benz.

Meanwhile, the Mercedes name came into existence on the Daimler side of the equation. Mercedes happened to be the name of the daughter of Emil Jellinek, the Austro-Hungarian Consul at Nice, France, around the turn of the century. In the final years of the 1890s, Jellinek had become an agent for Daimler, selling a small number of cars in southern France. Jellinek used the Mercedes name for a car he entered in the Nice Speed Week competition. By 1900, he suggested that Daimler develop a more modern motorcar, one that was lower in profile, faster and more powerful. He even agreed to accept the first three dozen, provided that he be granted full rights to sell them in France, Austro-Hungary, Belgium and even the U.S.; and also that the new car be named after his daughter.

Gottlieb Daimler

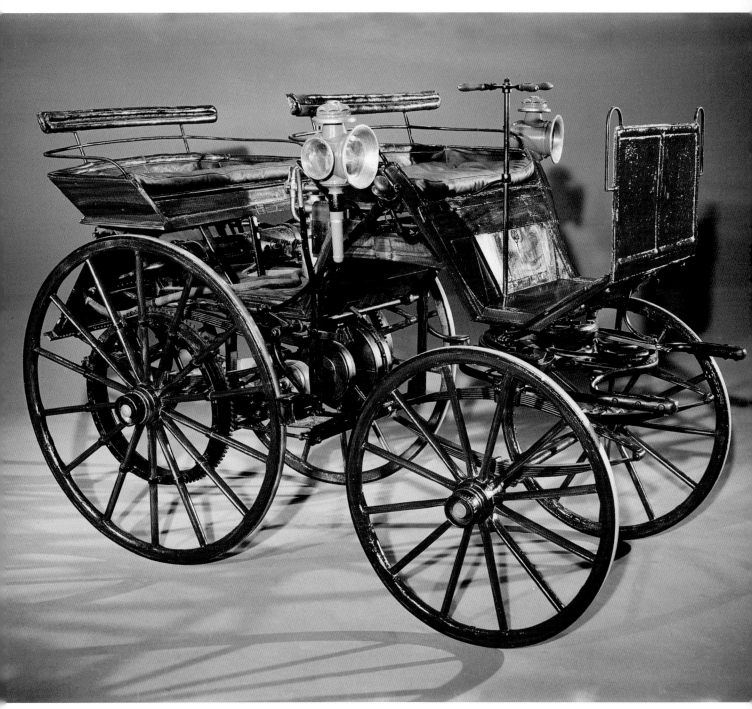

1886 Daimler motor carriage

Thus appeared the 1901 Mercedes, designed by Wilhelm Maybach and Paul Daimler, whose father Gottlieb had died in 1900. That first Mercedes sported a honeycomb radiator and angled steering column with a 5,913 cc T-head four-cylinder engine and gated four-speed transmission driving the rear wheels. By 1902, Daimler registered the Mercedes name as a trademark and it went onto all passenger cars, but not on trucks, which kept the Daimler designation. Expansion of the models available helped to strengthen the Mercedes reputation, to the point that many other companies began to replicate Mercedes vehicles. According to the World Guide to Automobile Manufacturers, companies as diverse as Fiat (Italy), Ariel (England), and Locomobile (U.S.) "based their 1904-5 models on Mercedes' patterns." Steinway in the U.S. also turned out Mercedes cars from 1904-07. Offerings from the Daimler/Mercedes firm itself ranged from modest 1.6-liter models all the way up to a trio of chain-driven behemoths, with engines displacing as much as 9.6 liters.

As for competition, a 120-bhp Mercedes won the Grand Prix at Dieppe, France in 1908. In 1912, Ralph

1986 Benz three-wheeler

de Palma drove a former Grand Prix Mercedes in the Indianapolis 500. Though he led the pack for a long time, de Palma suffered engine trouble near the end. Three years later, however, he won at Indy.

The three-pointed star also came from Daimler. It was said to represent the triple use possibilities of his engine on land, sea, and air. First registered in 1909, it appeared on Daimler's motorcars by about 1911.

In 1911, Daimler had a new model powered by an overhead valve, four-cylinder engine with three valves per cylinder and a V-shaped radiator. Production resumed quickly after World War I on 4-liter and 7.2-liter models. Early in the 1920s, Daimler (Mercedes) became the first manufacturer to install a supercharger on a production model. Supercharging was first used on the 6/25/40 1.6-liter four and also on the 10/40/65 2,614 cc engine. Following the retirement of Paul Daimler, his role as head engineer was taken over by

Karl Benz

1888 Velocispeed

Ferdinand Porsche, who designed a line of six-cylinder overhead-cam engines. Porsche remained with Mercedes until 1928.

Negotiations for the Daimler-Benz merger began as early as 1923, and were completed in 1926. The modern insignia was created by placing Daimler's three-pointed star inside the laurel wreath that had been seen on Benz vehicles. The first supercharged model produced after the merger was the 24/100/Type K—essentially an old model with a new name. Then came the 1926 Stuttgart (2-liter) and Mannheim (3-liter) L-head engines, followed by the Nürburg straight eight.

In 1928, Mercedes debuted the Type S—called the 26/120/180 in Germany—rated at 120 horsepower unblown and 180 with its supercharger in action. Displacement of the six-cylinder engine was 6,789 cc, and the motor rode in a lower chassis than the more ordinary Type K. The famed 7.1-liter SS and SSK cars were characterized by long hoods with three exhaust pipes.

Only about 173 of the Type SS and a mere 45 Type SSK (on a shorter chassis) were produced from 1928 to 1934.

Two very different Mercedes-Benz models emerged as the 1930s began. At the 1930 Paris Motor Show, Mercedes displayed a 7.7-liter straight-eight "Grosser." At the other extreme was the Type 170 with a 1.7-liter engine and four-wheel independent suspension, introduced in 1931. Then came the rear-engined 130H and 170H, on a backbone chassis. Mercedes introduced the 260D, the world's first diesel engine production car, in 1935, powered by a 2,545 cc four. In 1936, a new front-engined 170V on a tubular backbone frame replaced the original 170. At the upper end of the scale, later in the 1930s, was the dramatic 540K, with a supercharged 5401 cc straight eight under its massive hood. Developing 115 horsepower under ordinary conditions, the 540K had a blower that went into action when the driver stomped the gas pedal to the floor. Mercedes also

Emil Jelinek

Mercedes Jelinek

Wilhelm Maybach

produced similar models with 3.8- and 5-liter engines.

By early 1945, Stuttgart stood in ruins as a result of Allied bombing during World War II. Most of the Daimler-Benz factory was destroyed. Nevertheless, by February of 1946, a handmade prototype of the upcoming 170V sedan was created, ready for production in June of that year. In 1949, a diesel-engined counterpart of the 170 went into production, followed by a more

luxurious 170S edition with a larger gasoline engine.

Each of those 170 Series sedans displayed prewar styling, but the 220 and 300 introduced in 1951 had a more modern look, with overhead-cam six-cylinder engines under their hoods. Also in 1951, Daimler-Benz patented front/rear crush zones in a rigid passenger compartment.

Not surprisingly, Max Hoffman of New York became

1894 Benz Velo

1895 Hurtu-Benz

the first importer of postwar Mercedes-Benz models into the U.S., a service he would perform for a number of other European makes.

During 1953, a monocoque-bodied 180 replaced the 170 Series and was offered with both gasoline and, later, diesel engines. More important to Mercedes history were the 300SL racing cars created in 1952, with an alloy body on a multi-tubular space frame. Finishing in the top three spots at the Le Mans race, they attracted so much attention, especially in the U.S., that Daimler-Benz turned to a production version that became one of the most famous and distinctive sports cars of all time. A 240-bhp (SAE) version of the 300 sedan's 2,996 cc overhead-cam engine provided the power, making it the

1900-02 Mercedes race car

1899 Benz

1902 Simplex

1906 Touring

first gasoline-powered production car with fuel injection (a Bosch mechanical system). With at least a 130-mph top speed, some reports claimed much swifter velocities, the gullwing-door 300SL quickly became the fastest car in the world. A straight-eight engine powered the 300SLR racing car of 1955.

Gullwing production lasted only a few years, ceasing in 1957. The 300SL roadster's successor had conventional doors. A smaller 190SL edition, with an 1,897 cc four-cylinder engine, sold in far greater numbers through 1963.

By the late 1950s, Daimler-Benz established a connection with Studebaker-Packard in the U.S., whereby the latter company undertook distribution of Mercedes-Benz products. That tie lasted until the demise of Studebaker's operation at South Bend, Indiana in early 1964.

Daimler-Benz attempted to diversify in the late 1950s and early '60s, taking control of the Auto Union Company in 1958 and contributing to the design of the DKW models and the new Audis of the mid-1960s. By 1964, Daimler-Benz was losing interest in the DKW/Audi connection. Thus, Volkswagen became joint owner of the Audi operation and, by 1968, took it over completely.

By 1959, fuel injection was available on the 220SE sedan (E = injection). A year later, the 220 Series was wearing a new body. A 230SL roadster replaced the original 190SL/300SL duo in 1963 and could be ordered with an automatic transmission and removable

1907 Mercedes with double chain drive

hardtop. Also new was the massive and luxurious Type 600 sedan, on a 126-inch wheelbase and powered by a 6,329 cc V-8 capable of top speeds beyond 125 mph. A Pullman limousine version with six doors rode a vast 153.5-inch wheelbase, stretching 246 inches overall. This "Grosser" Mercedes ranked as the world's longest car. A lesser-known Landaulet variant also became available, used primarily by heads of states. More than a handful of the 600 sedans reached the U.S. between 1963 and 1980, out of the total of 2,190 sedans and 487 Pullmans built.

In the mid-1960s, the 230 and 250 Series sedans re-placed the former 220. Then, the 230SL roadster turned into the 250SL and, after only a year, transformed again into the 280SL. New bodies and revised suspensions were installed on smaller Mercedes-Benz models in 1968. These cars were known as the "New Generation." In addition, a new 280 Series with a 2,778 cc engine replaced the 250SE and 300SE. By the end of the de-cade, a 3,499 cc V-8 engine went into the 300SE, which displayed quad vertical headlamps. It was also used optionally for the 280 Series coupe and convertible. The big 6.3-liter V-8, as in the "Grosser," also became available in some 300 Series sedans. By this time, the

1909 Benz & Cie trademark

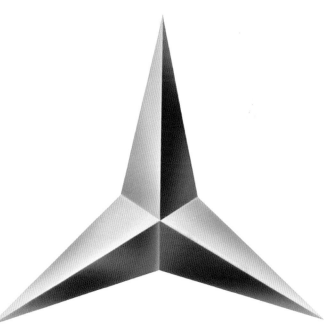

1909 star trademark

1916 three-pointed star

1926 new trademark

1926 merger poster

1927 K tourer

1926 Type 630

1927 Type 180K

1927 Type S tourer

1928 S cabriolet

1927 Mercedes S engine

1928 320 Pullman

1929 SSK

1831 770 Grand Mercedes

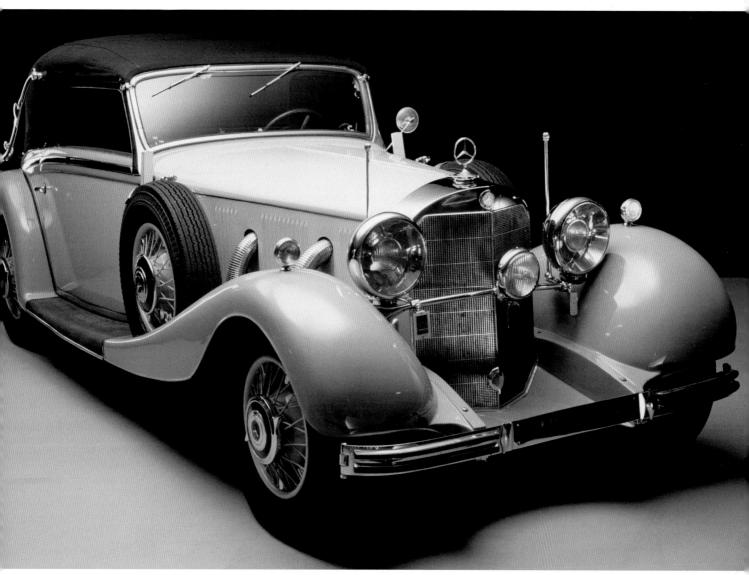

1934 500K cabriolet C

Mercedes-Benz lineup was growing quite complex, and most of the models produced were finding their way into the U.S. market.

A 350SL two-seat roadster replaced the 280SL in Europe in 1971, with a 3,499 cc V-8 under its hood. (U.S. versions turned to a bigger 4,520 cc V-8.) New S-Class sedans began to arrive in 1972, with "280" and "350" (Europe only) prefixes. Also new was the 450 Series, with the longer-stroke V-8 that displaced 4,520 cc on a 112.8-inch wheelbase. The 450SEL was longer yet.

Mercedes-Benz introduced its first five-cylinder diesel in 1974 under the hood of the 300D. A turbocharger became available in 1978, ranking the 300D as the world's first production car with turbodiesel power. Topping the engine scale was the 450SEL 6.9 with a 6,834 cc enlargement of the earlier 6.3-liter V-8.

In 1976, the smaller models got a reworking into a new W123 Series on a 110-inch wheelbase with lower and wider bodies. Station wagons were added two years later.

A new aluminum-alloy 4,973 cc V-8 went into the European 450SL roadster in 1978, then into all-new

1935 150 sport roadster

S-Class models. A 3,818 cc version also was produced. These S-Class bodies were lighter and more aerodynamic on a 115.6-inch (or longer) wheelbase. In European trim, a 500SE could do 140 mph, while a 280SE or 380SE might top 130 mph. As the 1980s began, an S-Class bodied 300SD Turbodiesel targeted the U.S. market.

Late in 1982 came a smaller 190 Series with a 1,997 cc four-cylinder engine. That was followed by a 16-valve, 2.3-liter version of the 190 engine developed by Cosworth, which went into U.S. versions. A new 124

Series body replaced the W123 versions at mid-decade, using the 190's rear suspension and a 110.2-inch wheelbase. Late in 1985, Mercedes introduced a set of revised S-Class engines up to the 5,549 cc V-8. Daimler-Benz also developed 4Matic four-wheel-drive, which engaged as soon as wheel slip was detected. It was introduced on the 300E/TE. By the end of the decade, the eagerly awaited replacement for the long-lived SL Series sports cars finally arrived in both six-cylinder and V-8 form as the 300SL and 500SL.

Through all the postwar years, Mercedes-Benz ex-

1935 500 K

1936 260D

1936 500K special roadster

Current three-pointed star

ported most of its significant models to the U.S., though not always in precisely the same form or with the same engine ratings as examples marketed elsewhere in the world.

Model Number Note: As a rule, the numeric digits of each model designation indicate the number of liters (multiplied by 100) in the engine, but there were numerous exceptions. Suffix E denotes fuel injection (einspritzung), S indicates a senior (generally bigger, more costly) model. The SL suffix initially stood for super light (sehr leicht, or very light), though later SL convertibles added quite a few pounds and no longer literally qualified for that designation.

1936 500 K three-position convertible

1938 540 K phaeton

1937 Type 230 roadster

1937 170 V roadster

1937 Type 320 cabriolet

1939 Grosser

1938 770 K Grosser open limousine

1946-1950

170V/170S — FOUR — Prewar-style in appearance, the first postwar 170V four-door sedan had separate headlamps, rear-hinged front doors ("suicide" style), and front-hinged rear doors. A flat one-piece windshield was installed. Under the hood went a 1,697 cc L-head engine that developed 38 horsepower (DIN). Wheelbase was 112 inches, and a 170V could hit about 65 mph

A heavier 170S sedan was added in 1949, with 15-inch wheels and a larger (1,767 cc) engine that developed 52 horsepower (DIN). Styling was similar to the prewar Type 230, and the 170S became available in cabriolet as well as sedan form. In 1950, that bigger engine also went into the 170Va (170V successor), but detuned to 45 bhp Even so, it could travel about 10 mph faster than the original 170V (about 75 mph), and switched to tubular shock absorbers. Both the 170V and 170S rode a tubular oval-section cruciform chassis with tubular outriggers. Rear suspensions used coil springs and swing axles. Up front, the 170V had a transverse leaf spring, while the 170S switched to a wishbone/coil-spring setup with anti-sway bar.

170D — DIESEL FOUR — Allied forces initially prohibited production of a Mercedes with a diesel engine, but one became available during 1949. Styling was virtually identical to the gasoline-engine 170V sedan. The 1,697 cc overhead-valve four produced 38 bhp As in prewar diesels, fuel was injected into a pre-combustion chamber, with an electric glow plug to aid starting. Mercedes-Benz claimed a top speed of 62 mph

I.D. DATA: Chassis serial number for 170 Series is on a firewall plate. Engine number is on lower left of block.

ENGINES

Base Four (170V): Inline, L-head four-cylinder. Cast-iron block. Displacement: 103.5 cid (1,697 cc). Bore & Stroke: 2.89 x 3.94 in. (73.5 x 100 mm). Compression Ratio: 6.0:1. Brake horsepower: 38 (DIN) at 3,700 rpm. Three main bearings. Solid valve lifters. One downdraft carburetor.

Diesel Four (1949-up 170D): Inline, overhead-valve four-cylinder. Displacement: 103.5 cid (1,697 cc). Bore & stroke: 2.89 x 3.94 in. (73.5 x 100 mm). Compression ratio: 19.0:1. Brake horsepower: 38 (DIN) at 3,200 rpm. Three main bearings. Solid valve lifters.

Base Four (later 170Va, 170S): Inline, L-head four-cylinder. Cast-iron block. Displacement: 107.8 cid (1,767 cc). Bore & stroke: 2.95 x 3.94 in. (75 x 100 mm). Compression ratio: 6.5:1. Brake horsepower: (170Va) 45 at 3,650 rpm; (170S) 52 at 4,000 rpm. Three main bearings. Solid valve lifters. One downdraft carburetor.

1947 170 cabriolet

1947 170 sedan

CHASSIS

Wheelbase: 112 in. Overall length: 169 in. Width: 64 in. Front tead: (170V) 51.6 in.; (170D) 51.8 in. Rear tread: (170V) 51.0 in.; (170D) 52.8 in. Standard tires: (1946-48 170V) 5.50x16; (1949-up 170V) 5.50x15; (170S) 6.40x15.

TECHNICAL

Layout: front-engine, rear-drive. Transmission: four-speed manual. Suspension (front): (170V) transverse leaf spring; (170S) wishbones and coil springs, with anti-sway bar. Suspension (rear): swing axles with coil springs. Brakes: hydraulic, front/rear drum. Body construction: steel body on tubular cruciform frame.

PERFORMANCE

Top Speed: (170V) 65 mph; (170S) 75 mph Acceleration (0-60 mph): N/A (factory claimed 0-60 mph acceleration in 36 sec. for 170V, and 32 sec. for 170S).

MANUFACTURER: Daimler-Benz AG, Stuttgart, West Germany.

DISTRIBUTOR: Hoffman Motors Corp., New York City.

HISTORY

The 170V sedan debuted in 1946. Its successor, the 170Va sedan debuted in May 1950 and was produced until May 1952. Production of the 170S sedan began in May 1949 and continued until March 1952. Original production of the 170V dated back to 1936. By 1950, Mercedes-Benz cars were using tubular shock absorbers.

MODEL	BODY TYPE & SEATING	ENGINE TYPE/CID	P.O.E. PRICE	WEIGHT (LBS.)	PRODUCTION TOTAL
170V	4-dr Sedan-5P	I4/103	Note 1	2,550	Note 2
170Va	4-dr Sedan-5P	I4/108	N/A	2,575	Note 2
170S	4-dr Sedan-5P	I4/108	Note 1	2,685	Note 2
170D (Diesel)	4-dr Sedan-5P	I4/103	N/A	2,750	Note 2

Note 1: Approximate price of the 170V sedan was $1,860; the 170S sedan, $2,400.
Note 2: A total of 214 Mercedes-Benz cars were produced during 1946, followed by 1,045 in 1947, 5,116 in 1948, 17,417 in 1949, and 33,906 in 1950.
Model Note: The 170S, produced until 1952, also came in cabriolet form (either two- or five-seat).

1951-1953

170 SERIES — FOUR — Production of the 170Va and 170S sedans continued into the early 1950s, with various technical changes. Early in 1952, the 170S got a column-mounted gearshift. During that year, the 170V added transverse vent slots in its hood. By 1952, Mercedes-Benz issued an improved 170Sb version of the 170S with hypoid rear axle, dashboard-mounted starter button, wider track, and improved heater. A similarly modified 170Vb also was introduced. Then, in mid-1953, a 170S-V sedan replaced both models, with a redesigned front transverse leaf spring and the earlier detuned 45-bhp engine (as in the 170V) intended to keep the selling price low.

170D SERIES — DIESEL FOUR — Diesel changes paralleled those on the gasoline-powered version of the 170 Series, starting during the 1950 model year with a jump to 1,767 cc displacement (and 40-bhp rating) with the 170Da. In 1952-53, the 170Db arrived with its bigger windshield and revised hood. The 170DS (1952-53) and 170S-D (1953-55) were diesel versions of the gasoline-engined 170S sedan, with a redesigned front transverse leaf spring. The 170DS had cloth and artificial leather door panels and seats. Diesels in this Series were built as late as September 1955, in 170S-D form. The earlier versions were dropped by the end of 1953.

180 — FOUR — A Type 180 sedan joined the Mercedes-Benz lineup in mid-1953, powered by a 52-bhp version of the 1,767 cc engine used in the 170S-V. Wheelbase was 104.3 inches, compared to 112 inches for the 170 Series. New and modern styling was evident atop a chassis coded W120. The conservative, boxy shape was similar to that which would appear on small Mercedes sedans for years to come. The traditional upright grille was angled back a bit with the Mercedes tri-star emblem on top. High sectional steel side members were welded to the floor platform with subframes for suspension and drivetrain.

220 SERIES — SIX — Debut of the midrange 220 Series took place in mid-1951, ahead of the 300 Series. Both a sedan and cabriolet were introduced, with large grilles and "suicide" front doors, but carrying on basic prewar styling (though with a rounded appearance). Sedans had built-in headlamps, while the cabriolet retained separate headlamps and included landau bars. An overhead-cam six-cylinder engine displaced 2,195 cc (134 cid) and developed 80 horsepower (DIN). Wheelbase was 112 inches, on what was essentially a 170 chassis. Both the 170 and 220 still had semaphore-type turn signals.

1951 cabriolet

300 SERIES — SIX — Introduced at the Frankfurt Auto Show in late 1951, the stately Type 300 was the first Mercedes-Benz model intended for export and aimed squarely at Americans. It was destined to last 11 years in the Mercedes lineup.

An overhead-cam six-cylinder engine with aluminum cylinder head displaced 2,996 cc (183 cid), and developed 115 horsepower (DIN) using twin Solex downdraft carburetors with a triple-jet system. The engine block had open sides covered by plates, allowing inspection of water jackets. Valve positions were staggered. The four-speed transmission was synchronized in all forward gears, controlled by a column gearshift lever.

Independent swing-axle rear suspension with coil springs also included auxiliary springs that cushioned the rear-axle movements, to improve riding qualities over rough roads. That auxiliary springing could be brought into or out of operation from the driver's seat, according to the load of the car, and the Type 300 was the first car to be fitted with such a device. Its hypoid bevel gear axle was the first such installation on a German automobile. Front suspension consisted of frictionless soft coil springs, telescopic shocks and forged A-arms. A new hydraulic steering damper consisted of a telescopic shock between the frame and a section of the three-piece steering linkage, to absorb road shocks. Wheelbase was 120 inches, and the top speed of 96 mph was claimed to be easily attainable. Type 300 models also had a switch for one-shot chassis lubrication.

Styling features of the 300 Series included a curved windshield and built-in headlamps for its "envelope" style body, which had a more modern appearance than the smaller models. The large grille was in traditional upright Mercedes style, with tight mesh pattern. Sweeping fenders faded into the front doors (which hinged at the front), passing alongside an expansive hood. In addition to a plain slim-pillar sedan with quarter windows, Mercedes-Benz offered a four-door Convertible D, with landau bars, along with a two-door convertible coupe. Three people fit in the rear seat of the 300. A column-mounted gearshift controlled the four-speed transmission. The two-spoke steering wheel held the familiar Mercedes horn ring. Both front and rear seats had fixed side armrests. Rear seats also had a center armrest that folded away. The dashboard contained a large locking glove box. A pushbutton-tuned radio was optional.

Standard 300 equipment included dual fog lamps, backup lights, a triple horn, electric clock, lighter, locking glove box, and octane-rating compensator switch. Interior features included door armrests, retracting center rear armrest, dual sun visors, and front door pockets. Sedans had two long handrails with sliding coat hooks. Cabriolets had two short handrails for the front seats, plus two holding straps for the rear compartment.

300S — SIX — The 300S was introduced in mid-1952 after an earlier appearance at the Paris Salon (in autumn 1951). Available initially with a convertible body or as a five-passenger sedan, the 300S blended features of both the upcoming SL sports car and the recently-introduced long-wheelbase 300 Series. Its

Model	Body Type & Seating	Engine Type/CID	P.O.E. Price	Weight (lbs.)	Production Total
170 SERIES (Gasoline)					
170Va	4-dr Sedan-5P	I4/108	N/A	2,575	Note 1
170Vb	4-dr Sedan-5P	I4/108	N/A	2,607	Note 1
170S	4-dr Sedan-5P	I4/108	N/A	2,685	Note 1
170Sb	4-dr Sedan-5P	I4/108	N/A	2,750	Note 1
170S-V	4-dr Sedan-5P	I4/108	N/A	2,685	Note 1
170D SERIES (Diesel)					
170Da	4-dr Sedan-5P	I4/108	N/A	2,750	Note 1
170Db	4-dr Sedan-5P	I4/108	N/A	2,750	Note 1
170DS	4-dr Sedan-5P	I4/108	$3,590	2,805	Note 1
170S-D	4-dr Sedan-5P	I4/108	N/A	2,860	Note 1
180 SERIES					
180	4-dr Sedan-5P	I4/108	N/A	2,596	Note 1
220 SERIES					
220	4-dr Sedan-5P	I6/134	N/A	2,970	Note 2
220	2-dr Convertible Sedan-4P	I6/134	N/A	N/A	Note 2
220	2-dr Cabriolet-2/3P	I6/134	N/A	N/A	Note 2
220	2-dr Coupe	I6/134	N/A	N/A	Note 2
300 SERIES					
300	4-dr Sedan-5/6P	I6/183	N/A	3,916	Note 3
300	4-dr Cabriolet-5/6P	I6/183	N/A	N/A	Note 3
300	2-dr Coupe	I6/183	N/A	N/A	Note 3
300S	4-dr Sedan-5/6P	I6/183	$12,500	3,880	Note 4
300S	2-dr Cabriolet-2+2P	I6/183	$12,680	3,616	Note 4
300S	2-dr Coupe-2+2P	I6/183	N/A	2,845	Note 4
300S	2-dr Roadster-2+2P	I6/183	N/A	N/A	Note 4

Note 1: A total of 42,222 Mercedes-Benz passenger cars (all models) were produced during 1951, followed by 36,824 in 1952, and 34,975 in 1953. Production in 1952 included 3,034 cars in the 300 Series, 10,343 Type 220, and more than 23,000 Type 170.
Note 2: Approximately 16,154 first-Series 220 sedan and 2,360 open models were produced through mid-1955.
Note 3: A total of 6,214 Type 300 and subsequent 300b sedans (and 591 convertibles) were produced between late 1951 and summer 1955.
Note 4: Approximately 560 Type 300S models (216 sedans and 344 other bodies) were produced through August 1955.

1951 220 cabriolet

existence occurred virtually by accident, in fact, after the SL program was delayed. As on the basic 300 Series, handsome styling focused on long, flowing lines, with front fenders reached ahead of the upright radiator, with its three-pointed star. At the rear was a beautifully curved deck. Concealed running boards sat between the front and rear fenders.

A 150-bhp (DIN) hop-up of the Type 300's 2,996 cc engine breathed through two (later three) Solex carburetors, using 7.8:1 compression. Both floor and column-mounted gearshifts were available. The cruciform chassis consisted of oval tubes and tubular outriggers.

Functional landau bars decorated the cabriolet body, whose convertible top rode in a big rear bustle. A roadster (sans landau bars) also became available, with a top that disappeared completely. Each open style offered 2+2 seating with fold-down rear seats, and rolled/pleated leather upholstery. Customers had a choice of wood veneers: either straight-grain or burled walnut. Fitted luggage was available, too. Two spare tire wells sat in the trunk. On the dashboard was a control for ignition timing. Standard equipment included a signal-seeking radio, non-glare mirrors, vacuum-assisted brakes, backup lights, reclining seats, and windshield washers.

Top speed of the 300S was about 110 mph, and it could accelerate to 60 mph in about 14 seconds. Both the 300 and 300S had a turn signal combined with the horn ring, operated by rotating the ring. Each model also had turn-signal lights instead of the semaphore units still used on the 170/220 Series. Rear signal lights stood tall, at the top of back fenders (just below the beltline).

The 300S roadster appeared at the Paris Salon in late 1952, powered by the 150-bhp engine and with a claimed top speed of 110 mph Heavy chrome moldings went around the headlamps, with separately-mounted auxiliary lights above the bumper. A one-piece curved windshield was installed. Fender bulges extended a short distance into the doors. At the front was the usual upright grille topped by the Mercedes tri-star emblem, with long parking lights atop the fenders. According to Motor Trend, this model was called the "sister car to the 300SL model, which made such a terrific showing in the Mexican Road Race."

I.D. DATA: Chassis serial number is under the hood, on the right side of the firewall. Engine number is on lower left or right front of block.

ENGINES

Base Four (170/180 Gasoline SERIES): Inline, L-head four-cylinder. Cast-iron block. Displacement: 107.8 cid (1,767 cc). Bore & stroke: 2.95 x 3.94 in. (75 x 100 mm). Compression ratio: 6.5:1. Brake horsepower: (170Va/b, 170S-V) 45 at 3,650 rpm; (170S/Sb, 180) 52 at 4,000 rpm. Three main bearings. Solid valve lifters.

Base Diesel Four (170D SERIES): Inline, overhead-valve four-cylinder. Cast-iron block. Displacement: 107.8 cid (1,767 cc). Bore & stroke: 2.95 x 3.94 in. (75 x 100 mm). Compression ratio: 19.0:1. Brake horsepower: 40 at 3,200 rpm.

Base Six (220): Inline, overhead-cam six-cylinder. Cast-iron block. Displacement: 133.9 cid (2,195 cc). Bore & stroke: 3.15 x 2.87 in. (80 x 72.8 mm). Compression ratio: 6.5:1. Brake horsepower: 80 (DIN) at 3,600 rpm. Solid valve lifters. One carburetor.

Base Six (300): Inline, overhead-cam six-cylinder. Cast-iron block and aluminum head. Displacement: 182.8 cid (2,996 cc). Bore & stroke: 3.35 x 3.46 in. (85 x 88 mm). Compression ratio: 6.4:1. Brake horsepower: 115 (DIN) at 4,600 rpm. Torque: 144 lbs.-ft. at 2,500 rpm. Seven main bearings. Solid valve lifters. Two Solex 32 PAJAT carburetors.

Base Six (300S): Same as 2,996 cc six, with two or three Solex carburetors. Compression ratio: 7.5:1/7.8:1. Brake horsepower: 150 (DIN) at 4,850-5,100 rpm. Three Solex 40 PBJC carburetors.

CHASSIS

Wheelbase: (170) 112 in.; (180) 104.3 in.; (220 sedan) 112 in.; (300) 120 in.; (300S) 114 in. Overall length: (170) 169 in.; (170DS) 175.3 in.; (180) 176 in.; (220 sedan) 178 in.; (300) 195 in.; (300S) 181.1 in. Height: (170) 62.8-63.4 in.; (170DS) 63.3 in.; (180) 61 in.; (220 sedan) 63.4 in.; (300) 64.5 in.; (300S) 59.5 in. Width: (170) 63.5 in.; (170DS) 66.3 in.; (180) 69 in.; (220) 66.4 in.; (300) 72.5 in. Front tread: (170) 51.0 in.; (170DS) 51.8 in.; (180) 55.9 in.; (220) 51.8 in.; (300) 56.7 in.; (300S) 58.3 in. Rear tread: (170) 53.0 in.; (170DS) 56.5 in.; (180) 57.1 in.; (220) 56.5 in.; (300) 60.0 in.; (300S) 60.0 in. Standard tires: (170) 5.50x16; (180) 6.40x13; (220) 6.40x15; (300) 7.10x15; (300S) 6.70x15.

TECHNICAL

Layout: front-engine, rear-drive. Transmission: four-speed manual. Suspension (front): (170V, 170S-V) transverse leaf spring; (180/220) wishbones with coil springs; (300S) wishbones with coil springs and anti-roll bar. Suspension (rear):

1952 300

1952 300D

swing axles with coil springs. Brakes: hydraulic, front/rear drum. Body construction: steel body on steel frame except (180) steel unibody.

PERFORMANCE

Top Speed: (170S-V) 70 mph; (170DS) 62 mph; (180) 78 mph; (220) 90 mph; (300) 96-98 mph; (300S) 110 mph Acceleration (0-60 mph): (300) 16.1 sec.; (300S) 14 sec. Acceleration (quarter-mile): (300) 20 sec. Fuel mileage: (300) about 17 mpg (U.S.).

PRODUCTION/SALES: Approximately 288 Mercedes-Benz passenger cars were sold in the U.S. in 1953, including about 100 with diesel engines.

ADDITIONAL MODELS: In its first outing, at the Mille Miglia in May 1952, a 300SL racing car finished second (not far behind the winner). Late in 1952, both the 300SL Le Mans racing coupe and the 300S roadster appeared at the Paris Salon. The 300SL had a lightweight tubular frame, and was powered by a 183-cid six-cylinder engine that developed 175 horsepower at 5,200 rpm, on 8:1 compression with three Solex carburetors. Racers were developed by Rudolf Uhlenhaut. Wearing a Mercedes tri-star emblem in its oval grille, the 300SL had turned in a powerful one-two finish at the Carrera Panamericana race in Mexico. It led to the production version of 1954-57; see next listings for details.

Manufacturer: Daimler-Benz AG, Stuttgart, West Germany.

Distributor: Hoffman Motors Corp., New York City.

HISTORY:

Type 300 models were built at the coachworks in Sindelfingen. The 300's engine was the first overhead-cam design used on a Mercedes-Benz since 1932. The first-Series 300 sedan became available in late 1951 and lasted through March 1954. Production of the four-door convertible began in April 1952. Production of the 300S began in July 1952. Production of the 220 convertible and coupe continued through 1955. Both the 220 and 300 had engines designed by Josef Muller. The 220 was considered to be a replacement for the prewar 230 Series, while the 300 evolved from the prewar 320 and 500K sedans.

Road & Track noted that, "the 300S caused a quiet riot of enthusiasm with its low, sleek lines and its attitude of 'going' even when standing still." The magazine called it "one of the finest road vehicles in the world today." *Motor Trend* wasn't wholeheartedly impressed by the 170DS diesel, first pointing out that the body looked to be "about 1936 vintage, and not a very flashy '36 at that." When the engine fired up, the magazine added, it "breaks into a harsh clatter that sounds exactly as though you had just thrown three rods." On the other hand, they liked the car's luxury touches and ride quality, said to be "equal to virtually any Detroit car."

1954

170S-V — FOUR — Production of the 170S-V sedan continued into early 1955 with little change. All of the other 170 Series models with gasoline engines faded away during 1953.

170S-D — DIESEL FOUR — Production of the diesel-engine version of the 170 sedan also continued into 1955, with little change.

180/180D — GAS/DIESEL FOUR — The original 180 sedan, which remained in the Mercedes lineup until halfway through 1957, was joined this year by a diesel-powered edition. With the same 1,767 cc displacement as the gasoline engine, the diesel developed 40 horsepower.

220a SERIES — SIX — A new, more modern 220a sedan debuted in March 1954, edging aside the older-style 220 Series. This one had a more boxy profile, a much different fender line and smaller grille, with parking lights atop the fenders. Wheelbase was 111 inches (106 inches on some models).

300 SERIES — SIX — A 300b Series replaced the original 300 during the 1954 model year, with its 3.0-liter engine producing an additional 10 horsepower (now 125). Brakes also were larger. No change was evident in the 300S Series.

300SL — SIX — As of August 1954, the production version of the 300SL racing car was ready to become available

1954 220 coupe

1954 180D

to regular customers and, soon afterward, shipped to sports-car fans in the United States. Max Hoffman, importer of Mercedes-Benz cars into America, is generally credited with instigating the existence of the famed Gullwing coupe, by ordering 1,000 of the road-going editions ahead of time. The production 300SL first appeared at the New York Auto Show in February 1954.

The drive train and suspension were essentially the same as those used on the 300 Series sedans and coupes, on a chassis with 94.5-inch wheelbase. The "high-pivot" swing-axle rear suspension allowed extreme oversteering, a flaw that would later be corrected on the roadster follow-up of 1957. The front suspension consisted of upper and lower A-arms with coil springs and anti-roll bar. The 300SL used a multi-tube space-frame chassis, and was best known for the coupe's half-height Gullwing doors, which opened upward. In fact, the complex tubular space framework virtually demanded Gullwing doors. Though creating a dramatic appearance, those doors with their tall, wide sills also made it difficult to enter and exit. The car's steering wheel was hinged at the base of its hub, tilting down to ease entry/exit somewhat.

Although the 300SL prototype had inset door windows (a window within the window), the production version did not. The Mercedes-Benz tri-star emblem sat in the center of a horizontal bar across the wide grille. This was the only model lacking the traditional upright, tight-mesh grille. Of course, no one was likely to mistake a Gullwing 300SL for any other Mercedes, past or present. Other styling touches included long bulges over the wheel openings, longitudinal hood bulges and anodized aluminum beltline trim moldings. Large, angled, openings in the front fenders at the cowl were almost as noticeable a feature as the Gullwing doors, and would appear on other cars in later years. A small, round insignia was located

at the front of the hood. Round parking lamps went below the headlamps. Horizontal wraparound taillamps sat just above the back bumper.

The 300SL's single-overhead-cam, 2,996 cc (182.8 cid) six-cylinder engine developed 215 horsepower DIN (240 SAE at 6,100 rpm). Torque output was 210 lbs.-ft. (SAE). The engine was inclined 50-degrees, contained a forged-steel crankshaft, and used dry-sump lubrication. Bosch mechanical fuel injection replaced the usual carburetors. A remote oil tank sat in the left fender and the oil cooler sat next to the regular radiator. A four-speed, all-synchro manual transmission and drum brakes were installed. Early models had a long, bent gearshift lever that extended from the transmission tunnel. In 1955, that would change to remote-control linkage. A ZF self-locking differential contained a standard 3.64:1 axle ratio on U.S. models (but other ratios were available, from 3.25:1 to 4.11:1). With 3.25:1 gearing, the speedometer read up to 180 mph; others had a 160-mph speedometer installed. The gas tank held 34.5 gallons (45 gallons on racing models). Tires were size 6.

Aluminum was used for the doors, forward-opening hood, trunk lid, rocker panels, belly pan, and interior sheet metal, but the balance of the body was made of steel. All-aluminum competition bodies were available on special order. A total of 29 aluminum-bodied 300SLs were built. Those aluminum-bodied cars used Plexiglas windows but a glass windshield, and had Rudge center-lock wheels. Steel bodies could be ordered with competition springs, which were standard on aluminum-bodied cars.

I.D. DATA: Chassis serial number is under the hood, on the right side of the firewall. Engine number is on lower left or right front of block.

Model	Body Type & Seating	Engine Type/CID	P.O.E. Price	Weight (lbs.)	Production Total
170 SERIES					
170S-V	4-dr Sedan-5P	I4/108	N/A	2,685	Note 1
170S-D (Diesel)	4-dr Sedan-5P	I4/108	N/A	2,860	Note 1
180 SERIES					
180	4-dr Sedan-5P	I4/108	$3,350	2,535	Note 1
180D (Diesel)	4-dr Sedan-5P	I4/108	$3,575	2,535	Note 1
220a SERIES					
220a	4-dr Sedan-5P	I6/134	$4,175	2,860	Note 1
220a	2-dr Conv Sedan-4P	I6/134	$5,600	2,860	Note 1
220a	2-dr Cabriolet-2/3P	I6/134	$6,150	2,860	Note 1
220a	2-dr Coupe	I6/134	N/A	2,860	Note 1
300 SERIES					
300	4-dr Sedan-5/6P	I6/183	$6,780	3,916	Note 2
300	4-dr Cabriolet-5/6P	I6/183	$8,111	3,902	Note 2
300	2-dr Coupe-4/5P	I6/183	N/A	N/A	Note 2
300b	4-dr Sedan-5/6P	I6/183	N/A	3,916	Note 2
300b	4-dr Cabriolet-5/6P	I6/183	N/A	N/A	Note 2
300b	2-dr Coupe-4/5P	I6/183	N/A	N/A	Note 2
300S	4-dr Sedan-5/6P	I6/183	N/A	3,880	Note 3
300S	2-dr Cabriolet-2+2P	I6/183	$12,500	3,800	Note 3
300S	2-dr Coupe-2+2P	I6/183	$12,500	3,800	Note 3
300S	2-dr Roadster-2+2P	I6/183	$12,500	3,800	Note 3
300SL					
300SL	2-dr Coupe-2P	I6/183	$11,000	2,750	Note 4

Note 1: A total of 48,816 Mercedes-Benz cars (all models) were produced during 1954. That production included 1,455 Type 300 models.
Note 2: A total of 6,214 Type 300 and 300b sedans (and 591 convertibles) were produced between late 1951 and summer 1955.
Note 3: Approximately 560 Type 300S models (216 sedans and 344 other bodies) were produced through August 1955).
Note 4: A total of 1,400 Type 300SL Gullwing coupes were produced from 1954-57 (146 in 1954, 867 in 1955, 311 in 1956, and 76 in 1957).
Price Note: 300SL figure is early price; sales in U.S. did not begin until 1955, when the price dropped to $7,463.

ENGINES

Base Four (170S-V): Inline, L-head four-cylinder. Cast-iron block. Displacement: 107.8 cid (1,767 cc). Bore & stroke: 2.95 x 3.94 in. (75 x 100 mm). Compression ratio: 6.5:1. Brake horsepower: 45 at 3,600 rpm. Three main bearings. Solid valve lifters.

Base Four (180): Same as 1,767 cc four above, except Compression ratio: 6.7:1. Brake horsepower: 52 at 4,000 rpm.

Base Diesel Four (170S-D, 180D): Inline, overhead-valve four-cylinder. Cast-iron block. Displacement: 107.8 cid (1,767 cc). Bore & stroke: 2.95 x 3.94 in. (75 x 100 mm). Compression ratio: 19.0:1. Brake horsepower: 40 at 3,200 rpm.

Base Six (220a): Inline, overhead-cam six-cylinder. Cast-iron block. Displacement: 133.9 cid (2,195 cc). Bore & stroke: 3.15 x 2.87 in. (80 x 72.8 mm). Compression ratio: 7.6:1. Brake horsepower: 85 (DIN) at 4,800 rpm. Solid valve lifters. One carburetor.

Base Six (300): Inline, overhead-cam six-cylinder. Cast-iron block and aluminum head. Displacement: 182.8 cid (2,996 cc). Bore & stroke: 3.35 x 3.46 in. (85 x 88 mm). Compression ratio: 6.4:1. Brake horsepower: 115 (DIN) at 4,600 rpm. Torque: 144 lbs.-ft. at 2,500 rpm. Seven main bearings. Solid valve lifters. Two Solex 32 PAJAT carburetors.

Base Six (300b): Same as 2,996 cc six above, except Compression ratio: 7.4:1. Brake horsepower: 125 (DIN). Two dual-barrel carburetors.

Base Six (300S): Same as 2,996 cc six above, with three Solex 40 PBJC carburetors. Compression ratio: 7.8:1. Brake horsepower: 150 (DIN) at 5,100 rpm.

Base Six (300SL): Same as 2,996 cc six, above, with Bosch mechanical fuel injection (code M198). Compression ratio: 8.5:1. Brake horsepower: 215 (DIN) at 5,800 rpm (240 SAE at 6,100 rpm). Torque: 206 lbs.-ft. (DIN) at 4,600 rpm (217 lbs.-ft. SAE at 4,800 rpm).

CHASSIS

Wheelbase: (170S-V) 112 in.; (180) 104.3 in.; (220a sedan) 111 in.; (300) 120 in.; (300S) 114 in.; (300SL) 94.5 in. Overall length: (170S-V) 175 in.; (180) 176 in.; (220a sedan) 185 in.; (300) 195 in.; (300S) 181 in.; (300SL) 180 in. Height: (170S-V) 65.5 in.; (180) 61.5 in.; (220a sedan) 62 in.; (300) 64 in.; (300S) 59.5 in.; (300SL) 49.8 in. Width: (170S-V) 64 in.; (180) 68.5 in.; (220a sedan) 69 in.; (300/S) 71.7 in.; (300SL) 70.5 in. Front tread: (170S-V) 51.8 in.; (180) 55.9 in.; (300) 52.8 in.; (300S) 58.3 in.; (300SL) 54.5. Rear tread: (170S-V) 56.5 in.; (180) 57.1 in.; (300) 60.0 in.; (300S) 60.0 in.; (300SL) 56.5. Standard tires: (170S-V) 5.50x16; (180) 6.40x13; (220a) 6.70x15; (300) 7.10x15; (300S) 6.70x15; (300SL) 6.50x15.

TECHNICAL

Layout: front engine, rear drive. Transmission: four-speed manual. Gear ratios for the first 300SL coupes: (1st) 3.14:1; (2nd) 1.85:1; (3rd) 1.31:1; (4th) 1.00:1. Gear ratios for

1954 220

subsequent 300SL coupes: (1st) 3.34:1; (2nd) 1.97:1; (3rd) 1.39:1; (4th) 1.00:1. Standard final drive ratio: (300SL) 3.64:1 on U.S. models (optional 3.25:1, 3.42:1, 3.89:1, and 4.11:1). Suspension (front): upper/lower A-arms with coil springs; (300S/SL) upper/lower A-arms with coil springs and anti-roll bar. Suspension (rear): swing axles with coil springs; (300SL) high-pivot swing axles with radius arms and coil springs. Brakes: hydraulic, front/rear drum. Body construction: steel body on steel frame except (180/220) steel unibody; (300SL) steel/aluminum body on tubular space frame. Fuel tank: (300SL) 34.5 gallons (45 gallons on racer).

Note: Twenty-nine 300SLs had an aluminum body.

PERFORMANCE

Top Speed: (300) 96 mph; (300S) 110 mph; (300SL coupe) 120-146 mph (as much as 160 mph claimed). Acceleration (0-60 mph): (300S) 14 sec.; (300SL) 7.6-8.8 sec. Acceleration (quarter-mile): (300SL) 16.1 sec. (84 mph).

PRODUCTION/SALES: Approximately 437 Mercedes-Benz passenger cars were sold in the U.S. in 1954.

ADDITIONAL MODELS: A total of nine 300SLR racing

versions were built, two with a coupe body. The 300SLR racer differed from an ordinary 300SL in various ways, though the tubular-truss chassis and 3.0-liter engine displacement were the same.

Manufacturer: Daimler-Benz AG, Stuttgart, West Germany.

Distributor: Hoffman Motors Corp., New York City.

HISTORY

"The effect is electrifying," declared the British magazine Autocar in describing second-gear acceleration of 300SL. Passengers "feel they are being rocketed through space." Its test car managed to accelerate to 60 mph in 8.8 seconds, and to 100 in 21 seconds, with a top speed beyond 120 mph *Motor Trend* found 300SL acceleration "a trifle disappointing," with a 0-60 time of 8.5 seconds; but expressed greater appreciation for the 16.1-second quarter-mile time. Its test car neared 135 mph Mercedes-Benz announced the 190SL roadster in 1954, along with the 300SL Gullwing coupe, and it was featured in magazines early that year; but production did not begin until 1955.

1955

170S-V, 170S-D — FOUR — Production of the gasoline and diesel engine 170 Series sedans ended during 1955. Little change was evident in this final season.

180/180D — FOUR — Production of the modern, boxy-styled Mercedes with gasoline or diesel engine continued with little change.

190SL — FOUR — By spring of 1955, Mercedes-Benz was ready with its second member of the SL generation: the 190SL two-seat touring sports roadster. Actually, the 190SL had been featured in magazine articles a year earlier, alongside the new 300SL coupe; but production did not commence until the beginning of 1955.

Power came from a single-overhead-cam four-cylinder engine with 1,897 cc (116 cid) displacement, developing 105 horsepower DIN (120 SAE) at 5,700 rpm. The same engine would go into 180 Series sedans in 1957. A four-speed manual gearbox was standard. Prototypes had a column gearshift, but production models turned to a floor shift. Prototypes also had a hood scoop but that, too, disappeared in production.

Wheelbase was 94.5 inches, and the 190SL was styled to resemble the 300SL; but intended as a sporty tourer rather than all-out sports car. The front end, in particular, was similar to the 300SL, but it had no fender vents. The 190SL had a rounded overall look with a low nose, wide grille with large tri-star in center, and long horizontal bulges above the wheel

1955 180

Model	Body Type & Seating	Engine Type/CID	P.O.E. Price	Weight (lbs.)	Production Total
170 SERIES					
170S-V	4-dr Sedan-5P	I4/108	N/A	2,685	Note 1
170S-D (Diesel)	4-dr Sedan-5P	I4/108	N/A	2,860	Note 1
180 SERIES					
180	4-dr Sedan-5P	I4/108	$3,395	2,596	Note 1
180D (Diesel)	4-dr Sedan-5P	I4/108	$3,595	2,684	Note 1
190SL					
190SL	2-dr Roadster-2P	I4/116	$3,998	2,550	Note 2
220a SERIES					
220a	4-dr Sedan-5P	I6/134	$4,588	2,860	Note 1
220a	2-dr Conv-4/5P	I6/134	N/A	N/A	Note 1
220a	2-dr Cabriolet-4/5P	I6/134	$6,290	N/A	Note 1
220a	2-dr Coupe-4/5P	I6/134	$6,450	N/A	Note 1
300 SERIES					
300b	4-dr Sedan-5/6P	I6/183	$6,988	3,916	Note 1
300b	4-dr Cabriolet-5/6P	I6/183	$8,328	N/A	Note 1
300b	2-dr Coupe	I6/183	N/A	N/A	Note 1
300S	4-dr Sedan-5/6P	I6/183	N/A	3,880	Note 3
300S	2-dr Cabriolet-2+2P	I6/183	$12,457	N/A	Note 3
300S	2-dr Coupe-2+2P	I6/183	$12,457	N/A	Note 3
300S	2-dr Roadster-2+2P	I6/183	$12,457	N/A	Note 3
300SL					
300SL	2-dr Coupe-2P	I6/183	$7,463	2,885	Note 4

Note 1: A total of 63,683 Mercedes-Benz cars (all models) were produced during 1955.
Note 2: A total of 25,881 190SL models were produced during the full model run, 1955-63 (1,727 built in 1955 alone).
Note 3: A total of 560 Type 300S models were produced during the full model run, from 1952-55 (216 coupes, 203 cabriolets and 141 roadsters).
Note 4: A total of 1,400 300SL Gullwing coupes were produced during the full model run, 1954-57 (867 in 1955 alone).

wells. A short horizontal trim strip decorated the front and rear fenders. The roadster had a rather long deck and ample trunk space, on a shortened version of the 180 (W120 Series) sedan platform, which debuted in 1953. This design (code W121 for the 190SL) had a steel unibody structure. The roadster's body was welded to its frame. The engine, transmission, and front axle were mounted in a removable front subframe. The all-independent suspension was similar to that used in the 180 sedan, and used single-pivot swing axles at the rear (different from the setup used on the 300SL).

The roadster came with a heater, roll-up windows, easy-to-operate convertible top, windshield washers, and backup lights. The gearbox was synchronized in all forward gears; a round tachometer and speedometer sat just ahead of the driver. *Road & Track* magazine said performance of the 190SL was "a function of intelligent use of the gearbox." A detachable steel hardtop soon became optional.

220a SERIES — SIX — Production of the 220a with 2,195 cc overhead-cam engine, in four body styles, continued with little change.

300 SERIES — SIX — Production of the 300b, introduced during 1954, continued with little change until it was replaced by the 300c late in 1955 (see next year for details). The 300S, with a more powerful version of the 3.0-liter engine, also continued with little change.

300SL — SIX — Introduced in 1954, the Gullwing coupe was officially on sale in the U.S. in 1955.

I.D. DATA: Chassis serial number is under the hood, on the right side of the firewall. Engine number is on lower left or right front of the block.

ENGINES

Base Four (170S-V, 180): Inline, L-head four-cylinder. Cast-iron block. Displacement: 107.8 cid (1,767 cc). Bore & stroke: 2.95 x 3.94 in. (75 x 100 mm). Compression ratio: 6.7:1. Brake horsepower: (170S-V) 50 at 3600 rpm; (180) 58 at 4,000 rpm. Torque: (180) 82 lbs.-ft. at 1,800 rpm. Three main bearings. Solid valve lifters. One carburetor.

Base Diesel Four (170S-D, 180D): Inline, overhead-valve four-cylinder. Displacement: 107.8 cid (1,767 cc). Bore & stroke: 2.95 x 3.94 in. (75 x 100 mm). Compression ratio: 19.0:1. Brake horsepower: 40/43 at 3,200 rpm.

Base Four (190SL): Inline, overhead-cam four-cylinder (code M121). Cast-iron block. Displacement: 116 cid (1,897 cc). Bore & stroke: 3.35 x 3.29 in. (85 x 83.6 mm). Compression ratio: 8.5:1. Brake horsepower: 105 (DIN) at 5,700 rpm (120 bhp SAE). Torque: 105 lbs.-ft. (DIN) at 3,200 rpm. Two Solex carburetors.

Base Six (220a): Inline, overhead-cam six-cylinder. Cast-iron block. Displacement: 133.9 cid (2,195 cc). Bore & stroke: 3.15 x 2.87 in. (80 x 72.8 mm). Compression ratio: 7.5:1. Brake horsepower: 92 at 4,800 rpm. Torque: 116 lbs.-ft. at 2,400 rpm. Solid valve lifters. One carburetor.

Base Six (300b): Inline, overhead-cam six-cylinder. Cast-iron block and aluminum head. Displacement: 183 cid (2,996 cc). Bore & stroke: 3.35 x 3.46 in. (85 x 88 mm). Compression ratio: 7.5:1. Brake horsepower: 136 at 4,500 rpm. Torque: 162 lbs.-ft. at 2,600 rpm. Seven main bearings. Solid valve lifters. Two Solex carburetors.

Base Six (300S): Same as 2,996 cc six, but with three Solex carburetors. Compression ratio: 7.8:1. Brake horsepower: 163

at 5,000 rpm. Torque: 170 lbs.-ft. at 3,800 rpm.

Base Six (300SL): Same as 2,996 cc six, above, with Bosch mechanical fuel injection. Compression ratio: 8.55:1. Brake horsepower: 215 (DIN) at 5,800 rpm (240 SAE at 6100 rpm). Torque: 206 lbs.-ft. (DIN) at 4,600 rpm (217 lbs.-ft. SAE at 4,800 rpm).

CHASSIS

Wheelbase: (170S-V) 112 in.; (180) 104.3 in.; (190SL) 94.5 in.; (220a sedan) 111 in.; (300b) 120 in.; (300S) 114.2 in.; (300SL) 94.5 in. Overall length: (170S-V) 175.3 in.; (180) 175.5 in.; (190SL) 166 in.; (220a sedan) 186 in.; (300b) 199 in.; (300S) 186 in.; (300SL) 178 in. Height: (170S-V) 62.7 in.; (180) 61.3 in.; (190SL) 52 in.; (220a sedan) 61.5 in.; (300b) 63 in.; (300S) 60 in.; (300SL) 51.3 in. Width: (170S-V) 66.3 in.; (180) 68.6 in.; (190SL) 68.5 in.; (220a sedan) 68.6 in.; (300b) 72.4 in.; (300S) 75.3 in.; (300SL) 71 in. Front tread: (170S-V) 51.8 in.; (180) 51.8 in.; (190SL) 56.3 in.; (220a) 56.3 in.; (300b) 58.3 in.; (300S) 58.3 in.; (300SL) 54.5. Rear tread: (170S-V) 56.7 in.; (180) 57.2 in.; (190SL) 57.9 in.; (220a) 57.9 in.; (300b) 60.0 in.; (300S) 60.0 in.; (300SL) 56.5. Standard tires: (170S-V) 5.50x16; (180) 6.40x13; (190SL) 6.40x13; (220a) 6.70x13; (300b) 7.10x15; (300S) 6.70x15; (300SL) 6.50x15.

TECHNICAL

Layout: front engine, rear drive. Transmission: four-speed manual. Suspension (front): upper/lower A-arms with coil springs; (190SL/300SL) upper/lower A-arms with coil springs and anti-roll bar. Suspension (rear): swing axles with coil springs; (190SL) single-joint swing axles as upper lateral arms, with radius arms and coil springs; (300SL) high-pivot swing axles with radius arms and coil springs. Brakes: hydraulic, front/rear drum. Body construction: steel body on steel frame except (180/220) steel unibody; (300SL) steel/aluminum body on tubular space frame.

MAJOR OPTIONS: Detachable hardtop (190SL). Automatic antenna (190SL). Sliding sunroof (180). Reclining seats (180).

1955 300 C cabriolet

PERFORMANCE

Top Speed: (190SL) 105-112 mph (factory claimed 111.8 mph); (300b) 100 mph; (300S) 110 mph; (300SL) 120-146 mph (as much as 160 mph claimed). Acceleration (0-60 mph): (190SL) 11.6-14.5 sec.; (300S) 14 sec.; (300SL) 7.4-8.8 sec. Acceleration (quarter-mile): (190SL) 18.7-18.9 sec. (76 mph). Fuel mileage: (190SL) 16-20 mpg.

ADDITIONAL MODELS: The 300SLR racing coupe evolved from the single-seat Grand Prix car, with a longer (93.3-inch) wheelbase and two seats. During 1955, the 300SLR was victorious at the Mille Miglia, Targa Florio, and Tourist Trophy events. As tested by *Motor Trend*, it was capable of traveling 176 mph and could accelerate to 60 mph in 6.8 seconds, using first and second gears. Accelerating to 100 mph took 13.6 seconds. The 2,976 cc inline eight-cylinder engine developed 296 horsepower at 7,450 rpm, and 228 lbs.-ft. of torque at 5,950 rpm.

Manufacturer: Daimler-Benz AG, Stuttgart, West Germany.

Distributor: Hoffman Motors Corp., New York City.

HISTORY

At the 1955 Le Mans race, a 300SLR driven by Pierre Levegh flew into the grandstand. This tragedy prompted Mercedes-Benz to withdraw from motor racing.

1955 300 SL

1955 300 SL

1955 190SL

1955 180

1956-1957

180 SERIES — FOUR — Production of the original 180 sedan continued with little change into mid-1957, when it was replaced by the 180a, with a larger (1,897 cc) engine. The earlier engine was a 1,767 cc L-head design. Diesel (180D) production continued into 1959 with the original smaller engine.

190 SERIES — FOUR — A 190 gasoline-engine sedan was added, with the same styling as the 180 but new single-pivot swing-axle rear suspension (on the W121 chassis). Power came from an overhead-cam, 1,897 cc four as in the 190SL roadster, but developing 75 horsepower (84 bhp SAE). Wheelbase was 104 inches.

190SL — FOUR — Production of the two-seat roadster continued with little change. A removable hardtop was optional (sometimes described as a coupe model). The coupe was available in a choice of colors, from classic black down to pale two-tone finishes. Second gear was claimed to be usable to 47 mph; third, to 75 mph; fourth, from 105-113 mph

219/220 SERIES — SIX — A new Series of sedans, coupes, and cabriolets (convertibles) joined the lineup during 1956. The Type 220S served as successor to the prior 220a, offered as a four-door sedan, two-door coupe, and two-door cabriolet. The 219 came only as a sedan with single rear window. Wheelbase was 108.3 inches (chassis code W105) for the 219, and 111 inches (chassis W180) for the 220S sedan. Two-door 220S models rode a W128 chassis with 106.3-inch wheelbase. Both models carried a 2,195 cc (134 cid) six-cylinder overhead-cam engine, but with different ratings. The engine initially developed 85 horsepower on 7.6:1 compression under Type 219 hoods; but that grew to 90 bhp during 1957, as a result of a compression boost to 8.7:1. In the Type 220, the engine used twin two-barrel carburetors.

300 SERIES — SIX — A 300c sedan, with automatic transmission, became available late in 1955, soon followed by a 300Sc Series with fuel-injected engine (replacing the 300S). The 300Sc Series came in sedan, cabriolet, and roadster form. Using Bosch direct fuel injection and 8.55:1 compression, its 2,996 cc engine developed 175 horsepower (DIN). The 300Sc introduced Hydrovac power brakes to the Mercedes-Benz line. Although the 300c engine used dual compound carburetion, it offered no increase in horsepower. Appearance of the 300Sc was similar to the former 300S, except for two extra horizontal trim strips along the former's hood.

1956 219

1957 300 SL Gullwing

300SL — SIX — Production of the Gullwing coupe continued through spring 1957. A new roadster entered production in August of that year. See next year for details.

I.D. DATA: Chassis serial number is on the right side of the firewall. Engine number is on top, or on right side of block.

ENGINES

Base Four (180): Inline, L-head four-cylinder. Cast-iron block. Displacement: 107.8 cid (1,767 cc). Bore & stroke: 2.95 x 3.94 in. (75 x 100 mm). Compression ratio: 6.7:1. Brake horsepower: 58 at 4,000 rpm. Torque: 82 lbs.-ft. at 1,800 rpm. Three main bearings. Solid valve lifters. One carburetor.

Diesel Note: The overhead-valve diesel version of the 1,767 cc engine produced 46 horsepower (SAE) at 3,500 rpm, on 19:1 compression.

Base Four (180a): Inline, overhead-cam four-cylinder. Cast-iron block. Displacement: 116 cid (1,897 cc). Bore & stroke: 3.35 x 3.29 in. (85 x 83.6 mm). Compression ratio: 6.8:1. Brake horsepower: 74 at 4,700 rpm. Torque: 104 lbs.-ft. at 2,800 rpm. Solid valve lifters.

Base Four (190SL): Same as 1,897 cc four above, except Compression ratio: 8.5:1. Brake horsepower: 105 (DIN) at 5,700 rpm (120 SAE at 5,800 rpm). Torque: 105 lbs.-ft. (DIN) at 3,200 rpm. Two Solex horizontal compound carburetors.

Base Four (190 sedan): Same as 1,897 cc four above, except Compression ratio: 7.5:1. Brake horsepower: 84 (SAE) at 4,800 rpm.

Base Six (219, 220S): Inline, overhead-cam six-cylinder. Cast-iron block. Displacement: 133.9 cid (2,195 cc). Bore & stroke: 3.15 x 2.87 in. (80 x 72.8 mm). Compression ratio: (early) 7.6:1; (late) 8.7:1. Brake horsepower: (219) 85/90 (up to 100 SAE at 5,000 rpm); (220S) 100/106 (112/120 SAE at 5,000/5,200 rpm). Torque: (late 220S) 128.8 lbs.-ft. at 3,800 rpm. Solid valve lifters. One carburetor except (220S) dual two-barrel carburetors.

Base Six (300c): Inline, overhead-cam six-cylinder. Cast-iron block and aluminum head. Displacement: 183 cid (2,996 cc). Bore & stroke: 3.35 x 3.46 in. (85 x 88 mm). Compression ratio: 7.5:1. Brake horsepower: 115 DIN (136 SAE at 4,500 rpm). Seven main bearings. Solid valve lifters. Two carburetors.

Base Six (300Sc): Same as 2,996 cc six above, but with Bosch fuel injection. Compression ratio: 8.55:1. Brake horsepower: 175 (DIN) at 5,400 rpm. Torque: 188/191 lbs.-ft. at 4,300 rpm.

Base Six (300SL): Same as 2,996 cc six, above, with Bosch fuel injection. Compression ratio: 8.55:1. Brake horsepower: 215 (DIN) at 5,800 rpm (240 SAE at 6,100 rpm). Torque: 206 lbs.-ft. (DIN) at 4,600 rpm (217 lbs.-ft. SAE at 4,800 rpm).

Model	Body Type & Seating	Engine Type/CID	P.O.E. Price	Weight (lbs.)	Production Total
180 SERIES					
180	4-dr Sedan-5P	I4/108	$3,150	2,535	Note 1
180D (Diesel)	4-dr Sedan-5P	I4/108	$3,438	2,645	Note 1
190 SERIES					
190	4-dr Sedan-5P	I4/116	$3,298	2,645	Note 1
190SL	2-dr Roadster-2P	I4/116	$3,998	2,510	Note 2
190SL	2-dr HT Coupe-2P	I4/116	$4,295	2,510	Note 2
219 SERIES					
219	4-dr Sedan-6P	I6/134	$3,680	2,780	Note 4
220 SERIES					
220a	4-dr Sedan-5/6P	I6/134	N/A	N/A	Note 1
220S	4-dr Sedan-5/6P	I6/134	$4,494	2,955	Note 3
220S	2-dr Conv Coupe	I6/134	$7,138	3,142	Note 3
220S	2-dr Coupe	I6/134	N/A	N/A	Note 3
300 SERIES					
300c	4-dr Sedan-6P	I6/183	$7,078	4,210	Note 5
300c	4-dr Limo-6P	I6/183	$7,368	4,210	Note 5
300c	4-dr Cabriolet-6P	I6/183	N/A	N/A	Note 5
300c	2-dr Coupe	I6/183	N/A	N/A	Note 5
300S	4-dr Sedan-6P	I6/183	N/A	3,880	Note 1
300S	2-dr Cabriolet-3P	I6/183	$12,898	3,925	Note 1
300S	2-dr Coupe-3P	I6/183	$12,898	3,925	Note 1
300S	2-dr Roadster-3P	I6/183	$12,898	3,925	Note 1
300Sc	4-dr Sedan-6P	I6/183	N/A	N/A	Note 6
300Sc	2-dr Cabriolet-3P	I6/183	N/A	N/A	Note 6
300Sc	2-dr Roadster-3P	I6/183	N/A	N/A	Note 6
300SL					
300SL	2-dr Coupe-2P	I6/183	$7,295	3,000	Note 7

Note 1: A total of 69,601 Mercedes-Benz cars (all models) were produced during 1956 and 80,899 in 1957.
Note 2: A total of 25,881 190SL models were produced during the full model run, 1955-63.
Note 3: Total 220S production over the full model run (1956-59) included 55,279 four-door sedans and 3,429 coupes/convertibles.
Note 4: A total of 27,845 Type 219 sedans were produced from 1956-59.
Note 5: A total of 1,432 Type 300c sedans and 51 other bodies were produced from late 1955 into mid-1956.
Note 6: A total of 200 Type 300Sc models were produced over the full model run, from late 1955 to early 1958 (98 sedans, 49 cabriolets and 53 roadsters).
Note 7: A total of 1,400 300SL Gullwing coupes were produced during the full model run, 1954-57.
Model Note: Official production of the 300S Series halted late in 1955, but they remained on lists of models sold in the U.S. for the following year.
Price Note: Figures shown were valid in 1956. In 1957, the 190SL sold for $4,652 ($4,949 with hardtop), and the 300SL for $7,967. Other models rose in price by smaller amounts.

1957 300 SL

1957 300SL roadster

CHASSIS

Wheelbase: (180) 104.3 in.; (190 sedan) 104.3 in.; (190SL) 94.5 in.; (220S sedan) 111 in.; (220S conv) 106.3 in.; (219) 108.25 in.; (300c sedan) 120 in.; (300S) 114.25 in.; (300SL) 94.5 in. Overall length: (180) 175.6 in.; (190 sedan) 176.6 in.; (190SL) 165.3 in.; (220S sedan) 185.5 in.; (220S conv) 185 in.; (219) 182.7 in.; (300c sedan) 199 in.; (300S) 185 in.; (300SL) 178 in. Height: (180) 61.4 in.; (190 sedan) 61.4 in.; (190SL) 52 in.; (219) 61.4 in.; (220S sedan) 61.6 in.; (220S conv) 60.3 in.; (300c sedan) 63 in.; (300S) 59.5 in.; (300SL) 51.4 in. Width: (180/190/190SL/219/220S sedan) 68.5 in.; (220S conv) 70 in.; (300c sedan) 72.4 in.; (300S sedan) 75.4 in.; (300SL) 70.5 in. Front tread: (180) 56.1 in.; (190/190SL/219/220S) 56.3 in.; (300c sedan) 58.3 in.; (300S) 58.3 in.; (300SL) 54.5 in. Rear tread: (180) 57.5 in.; (190/190SL/219/220S) 57.9 in.; (300c sedan) 60.0 in.; (300S) 60.0 in.; (300SL) 56.5 in. Standard tires: (180/190/190SL/219) 6.40x13; (220S sedan) 6.70x13; (300/S) 7.60x15; (300SL) 6.50x15/6.70x15.

TECHNICAL

Layout: front-engine, rear-drive. Transmission: four-speed manual (automatic on 300c Series). Suspension (front): upper/lower A-arms with coil springs. Suspension (rear): swing axles with coil springs. Brakes: hydraulic, front/rear drum. Body Construction: (180/220) steel unibody; (300SL) steel/aluminum body on tubular space frame.

MAJOR OPTIONS: Automatic transmission: 300 ($350). Sliding sunroof (180/190/219/220S sedans).

PERFORMANCE

Top Speed: (190SL) 105-113 mph; (220S) 100 mph; (219) 92 mph; (300c) 100 mph; (300Sc) 112+ mph; (300SL coupe) 145-165 mph Acceleration (0-60 mph): (300Sc) 12-13 sec.; (300SL coupe) 7.6-8.8 sec.

PRODUCTION/SALES: Approximately 3,000 Mercedes-Benz passenger cars were sold in the U.S. in 1957.

Manufacturer: Daimler-Benz AG, Stuttgart, West Germany.

Distributor: Mercedes-Benz Sales, Inc. (Studebaker-Packard Corp.), South Bend, Indiana.

HISTORY

"Whoever sees the Mercedes-Benz Type 190SL for the first time gets the urge to step in and speed away; such is the stunning beauty of this car." That was its beauty in the eyes of Mercedes-Benz copywriters, at any rate. By 1957, Studebaker-Packard was handling distribution of Mercedes-Benz automobiles in the U.S. The roadster version of the 300SL appeared at the London show in October 1957, and was available in the U.S. for the 1958 model year. Dealers complained when the 300 Series was about to be cancelled, so a 300d version arrived late in 1957. See next year for details on both models.

1958-1959

180 SERIES — FOUR — Production of the 180a sedan, introduced during 1957, continued with little change. The 1,897 cc engine developed 74 horsepower. Upholstery was new for 1958, including duo-tone door trim and padded sun visors. A 180b edition with extra horsepower debuted during the 1959 model year. Also introduced during the 1959 model year was a 180Db version of the diesel.

190 SERIES — FOUR — Little was new in the 190 sedan, except that a 190b edition with more power arrived late in the 1959 model year. A diesel version debuted during the 1958 model year, with a 55-bhp engine. In 1959, the 190SL engine was upgraded to 8.8:1 compression and the hardtop got a larger back window.

219/220 SERIES — SIX — Production of the 220S and 219 continued into 1958-59 with little change, powered by the more potent engines introduced during 1957. For the 1959 model year, they were joined by a 220SE Series (sedan, cabriolet, and coupe) with fuel-injected engine. Rear license plate lighting was now in the bumper guards. A Hydrak automatic clutch with fluid flywheel was optional, allowing two-pedal operation.

300 SERIES — SIX — After an absence of more than a year, a 300d version of the 300 Series debuted for 1958. Restyling gave it a more modern look, without sacrificing the "classic" design. New tail lamps went into rear fenders. The 300d had a fuel-injected engine and a slightly revised body, with longer

1958 300SC

1958 190 diesel

(124-inch) wheelbase. The roofline was flatter and more square; rear fenders longer; grille a tad wider. The sedan was now actually a four-door hardtop (without pillars). The fuel-injected engine developed 160 horsepower DIN (180 SAE). Either leather or fabric upholstery was available. A Borg-Warner three-speed automatic transmission was now standard (manual shift on special order). American versions got a 5.11:1 axle ratio for better acceleration. A total of 3,077 sedans were built through early 1962, but only 65 convertible sedans (all to special order). The 300Sc Series faded away early in 1958 (see previous year for details).

300SL — SIX — By the 1958 model year, a 300SL roadster replaced the Gullwing coupe. With its tubular frame lowered, the roadster used conventional front-hinged doors. Engine displacement remained the same, but the overhead-cam six got a 10-bhp boost via an increase in compression ratio (to 9.5:1). The roadster used a low-pivot swing axle with transverse compensating spring, as in the Mercedes W196 Grand Prix racing car, which improved handling. Parking lamps no longer were separate and round, but now sat in bright housings below the headlamps. European-spec cars had big "bubble" headlamp housings. The roadster's windshield was more rounded than that used in the Gullwing coupe. A removable steel hardtop became optional, with a deep sloping wraparound window. The standard 300SL roadster had a rear-axle ratio of 3.64:1. Four other ratios were available: 3.25:1, 3.42:1, 3.89:1, or 4.11:1.

I.D. DATA: Chassis serial number is on the right side of the firewall. Engine number is on top, or on right side of block.

ENGINES

Base Four (190SL): Inline, overhead-cam four-cylinder. Cast-iron block. Displacement: 116 cid (1,897 cc). Bore & stroke: 3.35 x 3.29 in. (85 x 83.6 mm). Compression ratio: 8.5:1 (8.8:1 in 1959). Brake horsepower: 105 (DIN) at 5,700 rpm (120 SAE at 5,800 rpm). Torque: 105 lbs.-ft. (DIN) at 3,200 rpm. Solid valve lifters. Two Solex carburetors.

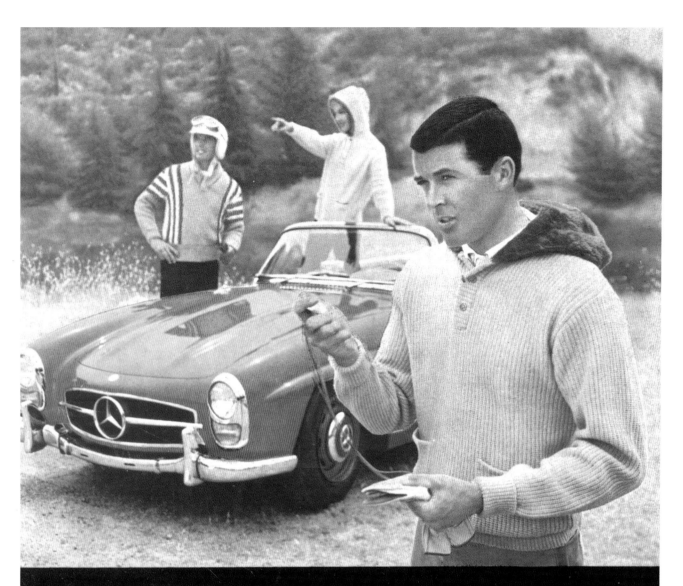

FOR EVERY STATE OF ACTION...

the california look of
Catalina® sweaters

Geared for the fast road—Catalina sweaters that qualify quick for race or rallye. Smart at every turn, they're warm, but light enough to leave you free for speed and action.

In the foreground is "Thunderhead," a ribbed, bulky knit with fleece-lined hood. $15.95

Standing in the 300SL, her sweater matches his to make a team —same smartness, same warm fleecy hood. $15.98

Then there's "Campus Leader," a brightly striped, masculine knit, with trim shawl collar. $16.95

Another bright new starter is Catalina's "Collegian Rambler"...trimmed inset, convertible shawl collar. $11.95

1958 Catalina sweater ad

Model	Body Type & Seating	Engine Type/CID	P.O.E. Price	Weight (lbs.)	Production Total
180 SERIES					
180a	4-dr Sedan-5/6P	I4/116	$3,240	2,570	Note 1
180D (Diesel)	4-dr Sedan-5/6P	I4/108	$3,517	2,645	Note 1
190 SERIES					
190	4-dr Sedan-5/6P	I4/116	$3,431	2,645	Note 1
190D (Diesel)	4-dr Sedan-5/6P	I4/116	$3,708	N/A	Note 1
190SL	2-dr Roadster-2P	I4/116	$5,020	2,515	Note 2
190SL	2-dr HT Coupe-2P	I4/116	$5,232	2,515	Note 2
219 SERIES					
219	4-dr Sedan-5/6P	I6/134	$3,823	2,780	Note 1
220 SERIES					
220S	4-dr Sedan-5/6P	I6/134	$4,283	2,955	Note 1
220S	2-dr Conv-2/3P	I6/134	$7,641	3,065	Note 1
220S	2-dr Conv-4/5P	I6/134	N/A	3,065	Note 1
220SE	4-dr Sedan-5/6P	I6/134	N/A	3,014	Note 3
220SE	2-dr Conv-2/3P	I6/134	N/A	N/A	Note 3
220SE	2-dr Conv-4/5P	I6/134	N/A	N/A	Note 3
300 SERIES					
300d	4-dr HT Sedan-6P	I6/183	$10,418	4,400	Note 1
300d	4-dr Conv-6P	I6/183	$13,655	N/A	Note 1
300SL					
300SL	2-dr Roadster-2P	I6/183	$10,928	3,000	Note 4

Note 1: A total of 99,209 Mercedes-Benz cars (all models) were produced during 1958 and 108,440 in 1959.
Note 2: A total of 25,881 190SL models were produced during the full model run, 1955-63.
Note 3: A total of 1,974 220SE four-door sedans were produced over the full model run (through 1960), plus 1,942 two-door models.
Note 4: A total of 1,858 300SL roadsters were produced during the full model run, from late 1957 into 1963.
Price Note: Figures shown were valid in 1958 and 1959, except 190D was not listed for sale in U.S. until 1959. A "convertible coupe" version of the 300SL roadster (with hardtop) sold for $11,106.
Production Note: See previous listing for additional breakdowns.

1958 190SL

Base Four (180a): Same as 1,897 cc four, except Compression ratio: 6.8:1. Brake horsepower: 74 (SAE) at 4,700 rpm. Torque: 104 lbs.-ft. at 2,800 rpm. Solex carburetor.

Base Four (190 sedan): Same as 1,897 cc four, except Compression ratio: 7.5:1. Brake horsepower: 84 (SAE) at 4,800 rpm. Torque: 107 lbs.-ft. at 2,500 rpm.

Note: A 190b sedan debuted during 1959 with a 90-bhp engine.

Diesel Note: The diesel version of the 1,897 cc engine produced 55 horsepower (SAE) at 4,000 rpm in the 190D on 21:1 compression. The 180D Series continued to use a 1,767 cc diesel rated at 46 horsepower (SAE) with 19:1 compression.

Base Six (219, 220S): Inline, overhead-cam six-cylinder. Cast-iron block. Displacement: 133.9 cid (2,195 cc). Bore & stroke: 3.15 x 2.87 in. (80 x 72.8 mm). Compression ratio: 8.7:1. Brake horsepower: (219) 100 (SAE) at 5,000 rpm; (220S) 120 (SAE) at 5,000 rpm. Torque: (219) 130 lbs.-ft. at 2,700 rpm; (220S) 137 lbs.-ft. at 3,600 rpm. Solid valve lifters. One carburetor except (220S) two Solex 32 PAJAT carburetors.

Base Six (220SE): Same as 2,195 cc six, but with Bosch mechanical fuel injection. Brake horsepower: 115 DIN (130 SAE at 5,000 rpm). Torque: 146 lbs.-ft. (SAE) at 3,800 rpm.

Base Six (300d): Inline, overhead-cam six-cylinder. Cast-iron block and aluminum head. Displacement: 182.8 cid (2,996 cc). Bore & stroke: 3.35 x 3.46 in. (85 x 88 mm). Compression ratio: 8.5:1. Brake horsepower: 160 DIN (180 SAE at 5,500 rpm). Torque: 191.7 lbs.-ft. (SAE) at 4,500 rpm. Seven main bearings. Solid valve lifters.

Base Six (300SL): Same as 2,996 cc six, above, with Bosch fuel injection. Compression ratio: 9.5:1. Brake horsepower: 225 (DIN) at 5,900 rpm (250 SAE at 6,200 rpm). Torque: 228 lbs.-ft. (SAE) at 5,000 rpm.

CHASSIS

Wheelbase: (180a) 104.3 in.; (190 sedan) 104.3 in.; (190SL) 94.5 in.; (220S sedan) 111 in.; (220S conv) 106.3 in.; (219) 108.25 in.; (300d) 124 in.; (300SL) 94.5 in. Overall length: (180a) 175.6 in.; (190 sedan) 176.6 in.; (190SL) 165 in.; (220S sedan) 185.5 in.; (220S conv) 185 in.; (219) 182.7 in.; (300d) 204.3 in.; (300SL) 178 in. Height: (180a) 61.4 in.; (190 sedan) 61.4 in.; (190SL) 52 in.; (220S sedan) 61.6 in.; (220S conv) 60.3 in.; (300d) 63.5 in.; (300SL) 51.3 in. Width: (180a/190/190SL/219/220S sedan) 68.5 in.; (220S conv) 70.5 in.; (300d) 73.25 in.; (300SL) 70.5 in. Front tread: (180a) 55.9 in.; (190 sedan) 54.1 in.; (190SL) 56 in.; (220S conv) 56.3 in.; (300d) 59.2 in.; (300SL) 53.5 in. Rear tread: (180a) 57.5 in.; (190 sedan) 57.9 in.; (190SL) 55 in.; (220S conv) 57.9 in.; (300d) 60.4 in.; (300SL) 57 in. Standard tires: (180/190/190SL/219) 6.40x13; (220S sedan) 6.70x13; (219) 6.40x13; (300D) 7.60x15; (300SL) 6.50/6.70x15.

1958 220S coupe

MERCEDES-BENZ

Perennial Favorite Famed for Beauty and Breeding... Mercedes-Benz cars. The evolution of Mercedes-Benz proceeds towards perfection with no wasteful haste. This new Mercedes-Benz 190 has many refinements invisible to the camera ...in the engine, running gear, suspension. The only visible change is in the grille where classic treatment has received but a touch more of modernity. Thus, by maintaining a steady tempo of superior engineering advances and design development, Mercedes-Benz is more than ever the car of connoisseurs, bearing the silver three-pointed star more triumphantly than ever.

MERCEDES-BENZ SALES, INC. (A Subsidiary of Studebaker-Packard Corporation)
Sedans, convertibles, sports cars...prices range from about $3,300 to $13,000.

1959 190 ad

1959 cabriolet

TECHNICAL
Similar to 1956-57.

MAJOR OPTIONS: Hydrak automatic clutch: 220S/219 ($165).

PERFORMANCE

Top Speed: (180D) 69 mph claimed; (190 sedan) 87 mph claimed; (190D) 75 mph; (190SL) 105-113 mph; (220S) 100 mph claimed; (300d) 105 mph; (300SL roadster) 129-155 mph claimed. Acceleration (0-60 mph): (190D) 31 sec.; (190SL) 11.0 sec.; (220S) about 15 sec.; (300SL) about 7 sec. Acceleration (quarter-mile): (190D) 28.9 sec. (57 mph).

PRODUCTION/SALES: Approximately 13,739 Mercedes-Benz passenger cars were sold in the U.S. in 1959.

Manufacturer: Daimler-Benz AG, Stuttgart, West Germany.

Distributor: Mercedes-Benz Sales, Inc. (Studebaker-Packard Corp.), South Bend, Indiana.

HISTORY

At the London Motor Show in October 1957, Mercedes-Benz literature explained that "the dynamic flow lines of its sprawling body are the outward promise of the pent-up power which the Type 300SL roadster can release within the second, in response to your command." *Sports Cars Illustrated* tested a 300SL roadster with 3.89:1 axle, achieving 0-60 mph acceleration in 7.8 seconds and hitting 100 mph in 19.2 seconds, with a 124-mph top speed. *Road & Track* managed to accelerate to 60 mph in 7.6 seconds, but took 20.5 seconds to reach 100 mph.

1960 SL roadster

1960-1962

180 SERIES — FOUR — The new 180b sedan had a slightly more powerful version of the 1,897 cc engine, as well as a lower hood, wider radiator, and larger tail lamp cluster than the 180a. The 180Db diesel differed little from its predecessor, but the 180Dc edition that arrived during 1961 added extra horsepower.

190 SERIES — FOUR — During 1959, a 190b sedan replaced the original 190, and a 190Db replaced the 190D diesel. Except for a horsepower increase in the gasoline engine, little was new for 1960. By this time, the 190SL's optional lift-off hardtop had a wraparound rear window. Restyling prior to the 1962 model year produced a 190c (and 190Dc) sedan with the same engines, but a more boxy body on a 106.3-inch wheelbase.

219/220 SERIES — SIX — By 1960, a 220b replaced the 219 sedan, a 220SB sedan replaced the 220S, and a 220SEb Series replaced the 220SE. The overhead-cam 2195 cc engine added a few horsepower in each version. All models had wraparound front and rear windows, with a vertically styled headlamp/parking-light unit, and horizontal tail lamps below subtle but sharp-edged tailfins.

300 SERIES — SIX — Production of the 300d sedan continued with little change, until early 1962. A 300SE Series was added during 1961, powered by a 160-bhp (185 bhp SAE) version of the 2,996 cc overhead-cam engine. Wheelbase was only 108.3 inches, comparable to the 220 Series.

300SL — SIX — Production of the two-seat roadster continued, with little change, into 1963.

I.D. DATA: Chassis serial number is on the right side of the firewall. Engine number is on top, or on right front of block.

ENGINES

Base Four (190SL): Inline, overhead-cam four-cylinder. Cast-iron block. Displacement: 116 cid (1,897 cc). Bore & stroke: 3.35 x 3.29 in. (85 x 83.6 mm). Compression ratio: 8.5:1 (8.8:1 in 1959). Brake horsepower: 105 (DIN) at 5,700 rpm (120 SAE at 5,800 rpm). Torque: 114 lbs.-ft. (SAE) at 3,800 rpm. Solid valve lifters. Two Solex carburetors.

Base Four (180b/180c): Same as 1,897 cc four, except Compression ratio: 7.0:1. Brake horsepower: 78 (SAE) at 4,500 rpm. Torque: 107 lbs.-ft. at 2,500 rpm.

Base Four (190b sedan): Same as 1,897 cc four, except Compression ratio: 8.5:1. Brake horsepower: 90 (SAE) at 5,000 rpm. Torque: 111 lbs.-ft. at 3,000 rpm.

Diesel Note: The diesel version of the 1,897 cc engine produced 55 horsepower (SAE) at 4,000 rpm in the 190D Series, on 21:1 compression. A 1,767 cc diesel was installed in the 180D Series until mid-1961, rated 43 horsepower DIN (46 SAE) with 19:1 compression. After that came 180Dc and 190Dc versions with 1,987 cc engines, rated 48/55 bhp DIN (52/60 bhp SAE).

Base Six (220 SERIES): Inline, overhead-cam six-cylinder. Cast-iron block. Displacement: 133.9 cid (2,195 cc). Bore & stroke: 3.15 x 2.87 in. (80 x 72.8 mm). Compression ratio: 8.7:1. Brake horsepower: (220b) 105 (SAE) at 5,000 rpm; (220Sb) 124 at 5,200 rpm; (220SEb) 134 at 5,000 rpm. Torque: (220b)

133 lbs.-ft. at 3,000 rpm; (220Sb) 139 lbs.- ft. at 3,700 rpm; (220SEb) 152 lbs.-ft. at 4,100 rpm. Solid valve lifters. Two Solex carburetors except (220SE). Bosch fuel injection.

Base Six (300d): Inline, overhead-cam six-cylinder. Cast-iron block and aluminum head. Displacement: 182.8 cid (2,996 cc). Bore & stroke: 3.35 x 3.46 in. (85 x 88 mm). Compression ratio: 8.5:1. Brake horsepower: 180 (SAE) at 5,500 rpm. Torque: 192 lbs.-ft. at 4,500 rpm. Seven main bearings. Solid valve lifters. Bosch fuel injection.

Base Six (300SE): Same as 2,996 cc six above, except Compression ratio: 9.0:1. Brake horsepower: 185 (SAE) at

5,200 rpm. Torque: 205 lbs.-ft. at 4,000 rpm.

Base Six (300SL): Same as 2,996 cc six, with Bosch fuel injection. Compression ratio: 9.5:1. Brake horsepower: 225 (DIN) at 5,900 rpm (250 SAE at 6,200 rpm). Torque: 228 lbs.-ft. (SAE) at 5,000 rpm.

CHASSIS

Wheelbase: (180b) 104.3 in.; (190b sedan) 104.3 in.; (190c sedan) 106.3 in.; (190SL) 94.5 in.; (220b/220Sb) 108.3 in.; (220SEb coupe/conv) 106.3 in.; (220SEb sedan) 108.3 in.; (300d) 124 in.; (300SE) 108.3 in.; (300SL) 94.5 in. Overall

MODEL	BODY TYPE & SEATING	ENGINE TYPE/CID	P.O.E. PRICE	WEIGHT (LBS.)	PRODUCTION TOTAL
180 SERIES					
180b	4-dr Sedan-5/6P	I4/116	$3,250	2,570	**Note 1**
180Db (Diesel)	4-dr Sedan-5/6P	I4/108	$3,527	2,670	**Note 1**
190 SERIES					
190b	4-dr Sedan-5/6P	I4/116	$3,441	2,645	**Note 1**
190Db (Diesel)	4-dr Sedan-5/6P	I4/116	$3,718	2,670	**Note 1**
190SL	2-dr Roadster-2P	I4/116	$5,032	2,500	**Note 2**
190SL	2-dr HT Coupe-2P	I4/116	$5,244	2,500	**Note 2**
220 SERIES					
220b	4-dr Sedan-5/6P	I6/134	$4,283	2,890	**Note 1**
220Sb	4-dr Sedan-5/6P	I6/134	$4,583	2,940	**Note 1**
220SEb	4-dr Sedan-5/6P	I6/134	$5,018	2,980	**Note 1**
220SEb	2-dr Coupe-4P	I6/134	$8,091	3,020	**Note 1**
220SEb	2-dr Conv	I6/134	$8,091	3,095	**Note 1**
300 SERIES					
300d	4-dr HT Sedan-6P	I6/183	$10,070	4,400	**Note 1**
300d	4-dr Conv Sedan-6P	I6/183	$12,644	4,585	**Note 1**
300SE	4-dr Sedan-6P	I6/183	N/A	3,650	**Note 1**
300SE	2-dr Cabriolet-5/6P	I6/183	N/A	N/A	**Note 1**
300SE	2-dr Coupe-5/6P	I6/183	N/A	N/A	**Note 1**
300SL					
300SL	2-dr Roadster-2P	I6/183	$10,950	3,000	**Note 3**

Note 1: A total of 122,684 Mercedes-Benz cars (all models) were produced during 1960, followed by 137,431 in 1961, and 146,393 in 1962.
Note 2: A total of 25,881 190SL models were produced during the full model run, 1955-63.
Note 3: A total of 1,858 300SL roadsters were produced during the full model run, 1957-63.
Price note: Figures shown were valid in 1960 and 1961.

1961 300SE

1962 300SE fintail

It's a diesel   ...it's a gas.

There is nothing prettier than a Mercedes-Benz.

Unless it's two of them. Consider the beauties above. Identical except for the wonderful power plants under the bonnets.

At left, the 190 D. The "D" stands for diesel and for extra distance.

At right, the similarly elegant 190, with gasoline engine.

Now, if you drive 20,000 to 30,000 miles per year the 190 D may be for you. Here's real class with smart, business-like economy.

Proved, too. One of the country's top petroleum marketers recently put this car through a 7,000 mile fuel consumption test in a big city.

The 190 D traveled up to 39 miles per gallon in regular city traffic and up to 43.9 miles per gallon over the big city expressways!

And remember—diesel fuel, available practically everywhere, costs about 40% less than gasoline.

But if the idea of a diesel is a little too advanced to digest right now, you might think of the 190.

Here is the same classic beauty. The same quiet, enduring design. Simply runs on gasoline (22 m.p.g., too). That's the difference.

Automatic transmission, if you want, both models.

MERCEDES-BENZ

GOING TO EUROPE? FOR TRAVEL GUIDE, WRITE HANS VON BROCKHUSEN, MERCEDES-BENZ OF NORTH AMERICA, INC., 158 LINWOOD PLAZA, FORT LEE, N. J., 07024
MERCEDES-BENZ OF NORTH AMERICA, INC. A SUBSIDIARY OF DAIMLER-BENZ A. G., GERMANY

190 ad

length: (180b) 177.2 in.; (190b sedan) 177.2 in.; (190SL) 166 in.; (220b/220Sb) 192.2 in.; (220SEb coupe/conv) 185 in.; (220SEb sedan) 192.2 in.; (300d) 204.3 in.; (300SE) 192 in.; (300SL) 179.9 in. Height: (180b/190b sedan) 61.4 in.; (190SL) 52 in.; (220Sb) 59.5 in.; (300d) 64 in.; (300SE) 57.5 in.; (300SL) 51.3 in. Width: (180b/190b/190SL) 68.5 in.; (220b) 70.7 in.; (300d) 73.25 in.; (300SL) 70.5 in. Front tread: (180b/190b) 56.3 in.; (190SL) 56.3 in.; (220Sb) 57.9 in.; (300d) 58.3 in.; (300SE) 58.3 in.; (300SL) 55.5 in. Rear tread: (180b/190b) 58.1 in.; (190SL) 57.9 in.; (220Sb) 58.5 in.; (300d) 60.0 in.; (300SE) 58.6 in.; (300SL) 57 in. Standard tires: (180b/190b/190SL) 6.40x13; (220Sb) 7.25x13; (300d) 7.60x15; (300SE) 7.50x13; (300SL) 6.50/6.70x15.

TECHNICAL

Layout: front-engine, rear-drive. Transmission: four-speed manual or (300 Series) three-speed automatic. Suspension (front): upper/lower A-arms with coil springs. Suspension (rear): swing axles with coil springs. Brakes: front/rear drum except (late 220S/SE) front disc, rear drum.

MAJOR OPTIONS: Automatic transmission: 300 Series ($985). Bench-type rear seat: 220SE ($93).

PERFORMANCE: Similar to 1958-59.

PRODUCTION/SALES: Approximately 14,435 Mercedes-Benz passenger cars were sold in the U.S. in 1960, 12,903 in 1961, and 11,075 in 1962.

Manufacturer: Daimler-Benz AG, Stuttgart, West Germany.

Distributor: Mercedes-Benz Sales, Inc. (Studebaker-Packard Corp.), South Bend, Indiana.

HISTORY

"The engineering and construction of Mercedes-Benz is aimed at perfection," claimed advertisements in 1961. "This 300SL, for example, starts its life as an entirely hand-built space frame. Its tubes are cut, balanced, and welded by devoted craftsmen. Its brakes and wheels are added carefully. Then its hand-welded body slips firmly over the geometric symmetry of its skeleton. Finally, its fuel-injection powerplant, fresh from its test bench, is lowered into place. Then the 300SL is road tested and checked with a thoroughness that leaves no secrets." Daimler-Benz celebrated its Diamond Jubilee in 1961, electing a new chairman: Walter Hitzinger.

A 300 Automatic, declared *Motor Trend* in 1961, "combines maximum dignity and impressiveness with minimum ostentation." Its "interior is a symphony in tasteful luxury." As for the 220S coupe, its "woodwork and leather are works of art."

1963

180 SERIES — FOUR — Production of the 180c sedan ceased in 1963, and the diesel version even earlier, though both continued to be listed in some directories of imported vehicles this year.

190 SERIES — FOUR — This would be the final year for the 190SL roadster. Production of the 190 Series sedans continued with little change.

220 SERIES — SIX — Production of the 'b' Series models continued with little change, each powered by a variant of the 2,195 cc overhead-cam engine.

230SL — SIX — In 1963, Mercedes-Benz introduced its replacement (more or less) for the 190/300SL. The "pagoda-roof" 230SL roadster (code W113) debuted at the Geneva Auto Show in Switzerland. Rather than a sports car per se, the 230SL ranked as a sports tourer, comparable to the 190SL in size and performance, but more posh. The engine and monocoque body/chassis came from the sedans that debuted in 1959. The overhead-cam six had been used in the 220SE, but bored to 2,308 cc displacement in this installation. Multi-point Bosch fuel injection was used instead of the former single-point system, boosting horsepower by 30 (DIN). The low-pivot swing-axle rear suspension included a transverse camber-compensating spring. Girling front disc brakes were installed, with rear drums (vacuum assisted). Though not much

longer than the 190SL, this new version was considerably heavier. It was also available with a four-speed Daimler-Benz semi-automatic transmission, which included a fluid coupling but no torque converter. The all-synchro four-speed manual gearbox remained standard. Styling was much more angular than on the 190/300SL, kin to the sedans, but the grille with its large center tri-star was similar to prior installations. The optional hardtop's "pagoda" roofline curved upward a bit at the side. Leather upholstery was included.

300 SERIES — SIX — The big 300d Series was gone, but the short 300SE continued, joined this year by a longer 300SEL on a 112.2-inch wheelbase.

300SL — SIX — This was the final year for the 300SL roadster.

I.D. DATA: Chassis serial number is on the right side of the firewall (230SL), or on right front fender skirt or hood lock panel. Engine number is on right front of block.

ENGINES

Base Four (190SL): Inline, overhead-cam four-cylinder. Cast-iron block. Displacement: 116 cid (1,897 cc). Bore & stroke: 3.35 x 3.29 in. (85 x 83.6 mm). Compression ratio: 8.8:1. Brake horsepower: 105 (DIN) at 5,700 rpm (120 SAE at 5,800 rpm). Torque: 105 lbs.-ft. (DIN) at 3,200 rpm.

Model	Body Type & Seating	Engine Type/CID	P.O.E. Price	Weight (lbs.)	Production Total
180 SERIES					
180c	4-dr Sedan-5/6P	I4/116	$3,484	2,429	**Note 1**
180Dc (Diesel)	4-dr Sedan-5/6P	I4/121	$3,704	2,550	**Note 1**
190 SERIES					
190c	4-dr Sedan-6P	I4/116	$3,844	2,629	**Note 1**
190Dc (Diesel)	4-dr Sedan-6P	I4/121	$4,047	2,739	**Note 1**
190SL	2-dr Roadster-2P	I4/116	$5,215	2,458	**Note 2**
190SL	2-dr HT Coupe-2P	I4/116	$5,443	2,505	**Note 2**
220 SERIES					
220b	4-dr Sedan-5/6P	I6/134	$4,349	2,739	**Note 1**
220Sb	4-dr Sedan-5/6P	I6/134	$4,818	2,833	**Note 1**
220SEb	4-dr Sedan-5/6P	I6/134	$5,187	2,877	**Note 1**
220SEb	2-dr Coupe	I6/134	$8,761	2,901	**Note 1**
220SEb	2-dr Conv	I6/134	$9,562	3,190	**Note 1**
230SL					
230SL	2-dr Roadster-2P	I6/141	N/A	2,900	**Note 3**
230SL	2-dr Coupe-2P	I6/141	N/A	N/A	**Note 3**
300 SERIES					
300SE	4-dr Sedan-6P	I6/183	$8,662	3,531	**Note 1**
300SE	2-dr Cabriolet-5P	I6/183	N/A	N/A	**Note 1**
300SE	2-dr Coupe-5P	I6/183	N/A	3,452	**Note 1**
300SEL	4-dr Sedan-6P	I6/183	N/A	3,600	**Note 1**
300SL					
300SL	2-dr Roadster-2P	I6/183	$11,099	2,811	**Note 4**

Note 1: A total of 153,182 Mercedes-Benz cars (all models) were produced during 1963.
Note 2: A total of 25,881 190SL models were produced during the full model run, 1955-63.
Note 3: A total of 19,831 230SL models were produced during the full model run, 1963-66.
Note 4: A total of 1,858 300SL roadsters were produced during the full model run, 1957-63.

The new Mercedes-Benz 220SE Coupe...and why aren't you in the picture?

This Mercedes-Benz Invites You to Europe as its Guest

More than 60,000 owners of Mercedes-Benz motorcars in this country can tell you about substantial savings in fuel, in routine maintenance, in repairs. They will happily confide that, instead of trading in every two or three years, they prefer to keep on enjoying their Mercedes-Benz and keep their money in the bank.

But you can enjoy still another advantage in Mercedes-Benz. Arrange with your dealer to take delivery in Europe...the dollar savings can pay for a glorious vacation.

We suggest you visit him, and ask for the figures. And while you are there, take a drive behind the three-pointed silver star!

Mercedes-Benz Sales, Inc.
(A Subsidiary of Studebaker Corporation)
South Bend, Indiana

1963 220SE ad

Base Four (180c): Same as 1,897 cc four above, except Compression ratio: 7.0:1. Brake horsepower: 78 (SAE) at 4,500 rpm. Torque: 107 lbs.-ft. at 2,500 rpm.

Base Four (190c sedan): Same as 1,897 cc four above, except Compression ratio: 8.7:1. Brake horsepower: 90 (SAE) at 5,000 rpm. Torque: 111 lbs.-ft. at 3,000 rpm.

Diesel Four (180Dc, 190Dc): Displacement: 121.2 cid (1,987 cc). Bore & stroke: 3.42 x 3.29 in. (87 x 83.6 mm). Compression ratio: 21:1. Brake horsepower: (180Dc) 52 at 3,800 rpm; (190Dc) 60 at 4,200 rpm.

Base Six (220 SERIES): Inline, overhead-cam six-cylinder. Cast-iron block. Displacement: 133.9 cid (2,195 cc). Bore & stroke: 3.15 x 2.87 in. (80 x 72.8 mm). Compression ratio: 8.7:1. Brake horsepower: (220b) 105 (SAE) at 5,000 rpm; (220Sb) 124 at 5,200 rpm; (220SEb) 134 at 5,000 rpm. Torque: (220b) 133 lbs.-ft. at 3,000 rpm; (220Sb) 139 lbs.- ft. at 3,700 rpm; (220SEb) 152 lbs.-ft. at 4,100 rpm. Four main bearings. Solid valve lifters. Two carburetors except (220SE) fuel injection.

Base Six (230SL): Inline, overhead-cam six-cylinder. Cast-iron block and aluminum head. Displacement: 140.8 cid (2,308 cc). Bore & stroke: 3.23 x 2.87 in. (82 x 73 mm). Compression ratio: 9.3:1. Brake horsepower: 170 (SAE) at 5,500 rpm. Torque: 159 lbs.-ft. at 4,500 rpm. Four main bearings. Solid valve lifters. Bosch multi-point fuel injection.

Base Six (300SE): Inline, overhead-cam six-cylinder. Cast-iron block and aluminum head. Displacement: 183 cid (2,996 cc). Bore & stroke: 3.35 x 3.46 in. (85 x 88 mm). Compression ratio: 9.0:1. Brake horsepower: 185 (SAE) at 5,200 rpm. Torque: 205 lbs.-ft. at 4,000 rpm. Seven main bearings. Solid valve lifters.

Base Six (300SEL): Same as 2,996 cc six above, except Compression ratio: 195 at 5,500 rpm. Torque: 203 lbs.-ft. at 4,100 rpm.

Base Six (300SL): Same as 2,996 cc six above, with Bosch fuel injection. Compression ratio: 9.5:1. Brake horsepower: 225 (DIN) at 5,900 rpm (250 SAE at 6,200 rpm). Torque: 228 lbs.-ft. (SAE) at 5,000 rpm.

CHASSIS

Wheelbase: (180) 104.5 in.; (190 sedan) 106.3 in.; (190SL) 94.5 in.; (220/220S) 108.3 in.; (230SL) 94.5 in.; (300SE) 108.3 in.; (300SEL) 112.2 in.; (300SL) 94.5 in. Overall length: (180) 177.2 in.; (190 sedan) 186.5 in.; (190SL) 166 in.; (220 sedan) 192.2 in.; (230SL) 169 in.; (300SE) 192.2 in.; (300SL) 179.9 in. Height: (190 sedan) 58.8 in.; (190SL) 52 in.; (220 sedan) 59.5 in.; (220 coupe) 56.0 in.; (300SE sedan) 57.5 in.; (300SE coupe) 55.7 in. Width: (180) 68.5 in.; (190 sedan) 68.5 in.; (190SL) 68.5 in.; (220) 70.7 in.; (230SL) 69.3 in.; (300SE) 73.25 in.; (300SL) 70.5 in. Standard tires: (180) 6.40x13; (190 sedan) 7.00x13; (190SL) 6.40x13; (220) 7.25x13; (230SL) 185x14; (300SE) 7.60x15; (300SL) 6.50x15.

TECHNICAL

Layout: front-engine, rear-drive. Transmission: four-speed manual (automatic standard on 300, optional on other models). Suspension (front): upper/lower A-arms with coil springs. Suspension (rear): swing axles with coil springs. Brakes: front/rear drum except (230SL) front disc, rear drum.

MAJOR OPTIONS: Automatic transmission.

PERFORMANCE: Top Speed: (230SL) 114-124 mph Acceleration (0-60 mph): (230SL) 9.9-10.7 sec. Acceleration (quarter-mile): (230SL) 17-18 sec.

PRODUCTION/SALES: Approximately 11,234 Mercedes-Benz passenger cars were sold in the U.S. in 1963.

Manufacturer: Daimler-Benz AG, Stuttgart, West Germany.

Distributor: Mercedes-Benz Sales, Inc. (Studebaker-Packard Corp.), South Bend, Indiana.

HISTORY

A 230SL won the Spa-Sofia-Liege rally in its first year. This would be the final year for distribution by the Studebaker-Packard dealer organization.

1964-1965

190 SERIES — FOUR — The 180 Series sedan was gone, but the 190 remained, in both gasoline- and diesel-powered form. This would be the final year for the 190 sedans.

220 SERIES — SIX — Three models (220b, 220Sb, and 220SEb) were identical in wheelbase and interior dimension, differing in equipment and performance. An automatic transmission was optional; front disc brakes were standard on 220S/SE. The 2,195 cc engine became available with fuel injection.

230SL — SIX — Production of the Mercedes two-seat sports car, introduced in 1963, continued with little change. As usual, the 'SL' suffix stood for Super Light, meaning that doors, trunk, and hood were made of aluminum. Under the hood was a 2,308 cc six-cylinder engine with fuel injection, hooked to a four-speed manual gearbox. A four-speed automatic transmission was optional, using a fluid coupling rather than a torque converter. The front end, with its large tri-star emblem in the center of the single horizontal grille bar, was similar to prior 190/300SL models, even though the angular body differed considerably from predecessors.

300SE — SIX — The full-size Mercedes came in four-door sedan, long four-door sedan, coupe, and convertible form. Standard equipment included an air suspension, automatic transmission, and power steering.

600/PULLMAN — GRAND MERCEDES — V-8 — Mercedes-Benz' largest model, the 600 Pullman seven-passenger limousine, rode a 153.5-inch wheelbase and measured 246 inches overall. Power came from a 6.3-liter V-8 engine that developed 300 horsepower. A shorter-wheelbase 600 also became available. Both were offered on special order in the U.S. market. Styling was similar to the 300SE, with a sharper-edged roofline and back window. The 600 Series lacked chrome bodyside trim strips, but front/rear wheel openings, rocker panels, and pillar posts all had chrome trim. A four-speed automatic transmission with column lever was standard.

I.D. DATA: Chassis serial number is on the right fender skirt or hood lock panel; or on the right side of the firewall (230SL). Engine number is on right side of block.

ENGINES

Base Four (190): Inline, overhead-cam four-cylinder. Cast-iron block and aluminum head. Displacement: 116 cid (1,897 cc). Bore & stroke: 3.35 x 3.29 in. (85 x 83.6 mm). Compression ratio: 8.7:1. Brake horsepower: 90 (SAE) at 5,200 rpm. Torque: 113 lbs.-ft. at 2,700 rpm. Three main bearings. Solid valve lifters.

Diesel Four (190D): Inline, overhead-cam four-cylinder. Displacement: 121.3 cid (1,988 cc). Bore & stroke: 3.43 x 3.29 in. (87 x 83.6 mm). Compression ratio: 21.0:1. Brake horsepower: 60 at 4,200 rpm. Torque: 87 lbs.-ft. at 2,400 rpm. Fuel injection.

Base Six (220, 220S, 220SE): Inline, overhead-cam six-cylinder. Cast-iron block and aluminum head. Displacement: 133.9 cid (2,195 cc). Bore & stroke: 3.15 x 2.87 in. (80 x 72.8 mm). Compression ratio: 8.7:1. Brake horsepower: (220S) 124 at 5,200 rpm; (220SE) 134 at 5,000 rpm. Torque: (220S) 139 lbs.-ft. at 3,700 rpm; (220SE) 152 lbs.-ft. at 4,100 rpm. Four main bearings. Solid valve lifters.

Base Six (230SL): Inline, overhead-cam six-cylinder. Cast-iron block and aluminum head. Displacement: 140.8 cid (2,308 cc). Bore & stroke: 3.23 x 2.87 in. (82 x 73 mm). Compression ratio: 9.3:1. Brake horsepower: 170 (SAE) at 5,600 rpm. Torque: 159 lbs.-ft. at 4,500 rpm. Four main bearings. Solid valve lifters. Bosch multi-point fuel injection.

MODEL	BODY TYPE & SEATING	ENGINE TYPE/CID	P.O.E. PRICE	WEIGHT (LBS.)	PRODUCTION TOTAL
190 SERIES					
190c	4-dr Sedan-5/6P	I4/116	$3,844	2,629	**Note 1**
190Dc (Diesel)	4-dr Sedan-5/6P	I4/121	$4,047	2,739	**Note 1**
220 SERIES					
220b	4-dr Sedan-5/6P	I6/134	$4,349	2,833	**Note 1**
220Sb	4-dr Sedan-5/6P	I6/134	$4,818	2,833	**Note 1**
220SEb	4-dr Sedan-5/6P	I6/134	$5,187	2,877	**Note 1**
220SEb	2-dr Coupe-5P	I6/134	$8,761	2,901	**Note 1**
220SEb	2-dr Conv-5P	I6/134	$9,562	3,190	**Note 1**
230SL					
230SL	2-dr Roadster-2P	I6/141	$7,506	2,749	**Note 2**
230SL	2-dr Coupe-2P	I6/141	$7,625	2,793	**Note 2**
230SL	2-dr Coupe/Roadster-2P	I6/141	$7,907	N/A	
300SE SERIES					
300SE	4-dr Sedan-5/6P	I6/183	$8,662	3,366	**Note 1**
300SE	2-dr Coupe-5P	I6/183	$11,770	N/A	**Note 1**
300SE	2-dr Conv-5P	I6/183	$12,573	N/A	**Note 1**
300SEL	4-dr Ext Sedan	I6/183	$9,910	N/A	**Note 1**
600/PULLMAN (GRAND MERCEDES)					
600	4-dr Sedan-5P	V8/386	$22,000	N/A	**Note 1**
Pullman	4-dr Sedan-7P	V8/386	$24,000	5,799	**Note 1**

Note 1: A total of 165,532 Mercedes-Benz passenger cars (all models) were produced during 1964, followed by 174,007 in 1965.
Note 2: A total of 19,831 230SL models were produced during the full model run, 1963-66.
Price Note: Model 600 figures shown are approximate.

1965 190

Base Six (300SE): Inline, overhead-cam six-cylinder. Aluminum alloy block and head. Displacement: 183 cid (2,996 cc). Bore & stroke: 3.35 x 3.46 in. (85 x 88 mm). Compression ratio: 9.0:1. Brake horsepower: 185 (SAE) at 5,200 rpm. Torque: 205 lbs.-ft. at 4,000 rpm. Seven main bearings. Solid valve lifters.

Base V-8 (600, Pullman): 90-degree, overhead-cam, eight-cylinder. Cast-iron block and aluminum heads. Displacement: 386.2 cid (6,329 cc). Bore & stroke: 4.05 x 3.74 in. (103 x 95 mm). Compression ratio: 9.0:1. Brake horsepower: 300 at 4,100 rpm. Torque: 369 lbs.-ft. at 2,800 rpm. Five main bearings. Solid valve lifters. Bosch fuel injection.

CHASSIS

Wheelbase: (190 sedan) 106.3 in.; (220S/SE) 108.3 in.; (230SL) 94.5 in.; (300SE) 108.3 in.; (300SEL) 112.2 in.; (600) 126 in.; (600 Pullman) 153.5 in. Overall length: (190 sedan) 186.5 in.; (220S/220SE) 192.2 in.; (230SL) 169 in.; (300SE) 192.2 in.; (600) 218 in.; (600 Pullman) 246 in. Height: (190 sedan) 58.8 in.; (220S) 59.5 in.; (220SE) 56.0 in.; (230SL) 51.7 in.; (300SE sedan) 57.5 in.; (300SE coupe) 55.7 in.; (600) 58.9 in.; (600 Pullman) 59.4 in. Width: (190 sedan) 68.5 in.; (220) 70.7 in.; (230SL) 69.3 in.; (300SE) 73.25 in.; (600) 76.8 in. Front tread: (190 sedan) 57.8 in.; (220S) 57.8 in.; (220SE) 58.4 in.; (230SL) 58.5 in.; (300SE) 58.4 in.; (600 Pullman) 62.4 in. Rear tread: (190 sedan) 58.5 in.; (220) 58.5 in.; (230SL) 58.5

Suspension (front): (220 Series, 230SL) unequal-length A-arms, coil springs and anti-roll bar; (300SE) wishbones with air springs, automatic leveling and anti-roll bar; (600) wishbones with air springs, automatic leveling and anti-roll bar. Suspension (rear): (220 Series, 230SL) single low-pivot swing axles with trailing arms and coil springs; (300SE, 600) swinging semi-axles with trailing lower radius arms, air springs, automatic leveling, and anti-roll bar. Brakes: (190) front/rear drum; (220S/SE, 230SL) front disc, rear drum; (300SE, 600) front/rear disc. Body construction: steel unibody with auxiliary front frame.

MAJOR OPTIONS: Automatic transmission. Power steering ($175). Air conditioning ($359-$400). Sunroof ($200).

PERFORMANCE

Top Speed: (190) about 90 mph; (220) about 96 mph; (220S) about 102 mph; (220SE) about 106 mph; (230SL) about 125 mph; (300SE) about 109 mph; (600) about 128 mph Acceleration (0-60 mph): (230SL) 9.9 sec. Acceleration (quarter-mile): (230SL) 17.0 sec. (83 mph). Fuel mileage: (190) about 22 mpg; (190D) about 35 mpg; (220) about 21 mpg; (230SL) near 19 mpg; (300SE) about 16-17 mpg.

PRODUCTION/SALES: A total of 2,190 Model 600 sedans and 487 long-wheelbase (Pullman) versions were produced between 1963 and 1982. Approximately 11,234 Mercedes-Benz passenger cars were sold in the U.S. in 1964, followed by 12,117 vehicles in 1965 (including tourist deliveries).

Manufacturer: Daimler-Benz AG, Stuttgart, West Germany.

Distributor: Mercedes-Benz Sales Inc., South Bend, Indiana; then Mercedes-Benz of North America Inc., Fort Lee, New Jersey.

HISTORY

By 1965, approximately 400 dealers in the U.S. sold Mercedes-Benz automobiles.

1965 220S ad

in.; (300SE) 58.7 in.; (600 Pullman) 62 in. Standard tires: (190 sedan) 7.00x13; (220) 7.25x13; (230SL) 185x14 or 7.25x14; (300SE) 7.50x13; (600/Pullman) 9.00x15.

TECHNICAL

Layout: front-engine, rear-drive. Transmission: four-speed manual except (300SE, 600) automatic standard; automatic optional on 220/230SL. Manual 230SL gear ratios: (1st) 4.42:1; (2nd) 2.28:1; (3rd) 1.53:1; (4th) 1.00:1; (rev) 3.92:1. Standard final drive ratio: (230SL) 3.75:1. Steering: recirculating ball.

1966

200 SERIES — FOUR — A new 200 four-door sedan replaced the former 190 Series, again powered by either a gasoline or diesel engine. The gasoline-powered 1,988 cc (121 cid) four developed 105 horsepower using two single-barrel carburetors. The diesel four produced 60 bhp

220SE — SIX — Only one model in the 220 Series remained for 1966, available in coupe and convertible form. The 2,195 cc (134 cid) six-cylinder engine developed 134 horsepower, using Bosch fuel injection.

230 SERIES — SIX — This new four-door sedan was similar in appearance to the 200, powered by a new 2,308 cc (141 cid), 118-bhp engine. The 230S version, which replaced the 220S, had the same rear fender design (with semi-tailfin) as the 200/230, but wore a front end like the 250 with single headlamps and an upper bumper guard bar. The 230S engine used twin two-barrel carburetors and produced 135 bhp

230SL — SIX — Production of the replacement for the original 190/300SL sports cars continued until late 1966, when it was superseded by the 250SL.

250S/SE — SIX — Another new model was the 250SE, which was built as a coupe, convertible or four-door sedan. Power came from a 2,496 cc (152.3 cid) engine, rated 170 bhp with Bosch fuel injection. A lower-priced 250S sedan used a carbureted version of the engine, rated 146 bhp These were the first examples of the "New Generation" body/chassis, which would be used on the full range of 220-280 Series sedans in 1968.

300SE — SIX — Production of the 300SE sedan continued, with a 2,996 cc (183 cid) engine under its hood.

600/PULLMAN — GRAND MERCEDES — V-8 — The largest Mercedes-Benz continued in limited production, and would remain so for another decade and a half.

I.D. DATA: Chassis serial number is on a plate under the hood, on the right side of the firewall. Starting serial number: (200) 160963; (200D) 225648; (230) 000001; (230S) 069693; (220SE coupe) 008909. Engine number is on right side of block.

ENGINES

Base Four (200): Inline, overhead-cam four-cylinder. Cast-iron block and aluminum head. Displacement: 121.3 cid (1,988 cc). Bore & stroke: 3.43 x 3.29 in. (87 x 83.6 mm). Compression ratio: 9.0:1. Brake horsepower: 105 (SAE) at 5,400 rpm. Torque: 123 lbs.-ft. at 3,800 rpm. Three main bearings. Solid valve lifters. Two Solex carburetors.

Diesel Four (200D): Inline, overhead-cam four-cylinder. Displacement: 121.3 cid (1,988 cc). Bore & stroke: 3.43 x 3.29 in. (87 x 83.6 mm). Compression ratio: 21.0:1. Brake horsepower: 60 at 4,200 rpm. Torque: 87 lbs.-ft. at 2,400 rpm. Fuel injection.

Base Six (220SE): Inline, overhead-cam six-cylinder. Cast-iron block and aluminum head. Displacement: 133.9 cid (2,195 cc). Bore & stroke: 3.15 x 2.87 in. (80 x 72.8 mm). Compression ratio: 8.7:1. Brake horsepower: 134 (SAE) at 5,000 rpm. Torque: 152 lbs.-ft. at 4,100 rpm. Four main bearings. Solid valve lifters. Bosch fuel injection.

Base Six (230, 230S, 230SL): Inline, overhead-cam six-cylinder. Cast-iron block and aluminum head. Displacement: 140.8 cid (2,308 cc). Bore & stroke: 3.23 x 2.87 in. (82 x 72.8 mm). Compression ratio: (230/S) 9.0:1; (230SL) 9.3:1. Brake horsepower: (230) 118 at 5400 rpm; (230S) 135 at 5,600 rpm; (230SL) 170 at 5,600 rpm. Torque: (230) 137 lbs.-ft. at 3,800 rpm; (230S) 145 lbs.-ft. at 4,200 rpm; (230SL) 159 lbs.-ft. at 4,500 rpm. Four main bearings. Solid valve lifters. Two Solex single-barrel carburetors (230); two twin-barrel carburetors (230S); or Bosch multi-point fuel injection (230SL).

Base Six (250S, 250SE): Inline, overhead-cam six-cylinder. Cast-iron block and aluminum head. Displacement: 152.3 cid (2,496 cc). Bore & stroke: 3.23 x 3.10 in. (82 x 78.8 mm). Compression ratio: 9.3:1. Brake horsepower: (250) 146 at 5,600 rpm; (250SE) 170 (SAE) at 5,600 rpm. Torque: 174 lbs.-ft. at 4,500 rpm. Four main bearings. Solid valve lifters. Two two-barrel carburetors (250S) or Bosch fuel injection (250SE).

Base Six (300SE): Inline, overhead-cam six-cylinder. Aluminum alloy block and head. Displacement: 183 cid (2,996 cc). Bore & stroke: 3.35 x 3.46 in. (85 x 88 mm). Compression ratio: 9.0:1. Brake horsepower: 185 (SAE) at 5,200 rpm. Torque: 205 lbs.-ft. at 4,000 rpm. Seven main bearings. Solid valve lifters. Fuel injection.

Base V-8 (600, Pullman): 90-degree, overhead-cam, eight-cylinder. Cast-iron block and aluminum heads. Displacement: 386.2 cid (6,329 cc). Bore & stroke: 4.05 x 3.74 in. (103 x 95 mm). Compression ratio: 9.0:1. Brake horsepower: 300 at 4,100 rpm. Torque: 435 lbs.-ft. at 3,000 rpm. Five main bearings. Solid valve lifters. Bosch fuel injection.

CHASSIS

Wheelbase: (200) 106.3 in.; (220SE) 108.3 in.; (230) 106.3 in.; (230S) 108.3 in.; (230SL) 94.5 in.; (250SE/300SE) 108.3 in.; (600) 126 in.; (600 Pullman) 153.5 in. Overall length: (200) 186.2 in.; (220SE) 192.1 in.; (230) 186.2 in.; (230S) 191.9 in.; (230SL) 169 in.; (250SE/300SE) 192 in.; (600) 218 in.; (600 Pullman) 245.7 in. Height: (200) 58.9 in.; (220SE) 55.9 in.; (230) 58.9 in.; (230S) 59.1 in.; (230SL) 51.3 in.; (250SE sedan) 56.7 in.; (600 Pullman) 59.4 in. Width: (200) 70.7 in.; (220SE) 72.7 in.; (230/S) 70.7 in.; (230SL) 69.2 in.; (250SE/300SE) 72.7 in.; (600 Pullman) 76.8 in. Front tread: (200) 58.4 in.; (220SE) 58.4 in.; (230/S) 58.4 in.; (230SL) 58.5 in.; (250SE/300SE) 58.4 in.; (600 Pullman) 62.4 in. Rear tread: (200) 58.5 in.; (220SE) 58.5 in.; (230SL) 58.5 in.; (230/S) 58.5 in.; (250SE) 58.5 in.; (300SE) 58.7 in.; (600 Pullman)

MODEL	BODY TYPE & SEATING	ENGINE TYPE/CID	P.O.E. PRICE	WEIGHT (LBS.)	PRODUCTION TOTAL
200 SERIES					
200	4-dr Sedan-5/6P	I4/121	$3,955	2,684	**Note 1**
200D (Diesel)	4-dr Sedan-5/6P	I4/121	$4,170	2,794	**Note 1**
220SE					
220SE	2-dr Coupe-5P	I6/134	$8,632	2,901	**Note 1**
220SE	2-dr Conv-5P	I6/134	$9,420	3,190	**Note 1**
230 SERIES					
230	4-dr Sedan-5/6P	I6/141	$4,140	2,750	**Note 1**
230S	4-dr Sedan-5/6P	I6/141	$4,785	2,816	**Note 1**
30SL					
230SL	2-dr Roadster-2P	I6/141	$6,185	2,855	**Note 2**
230SL	2-dr Coupe-2P	I6/141	$6,343	2,855	**Note 2**
230SL	2-dr Coupe/Roadster-2P	I6/141	$6,587	N/A	
250 SERIES					
250S	4-dr Sedan-5/6P	I6/152	$5,747	N/A	**Note 1**
250SE	2-dr Coupe-5P	I6/152	$8,959	3,063	**Note 1**
250SE	2-dr Conv-5P	I6/152	$9,748	3,352	**Note 1**
250SE	4-dr Sedan-5/6P	I6/152	$6,385	N/A	**Note 1**
300SE					
300SE	4-dr Sedan-5/6P	I6/183	$8,048	N/A	**Note 1**
600/PULLMAN (GRAND MERCEDES)					
600	4-dr Sedan-5P	V8/386	$22,299	N/A	**Note 1**
Pullman	4-dr Limo-7P	V8/386	$25,582	5,799	**Note 1**

Note 1: A total of 191,625 Mercedes-Benz passenger cars (all models) were produced during 1966.

Note 2: A total of 19,831 230SL models were produced during the full model run, 1963-66.

Model Note: Some directories also listed a 300SEL Series, priced at $9,946 for the sedan, $11,590 for the coupe, and $12,370 for the convertible.

62 in. Standard tires: (200) 7.00x13; (220SE) 7.25x13; (230) 7.00x13; (230S) 7.25x13; (230SL) 7.25x14; (250SE) 7.25x13; (600 Pullman) 9.00x15.

TECHNICAL

Layout: front-engine, rear-drive. Transmission: four-speed manual except (300SE, 600) automatic standard; automatic optional on other models. Steering: recirculating ball. Suspension (front): (200/220/230 Series) unequal-length A-arms, coil springs and anti-roll bar; (300SE, 600) wishbones with air springs, automatic leveling, and anti-roll bar. Suspension (rear): (200, 220SE, 230SL) single low-pivot swing axles with trailing arms and coil springs; (230/250 Series) single low-pivot swing axles with trailing arms, coil springs and automatic leveling; (300SE, 600) swinging semi-axles with trailing lower radius arms, air springs, automatic leveling and anti-roll bar. Brakes: (200/220/230/250 Series) front disc, rear drum; (300SE, 600) front/rear disc. Body Construction: steel unibody with auxiliary front frame.

MAJOR OPTIONS: Automatic transmission ($342). Power steering.

PERFORMANCE

Top Speed: (200) about 99 mph; (200D) about 85 mph; (220SE) about 106 mph; (230) about 109 mph; (230SL) 125 mph; (300SE) about 118 mph Acceleration (0-60 mph): (230SL) 9.9 sec. Acceleration (quarter-mile): (230SL) 17.0 sec. (83 mph). Fuel Mileage: (200) about 21 mpg; (200D) about 35 mpg; (220SE) about 22 mpg; (230) about 21 mpg; (230SL) about 17 mpg; (300SE) about 19 mpg.

PRODUCTION/SALES: Approximately 16,465 Mercedes-Benz vehicles were sold in the U.S. in 1966.

Manufacturer: Daimler-Benz AG, Stuttgart, West Germany.

Distributor: Mercedes-Benz of North America Inc., Fort Lee, New Jersey.

HISTORY

Production of the next generation of the Mercedes two-seater (250SL) began in 1966; see next year for details. By this time, the 220 and 300 Series were fading out of the lineup.

1967

200 SERIES — FOUR — Production of the smallest-engined Mercedes models continued with little change.

230 SERIES — SIX — Production of the sedan with 2,308 cc (141 cid) engine continued with little change.

250 SERIES — SIX — Only the four-door sedans were listed as available in the U.S. this year, in either 250S form (146 bhp) or as a 250SE (170 bhp). The former engine used two carburetors; the latter was fuel injected.

250SL — SIX — A larger engine went into the next edition of the Mercedes two-seat sports car, which would remain in production for only one year. The 2,496 cc overhead-cam six had a 6-mm longer stroke than its predecessor power plant, and produced the same horsepower (170). Torque output got a boost by 15, however, to 174 lbs.-ft. The new engine had seven main (crankshaft) bearings, versus four for the former version. Disc brakes were now used at both front and rear, and the 250SL had an axle ratio of 3.69:1. New standard equipment included a collapsible steering wheel.

600/PULLMAN — V-8 — The giant Mercedes-Benz "Grosser" sedan remained available on special order in the U.S., with little change evident.

I.D. DATA: Chassis serial number is on the right side of the firewall, or on the radiator cowl. Engine number is on right side of block.

ENGINES

Base Four (200): Inline, overhead-cam four-cylinder. Cast-iron block and aluminum head. Displacement: 121.3 cid (1,988 cc). Bore & stroke: 3.43 x 3.29 in. (87 x 83.6 mm). Compression ratio: 9.0:1. Brake horsepower: 105 (SAE) at 5,400 rpm. Torque: 123 lbs.-ft. at 3,800 rpm. Three main bearings. Solid valve lifters. Two Solex carburetors.

Diesel Four (200D): Inline, overhead-cam four-cylinder. Displacement: 121.3 cid (1,988 cc). Bore & stroke: 3.43 x 3.29 in. (87 x 83.6 mm). Compression ratio: 21.0:1. Brake horsepower: 60 at 4,200 rpm. Torque: 87 lbs.-ft. at 2,400 rpm. Fuel injection.

Base Six (230, 230S): Inline, overhead-cam six-cylinder. Cast-iron block and aluminum head. Displacement: 140.8 cid (2,308 cc). Bore & stroke: 3.23 x 2.87 in. (82 x 72.8 mm). Compression ratio: 9.0:1. Brake horsepower: (230) 118 at 5,400 rpm; (230S) 135 at 5,600 rpm. Torque: (230) 137 lbs.-ft. at 3,800 rpm; (230S) 145 lbs.-ft. at 4,200 rpm. Four main bearings. Solid valve lifters. Two single-barrel carburetors (230) or two two-barrel carburetors (230S).

Base Six (250S, 250SE): Inline, overhead-cam six-cylinder. Cast-iron block and aluminum head. Displacement: 152.3 cid (2,496 cc). Bore & stroke: 3.23 x 3.10 in. (82 x 78.8 mm). Compression ratio: 9.3:1. Brake horsepower: (250) 146 at 5,600 rpm; (250SE) 170 (SAE) at 5,600 rpm. Torque: 174 lbs.-ft. at 4,500 rpm. Four main bearings. Solid valve lifters. Two two-barrel carburetors (250S) or Bosch fuel injection (250SE).

Base Six (250SL): Inline, overhead-cam six-cylinder. Cast-iron block and aluminum head. Displacement: 152.3 cid (2,496 cc). Bore & stroke: 3.23 x 3.10 in. (82 x 78.8 mm). Compression ratio: 9.3:1. Brake horsepower: 170 (SAE) at 5,600 rpm. Torque: 174 lbs.-ft. at 4,500 rpm. Seven main bearings. Solid valve lifters. Bosch fuel injection.

Base V-8 (600, Pullman): 90-degree, overhead-cam, eight-cylinder. Cast-iron block and aluminum heads. Displacement: 386.2 cid (6,329 cc). Bore & stroke: 4.05 x 3.74 in. (103 x 95 mm). Compression ratio: 9.0:1. Brake horsepower: 300 at 4,100 rpm. Torque: 435 lbs.-ft. at 3,000 rpm. Five main bearings. Solid valve lifters. Bosch fuel injection.

CHASSIS

Wheelbase: (200) 106.3 in.; (230) 106.3 in.; (230S) 108.3 in.; (250SL) 94.5 in.; (250SE) 108.3 in.; (600 Pullman) 153.5 in. Overall length: (200) 186.2 in.; (230) 186.2 in.; (230S) 191.9 in.; (250SL) 168.7 in.; (250SE) 192 in.; (600 Pullman) 245.7 in. Height: (200) 58.9 in.; (230) 58.9 in.; (230S) 59.1 in.; (250SL) 52 in.; (250SE) 56.7 in.; (600 Pullman) 59.4 in. Width: (200) 70.7 in.; (230/S) 70.7 in.; (250SL) 69.2 in.; (250SE) 72.7 in.; (600 Pullman) 76.8 in. Front tread: (200) 58.4 in.; (230/S) 58.4 in.; (250SL) 58.4 in.; (600 Pullman) 62.4 in. Rear tread: (200) 58.5 in.; (230/S) 58.5 in.; (250SL) 58.5 in.; (250S/SE) 58.5 in.; (600 Pullman) 62 in. Standard tires: (200) 7.00x13; (230) 7.00x13; (230S) 7.25x13; (250SL) 7.25x14 or 185x14; (250SE) 7.25x13; (600 Pullman) 9.00x15.

TECHNICAL

Layout: front-engine, rear-drive. Transmission: four-speed manual except (600) automatic standard; automatic optional on other models. Steering: recirculating ball. Suspension (front): (200/230/250 Series) unequal-length A-arms, coil springs, and anti-roll bar; (600) wishbones with air springs, automatic leveling, and anti-roll bar. Suspension (rear): (200, 250SL) single low-pivot swing axles with trailing arms and coil springs; (230/250 Series) single low-pivot swing axles with trailing arms, coil springs and automatic leveling; (600) swinging semi-axles with trailing lower radius arms, air springs, automatic leveling, and anti-roll bar. Brakes: (200/230/250 Series) front disc, rear drum; (250SL, 600) front/ rear disc. Body Construction: steel unibody with auxiliary front frame.

MAJOR OPTIONS: Automatic transmission ($342). Power steering.

PERFORMANCE: Similar to 1966.

PRODUCTION/SALES: Approximately 20,691 Mercedes-Benz vehicles were sold in the U.S. in 1967.

Manufacturer: Daimler-Benz AG, Stuttgart, West Germany.

Distributor: Mercedes-Benz of North America Inc., Fort Lee, New Jersey.

Model	Body Type & Seating	Engine Type/CID	P.O.E. Price	Weight (lbs.)	Production Total
200 SERIES					
200	4-dr Sedan-5/6P	I4/121	$4,084	2,684	**Note 1**
200D (Diesel)	4-dr Sedan-5/6P	I4/121	$4,305	2,794	**Note 1**
230 SERIES					
230	4-dr Sedan-5/6P	I6/141	$4,280	2,750	**Note 1**
230S	4-dr Sedan-5/6P	I6/141	$4,910	2,816	**Note 1**
250 SERIES					
250S	4-dr Sedan-5/6P	I6/152	$5,747	3,014	**Note 1**
250SE	4-dr Sedan-5/6P	I6/152	$6,385	3,080	**Note 1**
250SL					
250SL	2-dr Roadster-2P	I6/152	$6,485	2,749	**Note 2**
250SL	2-dr Coupe-2P	I6/152	$6,647	2,793	**Note 2**
250SL	2-dr Coupe/Roadster-2P	I6/152	$6,897	2,848	
600/PULLMAN (GRAND MERCEDES)					
600	4-dr Sedan-5P	V8/386	$22,299	N/A	**Note 1**
Pullman	4-dr Limo-7P	V8/386	$25,582	5,799	**Note 1**

Note 1: A total of 200,470 Mercedes-Benz passenger cars (all models) were produced during 1967.
Note 2: A total of 5,196 250SL models were produced during the full (short) model run, 1966-67.
Model Note: Leftover 230SL sports cars were listed in U.S. directories in 1967, priced as in 1966 (their final production year).

1968-1969

200/220 SERIES — FOUR — Production of the 200 sedans (gas and diesel) continued into early 1968, when they were replaced by the "New Generation" 220 and 220D. A total restyling of the Mercedes sedan lineup followed the design introduced in 1966 with the 250 Series. The new grille kept the traditional look, but was considerably lower and wider. No evidence of vestigial tailfins remained. The new sedans had a lower hood, deeper beltline, and flatter rear deck. This new chassis rode a 108.3-inch wheelbase. For these "junior" Mercedes models, the new chassis was designated W114/115 and had thinner C-pillars than on the senior models. Each Mercedes sedan had huge amber parking lights below each headlamp.

230 SERIES — SIX — The six-cylinder version of the "junior" Mercedes also benefited from "New Generation" styling, powered by a 2,308 cc (141 cid) engine.

250 SERIES — SIX — Since this was the first Series to adopt the new styling, it continued with less change than the other Mercedes sedans.

280 SERIES — SIX — Known as the S-Class, the upper-level Mercedes' version of the "New Generation" got the designation W108. Under the hood was a 2,778 cc engine that developed 157 horsepower in "S" form, or 180 bhp with Bosch fuel injection in the 280SE.

280SL — SIX — After only one year with a 2,496 cc engine,

the Mercedes two-seat sports car moved up to a 2,778 cc six, as the result of an increase in bore dimension. That boosted output by 10 bhp, to 180 horsepower (SAE); and torque rose by 19 pound-feet, to 193. Also new was an optional ZF five-speed manual gearbox, with a $500 price tag. The U.S. version of the 280SL had a 4.08:1 final-drive ratio, with 3.69:1 and 3.92:1 available on request. Side-marker lights also were installed.

300SEL — 2.8 — SIX — A longer-wheelbase (W109) chassis was used for the largest standard Mercedes, measuring 112.2 inches between the wheels. Power came from the same 2.8-liter engine used in the 280SL sports car.

600/PULLMAN — V-8 — The giant Mercedes-Benz seven-passenger sedan remained available in the U.S., with little change evident. An automatic transmission was standard.

I.D. DATA: Chassis serial number is on the right side of the firewall, or on the radiator cowl. Engine number is on right side of block. Starting serial number (1968): 000001. Beginning in 1969, the serial number consists of 14 symbols. The first six symbols (all digits) indicate the model; the next two indicate standard (10) or automatic (12) transmission. The final six digits form the sequential production number.

ENGINES

Base Four (220): Inline, overhead-cam four-cylinder. Cast-iron block and aluminum head. Displacement: 134 cid (2,195

Model	Body Type & Seating	Engine Type/CID	P.O.E. Price	Weight (lbs.)	Production Total
220 SERIES					
220	4-dr Sedan-5P	I4/134	$4,360	2,948	**Note 1**
220D (Diesel)	4-dr Sedan-5P	I4/134	$4,494	3,036	**Note 1**
230 SERIES					
230	4-dr Sedan-5P	I6/141	$4,544	3,036	**Note 1**
250 SERIES					
250	4-dr Sedan-5P	I6/152	$5,060	3,080	**Note 1**
280 SERIES					
280S	4-dr Sedan-5P	I6/169	$5,897	3,278	**Note 1**
280SE	4-dr Sedan-5P	I6/169	$6,222	3,344	**Note 1**
280SE	2-dr Coupe-5P	I6/169	$9,174	3,454	**Note 1**
280SE	2-dr Conv-5P	I6/169	$9,967	3,630	**Note 1**
280SEL	4-dr Sedan-5P	I6/169	$6,622	N/A	**Note 1**
280SL					
280SL	2-dr Roadster-2P	I6/169	$6,485	3,102	**Note 2**
280SL	2-dr Coupe-2P	I6/169	$6,647	3,102	**Note 2**
280SL	2-dr Coupe/Roadster-2P	I6/169	$6,897	3,102	
300 SERIES					
300SEL 2.8	4-dr Sedan-5/6P	I6/169	$9,400	N/A	**Note 1**
600/PULLMAN (GRAND MERCEDES)					
600	4-dr Sedan-5P	V8/386	$22,299	N/A	**Note 1**
Pullman	4-dr Limo-7P	V8/386	$25,582	5,799	**Note 1**

Note 1: A total of 216,284 Mercedes-Benz passenger cars (all models) were produced during 1968, followed by 256,713 in 1969.

Note 2: A total of 23,885 280SL models were produced during the full model run, 1967-71.

Price Note: Figures shown were valid in 1968. Prices rose for 1969, ranging from $4,560 for the 220 sedan to $6,802 for the 280SL roadster (convertible) and $10,472 for the 280SE convertible.

1968 280SL roadster

cc). Bore & stroke: 3.15 x 2.87 in. (80 x 72.8 mm). Compression ratio: 9.0:1. Brake horsepower: 116 at 5,200 rpm. Torque: 142 lbs.-ft. at 3,000 rpm. Five main bearings. Solid valve lifters. Two carburetors.

Diesel Four (220D): Inline, overhead-cam four-cylinder. Displacement: 134 cid (2,195 cc). Bore & stroke: 3.15 x 2.87 in. (80 x 72.8 mm). Compression ratio: 21.0:1. Brake horsepower: 65 at 4,200 rpm. Torque: 96 lbs.-ft. at 2,400 rpm. Fuel injection.

Base Six (230): Inline, overhead-cam six-cylinder. Cast-iron block and aluminum head. Displacement: 140.7 cid (2,308 cc). Bore & stroke: 3.23 x 2.87 in. (82 x 72.8 mm). Compression ratio: 9.0:1. Brake horsepower: 135 at 5,600 rpm. Torque: 145 lbs.-ft. at 3,800 rpm. Four main bearings. Solid valve lifters. Two carburetors.

Base Six (250): Inline, overhead-cam six-cylinder. Cast-iron block and aluminum head. Displacement: 152.3 cid (2,496 cc). Bore & stroke: 3.23 x 3.10 in. (82 x 78.8 mm). Compression ratio: 9.0:1. Brake horsepower: 146 at 5,600 rpm. Torque: 161 lbs.-ft. at 3,800 rpm. Solid valve lifters. Two carburetors.

Base Six (280S): Inline, overhead-cam six-cylinder. Cast-iron block and aluminum head. Displacement: 169.5 cid (2,778 cc). Bore & stroke: 3.41 x 3.10 in. (86.6 x 78.8 mm). Compression ratio: 9.0:1. Brake horsepower: 157 at 5,400 rpm. Torque: 181 lbs.-ft. at 3,800 rpm. Seven main bearings. Solid valve lifters. Two carburetors.

Base Six (280SE/SEL, 280SL, 300SEL): Same as 2,778 cc six above, except Compression ratio: 9.5:1. Brake horsepower: 180 at 5,750 rpm. Torque: 193 lbs.-ft. at 4,500 rpm. Bosch fuel injection.

Base V-8 (600, Pullman): 90-degree, overhead-cam, eight-cylinder. Cast-iron block and aluminum heads. Displacement: 386.2 cid (6,329 cc). Bore & stroke: 4.05 x 3.74 in. (103 x 95 mm). Compression ratio: 9.0:1. Brake horsepower: 300 at 4,100 rpm. Torque: 434 lbs.-ft. at 3,000 rpm. Five main bearings. Solid valve lifters. Bosch fuel injection.

CHASSIS

Wheelbase: (220/230/250/280) 108.3 in.; (280SL) 94.5 in.; (300SEL) 112.2 in.; (600) 126 in.; (600 Pullman) 153.5 in. Overall length: (220/230/250) 184.5 in.; (280) 192.9 in.; (280SL) 168.7 in.; (300SEL) 197 in.; (600) 218 in.; (600 Pullman) 245.7 in. Height: (220/ 230/250/280) 56.7 in.; (280SL) 52.0 in.; (300SEL) 55.7 in.; (600) 58.5 in.; (600 Pullman) 59.1 in. Width: (220/230/250) 69.7 in.; (280) 71.3 in.; (280SL) 69.3 in.; (300SEL) 71.3 in.; (600) 76.8 in. Front tread: (220/230/250) 56.8 in.; (280) 58.4 in.; (280SL) 58.4 in.; (300SEL) 58.4 in.; (600) 62.5 in. Rear tread: (220/230/250) 56.7 in.; (280) 58.5 in.; (280SL) 58.5 in.; (300SEL) 58.7 in.; (600) 62.2 in. Standard tires: (220/230/250) 6.95x14; (280) 7.35x14; (280SL) 185x14; (300SEL) 7.35x13; (600 Pullman) 9.00x15.

TECHNICAL

Layout: front-engine, rear-drive. Transmission: four-speed manual except (600) automatic standard; automatic optional on other models; ZF five-speed optional on 280SL. Steering: recirculating ball. Suspension (front): (220/230/250/280 Series) unequal-length A-arms, coil springs, and anti-roll bar; (600) wishbones with air springs, automatic leveling, and anti-roll bar. Suspension (rear): (220, 280SL) single low-pivot swing axles with trailing arms and coil springs; (230/250 Series) single low-pivot swing axles with trailing arms, coil springs, and automatic leveling; (600) swinging semi-axles with trailing lower radius arms, air springs, automatic leveling, and anti-roll bar. Brakes: (200/230/250/280 Series) front disc, rear drum (later, four-wheel disc); (280SL, 600) front/rear disc. Body construction: steel unibody with auxiliary front frame.

MAJOR OPTIONS: Four-Speed automatic transmission ($342). Power steering ($171- $200). Air conditioning ($417- $562). Sliding steel sunroof. Leather upholstery. Power windows. AM/FM radio. Whitewall tires. Tinted glass. Rear jump seat (280SL). Roof ski brackets (280SL). Removable steel hardtop (280SL).

PRODUCTION/SALES: Approximately 24,553 Mercedes-Benz vehicles were sold in the U.S. in 1968, followed by 26, 193 in 1969.

Manufacturer: Daimler-Benz AG, Stuttgart, West Germany.

Distributor: Mercedes-Benz of North America Inc., Fort Lee, New Jersey.

HISTORY

Mercedes-Benz promoted the 280SL as "the sum total of everything the Mercedes-Benz engineers have learned about high-performance sporting machinery."

1969 600 Pullman

1970

220 SERIES — FOUR — Production of the gas and diesel engine "junior" Mercedes models continued with little change.

250 SERIES — SIX — A new 250C hardtop coupe with all-disc brakes joined the 250 sedan this year. Under the coupe's hood was the 2,778 cc (169.5 cid) six-cylinder engine, whereas the sedan kept the smaller 2,496 cc six. Otherwise, little change was evident.

280 SERIES — SIX — Production of the six-cylinder 280 Series continued with minimal change. The 280S carried a carbureted 169.5 cid engine that developed 157 horsepower; the 280SE/SEL had a 180-bhp version, as in the 280SL sports car.

280SE — 3.5 — V-8 — A new 213.5 cid V-8 engine with Bosch fuel injection that developed 230 horsepower went into the 280SE coupe and convertible. Power steering, air conditioning, and a radio were standard.

280SL — SIX — Production of the Mercedes two-seat sports car continued with little change.

300SEL — 3.5/6.3 — V-8 — Automatic transmission, power steering, air conditioning and radio were standard in the upper-ranked Mercedes sedan, which could have either the 213.5 cid V-8 or the big 386 cid V-8 (as in the 600 Pullman).

600/PULLMAN — V-8 — The giant Mercedes-Benz seven-passenger sedan remained available in the U.S., with little change evident. A shorter wheelbase version also was available. An automatic transmission, power steering, air conditioning,w and radio were standard.

I.D. DATA: Chassis serial number is under the hood on the right side of the firewall, or at the left front near the A-pillar. The chassis serial number consists of 14 symbols. The first six symbols (all digits) indicate the model; the next two indicate standard (10) or automatic (12) transmission. The final six digits form the sequential production number. Starting serial number: (220) 037069; (220D) 084964; (250) 033533; (250C) 000001; (280S) 035214; (280SE/SEL sedan) 036081; (280SL) 011948; (280SE cpe/conv) 003549; (300SEL 3.5 sedan) 002221; (300SEL 6.3 sedan) 002839; (600 sedan) 001435.

ENGINES

Base Four (220): Inline, overhead-cam four-cylinder. Cast-iron block and aluminum head. Displacement: 134 cid (2,195 cc). Bore & stroke: 3.15 x 2.87 in. (80 x 72.8 mm). Compression ratio: 9.0:1. Brake horsepower: 116 at 5,200 rpm. Torque: 142 lbs.-ft. at 3,000 rpm. Five main bearings. Solid valve lifters.

Diesel Four (220D): Inline, overhead-cam four-cylinder. Displacement: 134 cid (2,195 cc). Bore & stroke: 3.15 x 2.87 in. (80 x 72.8 mm). Compression ratio: 21.0:1. Brake horsepower: 65 at 4,200 rpm. Torque: 96 lbs.-ft. at 2,400 rpm. Fuel injection.

Base Six (250): Inline, overhead-cam six-cylinder. Cast-iron block and aluminum head. Displacement: 152.3 cid (2,496 cc). Bore & stroke: 3.23 x 3.10 in. (82 x 78.8 mm). Compression ratio: 9.0:1. Brake horsepower: 146 at 5,600 rpm. Torque: 161 lbs.-ft. at 3,800 rpm. Four main bearings. Solid valve lifters.

Base Six (250C, 280S): Inline, overhead-cam six-cylinder. Cast-iron block and aluminum head. Displacement: 169.5 cid (2,778 cc). Bore & stroke: 3.41 x 3.10 in. (86.6 x 78.8 mm). Compression ratio: 9.0:1. Brake horsepower: 157 at 5,400 rpm. Torque: 181 lbs.-ft. at 3,800 rpm. Seven main bearings. Solid valve lifters.

Base Six (280SE/SEL, 280SL): Same as 2,778 cc six above, except Compression ratio: 9.5:1. Brake horsepower: 180 at 5,750 rpm. Torque: 193 lbs.-ft. at 4,500 rpm.

Base V-8 (280SE 3.5 coupe/conv, 300SEL 3.5): 90-degree, overhead-cam, eight-cylinder. Cast-iron block and aluminum heads. Displacement: 213.5 cid (3,499 cc). Bore & stroke: 3.62 x 2.59 in. (92 x 65.8 mm). Compression ratio: 9.5:1. Brake horsepower: 230 at 6,050 rpm. Torque: 231 lbs.-ft. at 4,200 rpm. Five main bearings. Solid valve lifters. Bosch fuel injection.

Base V-8 (300SEL 6.3, 600, Pullman): 90-degree, overhead-cam, eight-cylinder. Cast-iron block and aluminum heads. Displacement: 386.2 cid (6,329 cc). Bore & stroke: 4.05 x 3.74 in. (103 x 95 mm). Compression ratio: 8.1:1. Brake horsepower: 300 at 4,100 rpm. Torque: 434 lbs.-ft. at 3,000 rpm. Five main bearings. Solid valve lifters. Bosch fuel injection.

CHASSIS

Wheelbase: (220/250/280) 108.3 in.; (280SL) 94.5 in.; (280SEL, 300SEL) 112.2 in.; (600) 126 in.; (600 Pullman) 153.5 in. Overall length: (220/250) 184.5 in.; (280) 192.9 in.; (280SL) 168.7 in.; (280SEL, 300SEL) 197 in.; (600) 218 in.; (600 Pullman) 245.7 in. Height: (220/250/280 sedan) 56.7 in.; (250C) 54.9 in.; (280SL) 52 in.; (280SE 3.5 coupe/conv) 55.9 in.; (300SEL) 55.5-55.9 in.; (600) 58.5 in.; (600 Pullman) 59 in. Width: (220/250) 69.7 in.; (250C) 70.5 in.; (280) 71.3 in.; (280SL) 69.3 in.; (280SE 3.5 coupe/conv) 72.6 in.; (300SEL) 71.3 in.; (600) 76.8 in. Front tread: (220/250) 56.8 in.; (280) 58.4 in.; (280SL) 58.4 in.; (280SE 3.5 coupe/conv) 58.3 in.; (300SEL 3.5) 58.3 in.; (300SEL 6.3) 58.7 in.;

(600) 62.5 in. Rear tread: (220/250) 56.7 in.; (280) 58.5 in.; (280SL) 58.5 in.; (280SE 3.5 coupe/conv) 58.7 in.; (300SEL 3.5) 58.7 in.; (300SEL 6.3) 58.5 in.; (600) 62.2 in. Standard tires: (220/230/250) 6.95x14; (280) 7.35x14; (280SL) 185x14; (280SE 3.5 coupe/conv) 7.35x14; (300SEL 3.5) 7.35x14; (300SEL 6.3) 195x14; (600 Pullman) 9.00x15.

TECHNICAL

Layout: front-engine, rear-drive. Transmission: four-speed manual except (300SEL, 600) automatic standard; automatic optional on other models; ZF five-speed optional on 280SL. Steering: recirculating ball. Suspension (front): unequal-length A-arms, coil springs, and anti-roll bar; (600) wishbones with air springs, automatic leveling, and anti-roll bar. Suspension (rear): single low-pivot swing axles with coil springs and anti-roll bar; (600) swinging semi-axles with trailing lower radius arms, air springs, automatic leveling, and anti-roll bar. Brakes: front/rear disc. Body construction: steel unibody with auxiliary front frame.

MAJOR OPTIONS: Automatic transmission. Power steering. Air conditioning.

PRODUCTION/SALES: Approximately 29,108 Mercedes-Benz vehicles were sold in the U.S. in 1970.

Manufacturer: Daimler-Benz AG, Stuttgart, West Germany.

Distributor: Mercedes-Benz of North America Inc., Fort Lee, New Jersey.

MODEL	BODY TYPE & SEATING	ENGINE TYPE/CID	P.E. PRICE	WEIGHT (LBS.)	PRODUCTION TOTAL
220 SERIES					
220	4-dr Sedan-5P	I4/134	$4,680	2,948	**Note 1**
220D (Diesel)	4-dr Sedan-5P	I4/134	$4,782	3,036	**Note 1**
250 SERIES					
250	4-dr Sedan-5P	I6/152	$5,208	3,080	**Note 1**
250C	2-dr Coupe-5P	I6/169	$6,260	3,100	**Note 1**
280 SERIES					
280S	4-dr Sedan-5P	I6/169	$6,273	3,278	**Note 1**
280SE	4-dr Sedan-5P	I6/169	$6,561	3,344	**Note 1**
280SEL	4-dr Sedan-5P	I6/169	N/A	N/A	**Note 1**
280SE 3.5	2-dr Coupe-5P	V8/213	$11,111	3,454	**Note 1**
280SE 3.5	2-dr Conv-5P	V8/213	$11,924	3,630	**Note 1**
280SL					
280SL	2-dr Roadster-2P	I6/169	$6,952	3,102	**Note 2**
280SL	2-dr Coupe-2P	I6/169	$7,118	3,102	**Note 2**
280SL	2-dr Coupe/Roadster-2P	I6/169	$7,374	3,102	**Note 2**
300SEL					
3.5	4-dr Sedan-5/6P	V8/213	$11,327	N/A	**Note 1**
6.3	4-dr Sedan-5/6P	V8/386	$15,122	N/A	**Note 1**
600/PULLMAN (GRAND MERCEDES)					
600	4-dr Sedan-5P	V8/386	$24,600	N/A	**Note 1**
Pullman	4-dr Limo-7P	V8/386	$28,120	5,820	**Note 1**

Note 1: A total of 280,419 Mercedes-Benz passenger cars (all models) were produced during 1970.
Note 2: A total of 23,885 280SL models were produced during the full model run, 1967-71.
Price Note: Figures shown for 300SEL and 600 include dealer preparation charges.

1971 300SEL 6.3 AMG

1971

220 SERIES — FOUR — Production of the only four-cylinder Mercedes-Benz sedans continued with little change, except for a substantial price hike this year. Both engines were 134 cid displacement, developing 116 horsepower (gasoline) or 65 bhp (diesel). Even these least-expensive models had fully independent suspension and all-disc brakes. An automatic transmission was optional; four-speed manual gearbox standard.

250 SERIES — SIX — A substantial price hike was the major change for the 250 coupe and sedan, both now powered by a 2,778 cc (169.5 cid) six-cylinder engine that developed 157 horsepower. Dimensions were virtually identical to the four-cylinder 220 Series.

280 SERIES — SIX — Production of the 280S, SE, and SEL sedans continued with little change. Each was powered by a 169.5 cid six-cylinder engine, but the latter two had 180 horsepower available and the 280S had only 157 bhp

280SE 3.5 — V-8 — A fuel-injected 213.5 cid V-8 engine powered the coupe and convertible of the 280 Series, which were similar in size to their six-cylinder sedan mates. Not all U.S. directories of imported models listed the coupe and convertible this year.

280SL — SIX — This would be the final season in America for the 280SL sports car. Late in 1971, a new R107 generation emerged, to be named 350SL, taking advantage of technical advances from Daimler-Benz.

300SEL — 3.5/6.3 — V-8 — Two very different V-8 engines were available under the hood of the 112.2-inch wheelbase 300SEL. The 300SEL 3.5 used a 213.5 cid V-8 that developed 230 horsepower, while the 300SEL 6.3 adopted the big 386 cid V-8 as installed in the mighty 600 Series.

600/PULLMAN — V-8 — The giant Mercedes seven-passenger sedan and its five-passenger counterpart remained minimally available in the U.S. with little change evident.

I.D. DATA: Depending on the model, the Mercedes-Benz chassis serial number is under the hood on the right side of the firewall, on right front frame rail, on the radiator cowl, at the B-pillar, or atop the instrument panel. The chassis serial number consists of 14 symbols. The first six symbols (all digits) indicate the model; the next two indicate standard (10) or automatic (12) transmission. The final six digits form the sequential production number. Starting serial number: (220) 057330; (220D) 142680; (250) 000001; (250C) 002362; (280S) 054244; (280SE) 059236; (280SL) 018506. Engine number is on right side of block.

1971 | 79

MODEL	BODY TYPE & SEATING	ENGINE TYPE/CID	P.E. PRICE	WEIGHT (LBS.)	PRODUCTION TOTAL
220 SERIES					
220	4-dr Sedan-5P	I4/134	$5,312	2,880	**Note 1**
220D (Diesel)	4-dr Sedan-5P	I4/134	$5,419	2,961	**Note 1**
250 SERIES					
250	4-dr Sedan-5P	I6/169	$6,378	2,989	**Note 1**
250C	2-dr Coupe-5P	I6/169	$7,373	2,993	**Note 1**
280 SERIES					
280S	4-dr Sedan-5P	I6/169	$7,370	3,148	**Note 1**
280SE	4-dr Sedan-5P	I6/169	$7,661	3,206	**Note 1**
280SEL	4-dr Sedan-5P	I6/169	$8,492	3,298	**Note 1**
280SE 3.5	2-dr Coupe-5P	V8/213	$13,766	3,687	**Note 1**
280SE 3.5	2-dr Convertible-5P	V8/213	$14,509	3,687	**Note 1**
280SL					
280SL	2-dr Roadster-2P	I6/169	$7,469	2,891	**Note 2**
280SL	2-dr Coupe-2P	I6/169	$7,642	2,891	**Note 2**
280SL	2-dr Coupe/Roadster-2P	I6/169	$7,909	2,891	**Note 2**
300SEL					
3.5	4-dr Sedan-5P	V8/213	$12,886	3,838	**Note 1**
6.3	4-dr Sedan-5P	V8/386	$16,275	4,070	**Note 1**
600/PULLMAN (GRAND MERCEDES)					
600	4-dr Sedan-5P	V8/386	$26,530	5,469	**Note 1**
Pullman	4-dr Limo-7P	V8/386	$30,120	6,031	**Note 1**

Note 1: A total of 284,230 Mercedes-Benz cars (all models) were produced during 1971.
Note 2: A total of 23,885 280SL models were produced during the full model run, 1967-71.
Model Number Note: Some directories included an /8 suffix with each model number (e.g., 220/8).
Weight Note: Figures shown for 280SE 3.5 and 300SEL are "unladen" amounts; others are shipping weights.

1971 300SEL, right-hand drive

ENGINES

Base Four (220): Inline, overhead-cam four-cylinder. Cast-iron block and aluminum head. Displacement: 134 cid (2,195 cc). Bore & stroke: 3.15 x 2.87 in. (80 x 72.8 mm). Compression ratio: 9.0:1. Brake horsepower: 116 at 5,200 rpm. Torque: 142 lbs.-ft. at 3,000 rpm. Five main bearings. Solid valve lifters.

Diesel Four (220D): Inline, overhead-cam four-cylinder. Displacement: 134 cid (2,195 cc). Bore & stroke: 3.15 x 2.87 in. (80 x 72.8 mm). Compression ratio: 21.0:1. Brake horsepower:

65 at 4,200 rpm. Torque: 96 lbs.-ft. at 2,400 rpm. Solid valve lifters. Fuel injection.

Base Six (250, 250C, 280S): Inline, overhead-cam six-cylinder. Cast-iron block and aluminum head. Displacement: 169.5 cid (2,778 cc). Bore & stroke: 3.41 x 3.10 in. (86.6 x 78.8 mm). Compression ratio: 9.0:1. Brake horsepower: 157 at 5,400 rpm. Torque: 181 lbs.-ft. at 3,800 rpm. Seven main bearings. Solid valve lifters.

1971 280SL convertible sportster, right-hand drive

Base Six (280SE, 280SEL, 280SL): Same as 2,778 cc six above, except Compression ratio: 9.5:1. Brake horsepower: 180 at 5,750 rpm. Torque: 193 lbs.-ft. at 4,500 rpm.

Base V-8 (280SE 3.5 coupe/conv, 300SEL 3.5): 90-degree, overhead-cam, eight-cylinder. Cast-iron block and aluminum heads. Displacement: 213.5 cid (3,499 cc). Bore & stroke: 3.62 x 2.59 in. (92 x 65.8 mm). Compression ratio: 9.5:1. Brake horsepower: 230 at 6,050 rpm. Torque: 231 lbs.-ft. at 4,200 rpm. Five main bearings. Solid valve lifters. Bosch fuel injection.

Base V-8 (300SEL 6.3, 600): 90-degree, overhead-cam, eight-cylinder. Cast-iron block and aluminum heads. Displacement: 386.2 cid (6,329 cc). Bore & stroke: 4.05 x 3.74 in. (103 x 95 mm). Compression ratio: 8.1:1. Brake horsepower: 300 at 4,100 rpm. Torque: 434 lbs.-ft. at 3,000 rpm. Five main bearings. Solid valve lifters. Bosch fuel injection.

CHASSIS

Wheelbase: (220/250/280) 108.3 in.; (280SL) 94.5 in.; (280SEL, 300SEL) 112.2 in.; (600) 126 in.; (600 Pullman) 153.5 in. Overall length: (220/250) 184.5 in.; (280) 192.9 in.; (280SL) 168.7 in.; (280SEL, 300SEL) 197 in.; (600) 218 in.; (600 Pullman) 245.7 in. Height: (220/250/280 sedan) 56.7 in.; (250C) 54.9 in.; (280SL) 52 in.; (280SE 3.5 coupe/conv) 55.9 in.; (300SEL 3.5) 55.5 in. (300SEL 6.3) 55.9 in.; (600) 58.5 in.; (600 Pullman) 59 in. Width: (220/250) 69.7 in.; (250C) 70.5 in.; (280) 71.3 in.; (280SL) 69.3 in.; (280SE 3.5 coupe/conv) 72.6 in.; (300SEL) 71.3 in.; (600) 76.8 in. Front tread: (220/250) 56.8 in.; (280) 58.4 in.; (280SL) 58.4 in.; (280SE 3.5 coupe/conv) 58.3 in.; (300SEL 3.5) 58.3 in.; (300SEL 6.3) 58.7 in.; (600) 62.5 in. Rear tread: (220/250) 56.7 in.; (280) 58.5 in.; (280SL) 58.5 in.; (280SE 3.5 coupe/conv) 58.7 in.; (300SEL 3.5) 58.7 in.; (300SEL 6.3) 58.5 in.; (600) 62.2 in. Standard tires: (220/250) 6.95x14; (280) 7.35x14; (280SL) 185x14; (280SE 3.5 coupe/conv) 7.35x14; (300SEL 3.5) 7.35x14; (300SEL 6.3) 195x14; (600 Pullman) 9.00x15.

TECHNICAL

Layout: front-engine, rear-drive. Transmission: (220, 280SL) four-speed manual, automatic optional; (others) automatic standard. Steering: recirculating ball. Suspension (front): unequal-length A-arms, coil springs, and anti-roll bar; (600) wishbones with air springs, automatic leveling, and anti-roll bar. Suspension (rear): single low-pivot swing axles with coil springs and anti-sway bar; (600) swinging semi-axles with trailing lower radius arms, air springs, automatic leveling, and anti-roll bar. Brakes: front/rear disc. Body construction: steel unibody with auxiliary front frame.

MAJOR OPTIONS: Automatic transmission ($392). Power steering ($198). Air conditioning ($597). Sunroof.

PRODUCTION/SALES: Approximately 35,192 Mercedes-Benz passenger cars were sold in the U.S. in 1971.

Manufacturer: Daimler-Benz AG, Stuttgart, West Germany.

Distributor: Mercedes-Benz of North America Inc., Fort Lee, New Jersey.

HISTORY

The 1971 models were introduced to the U.S. market on October 1, 1970. The 350SL replacement for the 280SL was in production in Europe, and would arrive in the U.S. for the 1972 model year.

1972

220 SERIES — FOUR — Except for a slight reduction in horsepower/torque ratings from the gasoline engine, little was new on the four-cylinder Mercedes-Benz models.

250 SERIES — SIX — Little change was evident on the 250 sedan and 250C coupe, powered by a 2,778 cc (169.5 cid) engine that developed 150 horsepower.

280SE — SIX — Only one version of the six-cylinder sedans in the 280 Series remained for 1972, with its engine producing 175 horsepower.

280SE/280SEL 4.5 — V-8 — Two V-8 versions of the 280 sedan got a displacement boost to 276 cid this year. The enlarged V-8 was rated 230 horsepower with 278 lbs.-ft. of torque.

300SEL 4.5 — V-8 — Like other models in the Mercedes lineup for 1972, the 300SEL gained displacement for its basic V-8 engine, now measuring 4.5 liters (276 cid). On the other hand, the former 6.3 version (386 cid) no longer was offered.

350SL — V-8 — A 4.5-liter (276 cid) V-8 engine went under the hood of the next Mercedes-Benz two-seat roadster, coded R107. It was longer, plusher, more expensive, and squarely aimed at American customers. This version used steel body panels instead of the former aluminum panels, adding several hundred pounds to the car's weight. Quad round headlamps went on U.S. versions. Some observers criticized the restyling as being overly "Americanized," but it became a strong seller and would remain in the lineup through the late 1980s, evolving into the

450SL, 380SL, and 560SL editions. European versions of the 350SL had the 3.5-liter V-8 engine, also rated at 230 bhp; but only the bigger 4.5 V-8 came to America.

600/PULLMAN — V-8 — Although the 600 "Grosser" Mercedes-Benz remained in production through 1980, it seldom appeared in listings of American imports after 1972.

I.D. DATA: Depending on the model, the Mercedes-Benz chassis serial number is atop the instrument panel (visible through the windshield), on the radiator cowl, or at the driver's door B-pillar. The chassis serial number consists of 14 symbols. The first six symbols (all digits) indicate the model; the next two indicate standard (10) or automatic (12) transmission. The final six digits form the sequential production number. Starting serial number: (220) 115.010-12-081308; (220D) 115.110-10-208608; (250) 114.011-12-007030; (250C) 114.023-12-005231; (280SE) 108.018-12-087244; (350SL) 107.044-12-000001. Engine number is on left front or right rear of block.

ENGINES

Base Four (220): Inline, overhead-cam four-cylinder. Cast-iron block and aluminum head. Displacement: 134 cid (2,195 cc). Bore & stroke: 3.15 x 2.87 in. (80 x 72.8 mm). Compression ratio: 8.0:1. Brake horsepower: 110 at 5,300 rpm. Torque: 127 lbs.-ft. at 3,300 rpm. Five main bearings. Solid valve lifters.

Diesel Four (220D): Inline, overhead-cam four-cylinder. Displacement: 134 cid (2,195 cc). Bore & stroke: 3.15 x 2.87 in.

Model	Body Type & Seating	Engine Type/CID	P.E. Price	Weight (lbs.)	Production Total
220 SERIES					
220	4-dr Sedan-5P	I4/134	$6,267	2,983	**Note 1**
220D (Diesel)	4-dr Sedan-5P	I4/134	$6,020	3,055	**Note 1**
250 SERIES					
250	4-dr Sedan-5P	I6/169	$7,218	3,159	**Note 1**
250C	2-dr Coupe-5P	I6/169	$8,069	3,159	**Note 1**
280SE					
280SE	4-dr Sedan-5P	I6/169	$9,503	3,386	**Note 1**
280SE 4.5	4-dr Sedan-5P	V8/276	$10,076	3,549	**Note 1**
280SEL 4.5	4-dr Sedan-5P	V8/276	$10,634	3,766	**Note 1**
300SEL					
4.5	4-dr Sedan-5P	V8/276	$13,768	3,877	**Note 1**
350SL					
350SL	2-dr Coupe/Roadster-2P	V8/276	$10,540	3,597	**Note 2**
600/PULLMAN (GRAND MERCEDES)					
600	4-dr Sedan-5P	V8/386	$32,695	5,469	**Note 1**
Pullman	4-dr Limo-7P	V8/386	$37,928	6,031	**Note 1**

Note 1: A total of 323,878 Mercedes-Benz cars (all models) were produced during 1972.

Note 2: A total of 15,304 350SL models were produced during the full model run, 1970-80 (sold as late as 1980 in the international market).

Model Number Note: Some directories included a /8 suffix with each model number (e.g., 220/8).

Price Note: Figure shown for 220D included manual transmission; automatic cost $393 more.

Weight Note: Figures shown for 280SEL 4.5 and 300SEL 4.5 are "unladen" amounts; others are shipping weights.

(80 x 72.8 mm). Compression ratio: 21.0:1. Brake horsepower: 65 at 4,200 rpm. Torque: 96 lbs.-ft. at 2,400 rpm. Solid valve lifters. Fuel injection.

Base Six (250, 250C): Inline, overhead-cam six-cylinder. Cast-iron block and aluminum head. Displacement: 169.5 cid (2,778 cc). Bore & stroke: 3.41 x 3.10 in. (86.6 x 78.8 mm). Compression ratio: 9.0:1. Brake horsepower: 150 at 5,300 rpm. Torque: 166 lbs.-ft. at 3,300 rpm. Seven main bearings. Solid valve lifters.

Base Six (280SE): Same as 2,778 cc six above, except Brake horsepower: 175 at 5,700 rpm. Torque: 174 lbs.-ft. at 4,500 rpm.

Base V-8 (280SE 4.5, 280SEL 4.5, 300SEL 4.5, 350SL): 90-degree, overhead-cam, eight-cylinder. Cast-iron block and aluminum heads. Displacement: 275.8 cid (4,520 cc). Bore & stroke: 3.62 x 3.35 in. (92 x 85 mm). Compression ratio: 8.0:1. Brake horsepower: 230 at 5,000 rpm. Torque: 278 lbs.-ft. at 3,200 rpm. Five main bearings. Solid valve lifters. Bosch fuel injection.

Base V-8 (600): 90-degree, overhead-cam, eight-cylinder. Cast-iron block and aluminum heads. Displacement: 386.2 cid (6,329 cc). Bore & stroke: 4.05 x 3.74 in. (103 x 95 mm). Compression ratio: 8.0:1. Brake horsepower: 270 at 4,200 rpm. Torque: 370 lbs.-ft. at 2,900 rpm. Five main bearings. Solid valve lifters. Bosch fuel injection.

CHASSIS

Wheelbase: (220/250/280) 108.3 in.; (280SE 4.5) 108.3 in.; (280SEL 4.5, 300SEL 4.5) 112.2 in.; (350SL) 96.9 in.; (600) 126 in.; (600 Pullman) 153.5 in. Overall length: (220/250) 184.5 in.; (280SE) 192.9 in.; (280SE/SEL 4.5) 196.8 in.; (300SEL 4.5) 196.9 in.; (350SL) 172.1 in.; (600) 218 in.; (600 Pullman) 245.7 in. Height: (220/250/280 sedan) 56.7 in.; (250C) 54.9 in.; (280SE/SEL 4.5) 56.7 in.; (300SEL 4.5) 55.5 in.; (350SL)

51.2 in.; (600) 58.5 in.; (600 Pullman) 59 in. Width: (220/250) 69.7 in.; (250C) 70.5 in.; (280 Series) 71.3 in.; (300SEL) 71.3 in.; (350SL) 70.5 in.; (600) 76.8 in. Front tread: (220/250) 56.8 in.; (280 Series) 58.4 in.; (300SEL 4.5) 58.3 in.; (350SL) 57.2 in.; (600) 62.5 in. Rear tread: (220/250) 56.7 in.; (280) 58.5 in.; (300SEL 4.5) 58.5 in.; (350SL) 56.7 in.; (600) 62.2 in. Standard tires: (220/250) 6.95x14; (280 Series) 7.35x14; (350SL) 205VR14; (600) 9.00x15.

TECHNICAL

Layout: front-engine, rear-drive. Transmission: (220D) four-speed manual, automatic optional; (others) automatic standard. Steering: recirculating ball. Suspension (front): unequal-length A-arms, coil springs, and anti-roll bar; (600) wishbones with air springs, automatic leveling, and anti-roll bar. Suspension (rear): single low-pivot swing axles with coil springs and anti-sway bar; (600) air springs, automatic leveling, and anti-roll bar. Brakes: front/rear disc. Body construction: steel unibody with auxiliary front frame.

MAJOR OPTIONS: Automatic transmission (220D). Power steering (220). Air conditioning. Sunroof. Leather seats.

PRODUCTION/SALES: Approximately 41,998 Mercedes-Benz passenger cars were sold in the U.S. in 1972.

Manufacturer: Daimler-Benz AG, Stuttgart, West Germany.

Distributor: Mercedes-Benz of North America Inc., Fort Lee, New Jersey.

HISTORY

The 1972 models were introduced to the U.S. market on August 2, 1971. The 350SL two-seater was not destined for long life in the Mercedes lineup, replaced by the 450SL for the 1973 model year.

1973

220 SERIES — FOUR — Advertised horsepower/torque figures were lower by 1973, as a result of the switch from SAE gross to SAE net standards. Otherwise, little change was evident in the four-cylinder Mercedes-Benz sedans, which again came with either a gasoline or diesel engine. Only the diesel four had a standard four-speed manual gearbox (automatic optional). All other Mercedes-Benz models had an automatic as standard equipment.

280 SERIES — SIX — Both a coupe and sedan were offered in the new 280 Series, (which replaced the 250 Series, wearing the same body), with a new 167.6 cid dual-overhead-cam six-cylinder engine producing 130 horsepower. An automatic transmission was standard. A radio and air conditioning were standard. The V-8 versions of the 280 Series were dropped, as was the 300SEL.

450SL — V-8 — After a brief stay in the Mercedes-Benz lineup, the 350SL two-seater was replaced by a 450SL. As it happened, this one was powered by the same 4.5-liter (276 cid) V-8 engine that went under the 350SL's hood in American trim. (The 3.5-liter edition had been marketed in Europe.) So in effect, little had changed. The 4.5-liter V-8 was rated 190 horsepower (SAE net) at 4,750 rpm, producing 240 pound-feet of torque. Appearance was similar to the 350SL, with the customary Mercedes-Benz tri-star emblem at the center

of a horizontal grille bar, flanked by quad round headlamps. Wheelbase was 96.9 inches. The two-seater measured 172.5 inches long overall and stood 51.2 inches tall, riding 205x14 tires.

450SE/SEL/SLC — V-8 — Mercedes-Benz now marketed a selection of body styles with the same 4.5-liter V-8 engine used in the 450SL two-seater: a 450SE four-door sedan, 450SEL sedan, and 450SLC coupe. Styling of these models was similar to the other Mercedes models, but wheelbases varied: 112.8 inches for the 450SE, 116.5 inches for the 450SEL, and 111 inches for the 450SLC.

Note: Although the 600 "Grosser" Mercedes remained in production through 1980, it seldom appeared in listings of American imports after 1972.

I.D. DATA: The Mercedes-Benz chassis serial number is atop the instrument panel (visible through the windshield), on the radiator cowl, or at the driver's door B-pillar; or for 450SE/SEL models, it may be at the center of the firewall, in the engine compartment. The chassis serial number consists of 14 symbols. The first six symbols (all digits) indicate the model; the next two indicate standard (10) or automatic (12) transmission. The final six digits form the sequential production number. Starting serial number: (220) 115.010-12-105672; (220D) 115.110-

MODEL	BODY TYPE & SEATING	ENGINE TYPE/CID	P.E. PRICE	WEIGHT (LBS.)	PRODUCTION TOTAL
220 SERIES					
220	4-dr Sedan-5P	I4/134	$6,889	2,960	**Note 1**
220D (Diesel)	4-dr Sedan-5P	I4/134	$6,662	3,000	**Note 1**
280 SERIES					
280	4-dr Sedan-5P	I6/168	$9,319	3,285	**Note 1**
280C	2-dr Coupe-5P	I6/168	$9,994	3,285	**Note 1**
450SL					
450SL	2-dr Coupe/Roadster-2P	V8/276	$12,773	3,555	**Note 2**
450 SERIES					
450SE	4-dr Sedan-5P	V8/276	$13,396	3,843	**Note 1**
450SEL	4-dr Sedan-5P	V8/276	$14,605	N/A	**Note 1**
450SLC	2-dr Coupe-4P	V8/276	$16,498	3,625	**Note 1**

Note 1: A total of 331,682 Mercedes-Benz cars (all models) were produced during 1973.

Note 2: A total of 66,298 450SL models were produced during the full model run, 1971-80.

Price Note: Figure shown for 220D included manual transmission; automatic cost $438 more.

10-277011; (280) 114.060-12-000001; (280C) 114.073-12-000001; (280SE) 108.067-12-014245; (450SL) 107.044-12-005794; (450SLC) 107.024-12-000001. Engine number is on left front or right rear of block.

ENGINES

Base Four (220): Inline, overhead-cam four-cylinder. Cast-iron block and aluminum head. Displacement: 134 cid (2,195 cc). Bore & stroke: 3.15 x 2.87 in. (80 x 72.8 mm). Compression ratio: 8.0:1. Brake horsepower: 85 at 4,500 rpm. Torque: 124 lbs.-ft. at 2,500 rpm. Five main bearings. Solid valve lifters.

Diesel Four (220D): Inline, overhead-cam four-cylinder. Displacement: 134 cid (2,195 cc). Bore & stroke: 3.15 x 2.87 in. (80 x 72.8 mm). Compression ratio: 21.0:1. Brake horsepower: 57 at 4,200 rpm. Torque: 88 lbs.-ft. at 2,400 rpm. Solid valve lifters. Fuel injection.

Base Six (280): Inline, dual-overhead-cam six-cylinder. Cast-iron block and aluminum head. Displacement: 167.6 cid (2,746 cc). Bore & stroke: 3.39 x 3.10 in. (86 x 78.8 mm). Compression ratio: 8.0:1. Brake horsepower: 130 at 5,000 rpm. Torque: 150 lbs.-ft. at 3,500 rpm. Seven main bearings. Solid valve lifters.

Base V-8 (450 SERIES): 90-degree, overhead-cam, eight-cylinder. Cast-iron block and aluminum heads. Displacement: 275.8 cid (4,520 cc). Bore & stroke: 3.62 x 3.35 in. (92 x 85 mm). Compression ratio: 8.0:1. Brake horsepower: 190 at 4,750 rpm. Torque: 240 lbs.-ft. at 3,000 rpm. Five main bearings. Solid valve lifters. Bosch fuel injection.

CHASSIS

Wheelbase: (220/280) 108.3 in.; (450SL) 96.9 in.; (450SE) 112.8 in.; (450SEL) 116.5 in.; (450SLC) 111 in. Overall length: (220/280) 184.5 in.; (450SL) 172.5 in.; (450SE) 195.3 in.; (450SEL) 199.2 in.; (450SLC) 186.6 in. Height: (220/280 sedan) 56.7 in.; (280C) 54.9 in.; (450SL) 51.2 in.; (450SE) 56.1 in.; (450SEL) 56.3 in.; (450SLC) 52.4 in. Width: (220/280 sedan) 69.7 in.; (280C) 70.5 in.; (450SL/SLC) 70.5 in.; (450SE) 73.4 in.; (450SEL) 73.4 in. Front tread: (220/280) 57 in.; (450SL/SLC) 57.2 in.; (450SE/SEL) 60 in. Rear tread: (220/280) 56.7 in.; (450SL) 56.7 in.; (450SE/SEL) 59.3 in.; (450SLC) 56.7 in. Standard tires: (220/280) 175x14; (450SL/SLC) 205x14; (450SE/SEL) 205x14.

TECHNICAL

Layout: front-engine, rear-drive. Transmission: (220D) four-speed manual, automatic optional; (others) automatic standard. Steering: recirculating ball. Suspension (front): unequal-length A-arms, coil springs, and stabilizer bar. Suspension (rear): diagonal swing axles with coil springs and stabilizer bar. Brakes: front/rear disc. Body construction: steel unibody with auxiliary front frame.

MAJOR OPTIONS: Automatic transmission (220D). Power steering (220/D). Air conditioning (220/D). Sunroof. Leather seats.

PRODUCTION/SALES: Approximately 41,865 Mercedes-Benz passenger cars (plus 540 trucks) were sold in the U.S. during 1973. The year's total included 10 Model 600 sedans (described in prior listings).

Manufacturer: Daimler-Benz AG, Stuttgart, West Germany.

Distributor: Mercedes-Benz of North America Inc., Montvale, New Jersey.

HISTORY

The 1973 models were introduced to the U.S. market on September 11, 1972, except the 280C, which debuted November 1, 1972.

1974 240D 3.0

1974

230 — FOUR — A new sedan with 141 cid four-cylinder engine became available for the 1974 model year. The engine produced 95 horsepower at 4,800 rpm. A four-speed automatic transmission with torque converter was standard. As in all the 2-Series models, roof pillars were redesigned to divert rain from side windows, and doors had a new "safety cone" lock. A lever to the left of the steering column controlled the turn signals, high/low beams, and wipers. Standard equipment included power steering, tinted glass, vinyl upholstery, and an electrically heated rear window.

240D — DIESEL FOUR — The 220 Series was gone, replaced by a 240D sedan (diesel engine only). The new 146.7 cid engine developed 62 horsepower. Standard equipment was similar to the gas-engine 230 sedan.

280 SERIES — SIX — As before, both a coupe and sedan were offered in the 280 Series, powered by a 167.6 cid dual-overhead-cam six-cylinder engine that developed 130 horsepower. A four-barrel carburetor handled the "breathing" duties, and a four-speed automatic transmission was standard. Standard equipment included air conditioning, front armrest, power steering, tinted glass, central locking, vinyl upholstery, AM/FM radio, halogen fog lamps, and an electrically heated rear window.

450SL — V-8 — Production of the Mercedes-Benz two-seat coupe/roadster continued with little change, with the 4.5-liter (276 cid) V-8 engine under its hood. A three-speed automatic transmission was standard. The 450SL could be driven as an open roadster, a convertible with the soft top erected, or with the steel hardtop fitted in position.

450SE/SEL/SLC — V-8 — Little change was evident in the trio of other Mercedes-Benz models with the 4.5-liter V-8 engine, rated at 190 horsepower and 240 lbs.-ft. of torque. Leather upholstery was standard on the 450SEL sedan and 450SLC coupe. All 450 Series models included a tachometer and quartz clock ahead of the driver. The 450SEL offered extra rear leg room and wider rear doors than its shorter 450SE companion. Each model had air conditioning, a three-speed automatic transmission, cruise control, central locking, halogen fog lamps, power windows, AM/FM stereo radio with automatic antenna, height-adjustable front seats, and radial tires. Upholstery was M-B Tex on the 450SE, leather on the 450SEL sedan and 450SLC coupe.

Note: Although the 600 "Grosser" Mercedes remained in production through 1980 and a handful were exported to the U.S., it seldom appeared in listings of American imports through the 1970s; See earlier listings for details.

I.D. DATA: The Mercedes-Benz chassis serial number is atop the instrument panel (visible through the windshield), on the radiator cowl, or at the driver's door B-pillar; or for 450SE/SEL models, it may be at the center of the firewall, in the engine compartment. The chassis serial number consists of 14 symbols. The first six symbols (all digits) indicate the model; the next two indicate standard (10) or automatic (12) transmission. The final six digits form the sequential production number. Starting serial number: (230) 115.017-12-000001; (240D) 115.117-

MODEL	BODY TYPE & SEATING	ENGINE TYPE/CID	P.E. PRICE	WEIGHT (LBS.)	PRODUCTION TOTAL
230					
230	4-dr Sedan-5P	I4/141	$8,420	3,040	**Note 1**
240D (Diesel)					
240D	4-dr Sedan-5P	I4/147	$8,715	3,080	**Note 1**
280 SERIES					
280	4-dr Sedan-5P	I6/168	$10,950	3,330	**Note 1**
280C	2-dr Coupe-5P	I6/168	$11,630	3,330	**Note 1**
450SL					
450SL	2-dr Coupe/Roadster-2P	V8/276	$15,450	3,580	**Note 2**
450 SERIES					
450SE	4-dr Sedan-5P	V8/276	$15,820	3,910	**Note 1**
450SEL	4-dr Sedan-5P	V8/276	$17,400	3,940	**Note 1**
450SLC	2-dr Coupe-4P	V8/276	$19,450	3,630	**Note 1**

Note 1: A total of 340,006 Mercedes-Benz cars (all models) were produced during 1974.

Note 2: A total of 66,298 450SL models were produced during the full model run, 1971-80.

Price Note: Figure shown for 240D included manual transmission; automatic cost $575 more.

10-000001; (280) 114.060-12-100666; (280C) 114.073-12-100168; (450SE) 116.032-12-013479; (450SEL) 116.033-12-013446; (450SL) 107.044-12-015082; (450SLC) 107.024-12-004128. Engine number is on left front or right rear of block.

Note: Various serial numbers that didn't follow the sequences listed above also were considered 1974 models.

ENGINES

Base Four (230): Inline, overhead-cam four-cylinder. Cast-iron block and aluminum head. Displacement: 140.8 cid (2,308 cc). Bore & stroke: 3.69 x 3.29 in. (94 x 83.6 mm). Compression ratio: 8.0:1. Brake horsepower: 95 at 4,800 rpm. Torque: 128 lbs.-ft. at 2,500 rpm. Five main bearings. Solid valve lifters.

Diesel Four (240D): Inline, overhead-cam four-cylinder. Cast-iron block and head. Displacement: 146.7 cid (2,404 cc). Bore & stroke: 3.58 x 3.64 in. (91 x 92.5 mm). Compression ratio: 21.0:1. Brake horsepower: 62 at 4,000 rpm. Torque: 97 lbs.-ft. at 2,400 rpm. Five main bearings. Solid valve lifters. Fuel injection.

Base Six (280): Inline, dual-overhead-cam six-cylinder. Cast-iron block and aluminum head. Displacement: 167.6 cid (2,746 cc). Bore & stroke: 3.39 x 3.10 in. (86 x 78.8 mm). Compression ratio: 8.0:1. Brake horsepower: 130 at 5,000 rpm. Torque: 150 lbs.-ft. at 3,500 rpm. Seven main bearings. Solid valve lifters. Four-barrel carburetor.

Note: California 280 Series engine was rated 123 bhp and 143 lbs.-ft.

Base V-8 (450 SERIES): 90-degree, overhead-cam, eight-cylinder. Cast-iron block and aluminum heads. Displacement: 275.8 cid (4,520 cc). Bore & stroke: 3.62 x 3.35 in. (92 x 85 mm). Compression ratio: 8.0:1. Brake horsepower: 190 at 4,750 rpm. Torque: 240 lbs.-ft. at 3,000 rpm. Five main bearings. Solid valve lifters. Bosch fuel injection.

Note: California 450 Series engine was rated 180 bhp and 232 lbs.-ft.

CHASSIS

Wheelbase: (230/240D/280) 108.3 in.; (450SL) 96.9 in.; (450SLC) 111.0 in.; (450SE) 112.8 in.; (450SEL) 116.7 in. Overall length: (230/240D/280) 195.5 in.; (450SL) 182.3 in.; (450SLC) 196.4 in.; (450SE) 205.5 in.; (450SEL) 209.4 in. Height: (230/240D/280 sedan) 56.7 in.; (280C) 54.9 in.; (450SL) 50.8 in.; (450SLC) 52.4 in.; (450SE) 56.1 in.; (450SEL) 56.3 in. Width: (230/240D/280) 69.7 in.; (450SL/SLC) 70.5 in.; (450SE/SEL) 73.6 in. Front tread: (230/240D/280) 57.0 in.; (450SL/SLC) 57.2 in.; (450SE/SEL) 60.0 in. Rear tread: (230/240D/280) 56.7 in.; (450SL/SLC) 56.7 in.; (450SE/SEL) 59.3 in. Standard tires: (230/240D/280) 175x14; (450 SL/SLC) 205/70x14; (450SE/SEL) 205/70x14.

TECHNICAL

Layout: front-engine, rear-drive. Transmission: (240D) four-speed manual, four-speed automatic optional; (230/280) four-speed automatic standard; (450 Series) three-speed automatic standard. Steering: recirculating ball. Suspension (front): unequal-length A-arms, coil springs, and stabilizer bar. Suspension (rear): diagonal swing axles with coil springs and stabilizer bar. Brakes: front/rear disc. Body construction: steel unibody.

MAJOR OPTIONS: Automatic transmission (240D). Air conditioning (230/240D). Sliding metal sunroof. Leather seats. Velour upholstery (280/280C). Automatic antenna. Power windows. Fitted luggage. Parcel nets (on front seatbacks). Front seats with orthopedic backrests. Central locking. Halogen foglamps. Signal-seeking Grand Prix radio (450SL). Light alloy wheels (450 Series).

PRODUCTION/SALES: Approximately 37,230 Mercedes-Benz passenger cars (plus 656 trucks) were sold in the U.S. during 1974, plus about 2,876 delivered to tourists in Europe.

Manufacturer: Daimler-Benz AG, Stuttgart, West Germany.

Distributor: Mercedes-Benz of North America Inc., Montvale, New Jersey.

HISTORY

The 1974 models were introduced to the U.S. market on September 30, 1973. This year's Mercedes-Benz catalog focused on safety features, pointing out that the company had "been concerned with automobile safety long before the public discussion began on the subject."

1975 450SEL 6.9

1975-1976

230 — FOUR — Production of the four-cylinder Mercedes with 141 cid engine continued with little change.

240D — FOUR — Mercedes' four-cylinder diesel remained in production with minimal change. The 146.7 cid engine developed 62 horsepower.

300D — FIVE — Mercedes turned to a five-cylinder power plant for its next diesel sedan. The 183.4 cid engine developed 77 hp and 115 lbs.-ft. of torque.

280 SERIES — SIX — Once again, a coupe and sedan were offered in the 280 Series, powered by a 167.6 cid dual-overhead-cam six-cylinder engine with four-barrel carburetor that developed 120 horsepower. This year, a 280S four-door sedan also was available, on a longer (112.2-inch) wheelbase. A four-speed automatic transmission was standard. Standard equipment was similar to 1974.

450SL — V-8 — Production of the two-seat coupe/roadster with removable hardtop continued with little change, powered by a 4.5-liter (276 cid) V-8 engine that developed 180 bhp An automatic transmission was standard.

450SE/SEL/SLC — V-8 — Each of the larger 450 Series models continued with little change, powered by the same engine used in the 450SL. Standard equipment was similar to 1974. By 1976, the 4.5-liter engine's fuel-injection system changed to Bosch K-Jetronic.

I.D. DATA: The Mercedes-Benz chassis serial number is atop the instrument panel (visible through the windshield), on the radiator cowl, or at the driver's door B-pillar; or for 450SE/SEL models, it may be at the center of the firewall, or in the engine compartment. The chassis serial number consists of 14 symbols. The first six symbols (all digits) indicate the model; the next two indicate standard (10) or automatic (12) transmission. The final six digits form the sequential production number. Starting serial number (1975 models): (230) 115.017-12-025972; (240D) 115.117-10-056706; (300D) 115.114-12-000001; (280) 114.060-12-112062; (280C) 114.073-12-103729; (280S) 116.020-12-029633; (450SE) 116.032-12-029673; (450SEL) 116.033-12-029418; (450SL) 107.044-12-021762; (450SLC) 107.024-12-008203. Engine number is on left front or right rear of block.

Note: Various serial numbers that didn't follow the sequences listed above also were considered 1975 models.

Model	Body Type & Seating	Engine Type/CID	P.E. Price	Weight (lbs.)	Production Total
230					
230	4-dr Sedan-5P	I4/141	$9,172	3,110	**Note 1**
240D/300D (Diesel)					
240D	4-dr Sedan-5P	I4/147	$9,811	3,100	**Note 1**
300D	4-dr Sedan-5P	I5/183	$12,194	3,340	**Note 1**
280 SERIES					
280	4-dr Sedan-5P	I6/168	$12,756	3,440	**Note 1**
280S	4-dr Sedan-5P	I6/168	$15,057	3,770	**Note 1**
280C	2-dr Coupe-5P	I6/168	$13,520	3,450	**Note 1**
450SL					
450SL	2-dr Coupe/Roadster-2P	V8/276	$17,653	3,640	**Note 2**
450 SERIES					
450SE	4-dr Sedan-5P	V8/276	$18,333	3,945	**Note 1**
450SEL	4-dr Sedan-5P	V8/276	$19,775	3,990	**Note 1**
450SLC	2-dr Coupe-4P	V8/276	$22,053	3,680	**Note 1**

Note 1: A total of 356,477 Mercedes-Benz cars (all models) were produced during 1975, followed by 370,348 in 1976.

Note 2: A total of 66,298 450SL models were produced during the full model run, 1971-80.

Price Note: Figure shown for 240D included manual transmission; automatic cost $639 more. Prices shown were valid during the 1975 model year; for 1976, they ranged from $9,930 for the 240D (manual shift) to $23,976 for the 450SLC coupe.

ENGINES

Base Four (230): Inline, overhead-cam four-cylinder. Cast-iron block and aluminum head. Displacement: 140.8 cid (2,308 cc). Bore & stroke: 3.69 x 3.29 in. (94 x 83.6 mm). Compression ratio: 8.0:1. Brake horsepower: 93 at 4,800 rpm. Torque: 125 lbs.-ft. at 2,500 rpm. Five main bearings. Solid valve lifters. Single-barrel carburetor.

Diesel Four (240D): Inline, overhead-cam four-cylinder. Cast-iron block and head. Displacement: 146.7 cid (2,404 cc). Bore & stroke: 3.58 x 3.64 in. (91 x 92.4 mm). Compression ratio: 21.0:1. Brake horsepower: 62 at 4,000 rpm. Torque: 97 lbs.-ft. at 2,400 rpm. Five main bearings. Solid valve lifters. Fuel injection.

Diesel Five (300D): Inline, overhead-cam five-cylinder. Cast-iron block and head. Displacement: 183.4 cid (3,005 cc). Bore & stroke: 3.58 x 3.64 in. (91 x 92.4 mm). Compression ratio: 21.0:1. Brake horsepower: 77 at 4,400 rpm. Torque: 115 lbs.-ft. at 2,400 rpm. Six main bearings. Solid valve lifters. Fuel injection.

Base Six (280): Inline, dual-overhead-cam six-cylinder. Cast-iron block and aluminum head. Displacement: 167.6 cid (2,746 cc). Bore & stroke: 3.39 x 3.10 in. (86 x 78.8 mm). Compression ratio: 8.0:1. Brake horsepower: 120 at 4,800 rpm. Torque: 143 lbs.-ft. at 2,800 rpm. Seven main bearings. Solid valve lifters. Four-barrel carburetor.

Base V-8 (450 SERIES): 90-degree, overhead-cam, eight-cylinder. Cast-iron block and aluminum heads. Displacement: 275.8 cid (4,520 cc). Bore & stroke: 3.62 x 3.35 in. (92 x 85 mm). Compression ratio: 8.0:1. Brake horsepower: 180 at 4,750 rpm. Torque: 220 lbs.-ft. at 3,000 rpm. Five main bearings. Solid valve lifters. Bosch fuel injection.

CHASSIS

Wheelbase: (230/240D/280/300D) 108.3 in.; (280S) 112.2 in.; (450SL) 96.9 in.; (450SLC) 111.0 in.; (450SE) 112.8 in.; (450SEL) 116.7 in. Overall length: (230/240D/280/300D) 195.5 in.; (450SL) 182.3 in.; (450SLC) 196.4 in.; (450SE) 205.5 in.; (450SEL) 209.4 in. Height: (230/240D/280/300D sedan) 56.7 in.; (280C) 54.9 in.; (280S) 56.1 in.; (450SL) 50.8 in.; (450SLC) 52.4 in.; (450SE) 56.1 in.; (450SEL) 56.3 in. Width: (230/240D/280/300D) 69.7 in.; (450SL/SLC) 70.5 in.; (450SE/SEL) 73.6 in. Front tread: (230/240D/280/300D) 57.0 in.; (450SL/SLC) 57.2 in.; (450SE/SEL) 60.0 in. Rear tread: (230/240D/280/300D) 56.7 in.; (450SL/SLC) 56.7 in.; (450SE/SEL) 59.3 in. Standard tires: (230/240D/300D) 175x14; (280 Series) 185x14; (450 Series) 205/70x14.

TECHNICAL

Layout: front-engine, rear-drive. Transmission: (240D) four-speed manual, four-speed automatic optional; (230/280/300D) four-speed automatic standard; (450 Series) three-speed automatic standard. Steering: recirculating ball. Suspension (front): unequal-length A-arms, coil springs and stabilizer bar. Suspension (rear): diagonal swing axles with coil springs and stabilizer bar. Brakes: front/rear disc. Body construction: steel unibody.

MAJOR OPTIONS: Similar to 1974.

PRODUCTION/SALES: Approximately 42,232 Mercedes-Benz passenger cars (plus 1,218 trucks) were sold in the U.S. during 1975, plus about 3,027 cars delivered to tourists in Europe, for a total of 45,259. Approximately 39,075 Mercedes-Benz cars were sold in the U.S. during 1976, plus 4,130 tourist deliveries, for a total of 43,205.

Manufacturer: Daimler-Benz AG, Stuttgart, West Germany.

Distributor: Mercedes-Benz of North America Inc., Montvale, New Jersey.

HISTORY

The 1975 models were introduced to the U.S. market in September 1974; the 1976 models in November 1975.

1977-1978

230 — FOUR — Wheelbase grew from 108.3 to 110 inches but overall length actually became shorter on the 230/240/280/300 sedans with their new W123 body/chassis. This was the first redesign of the basic Mercedes body since 1968, featuring a wider shape and wider radiator grille. Mechanically, production of the four-cylinder Mercedes with its 141 cid engine continued with little change, though horsepower dropped to 86. Cruise control became standard in 1978 on models with automatic transmissions.

240D — DIESEL FOUR — Only a modest change in dimensions was evident in Mercedes' four-cylinder diesel with its new body, again powered by a 146.7 cid engine that developed 62 horsepower.

300D SERIES — DIESEL FIVE — The most powerful Mercedes diesel sedan (until the turbocharged version arrived) used a five-cylinder engine, producing 77 horsepower. For the 1978 model year, a 300CD diesel coupe became available. Just a few months before the start of the 1979 model year, Mercedes introduced a 300SD turbodiesel sedan on a 112.8-inch wheelbase. The 300SD was powered by a more potent version of the five-cylinder engine, initially rated at 110 horsepower. Acceleration to 60 mph took less than 14 seconds.

280 SERIES — SIX — Only a pair of sedans remained of the 280 Series, on two different wheelbases: 110 inches for the 280E and 112.8 inches for the 280SE. The 168 cid six now developed 142 horsepower, using fuel injection instead of carburetion. For 1978 a headlamp-on buzzer was added. A 280CE coupe joined in 1978 with a roofline 1.5 inches lower than the sedan and a sharper-angled windshield and back window.

Body Note: W123 was the Mercedes-Benz internal code for the shorter-wheelbase 230/240/280/300 body group. Some 280/300 models rode a longer wheelbase and were actually part of the larger S-Class category.

450SL — V-8 — Production of the two-seat coupe/roadster with removable hardtop continued with little change. As before, the 4.5-liter (276 cid) V-8 engine developed 180 bhp and an automatic transmission was standard.

450SEL/SLC — V-8 — The 450SE sedan was dropped for 1977, but the other two variants remained. Power came again from the same 4.5-liter engine used in the 450SL coupe/roadster.

The Mercedes-Benz 450SL.
Secure, serene, understated.

You'll sense the quiet obviousness of the 450SL's good breeding at first sight. Now take the wheel. That first drive will confirm your initial impression. This car is every bit the thoroughbred. And it accomplishes brilliantly its primary purpose: to make your driving a pure pleasure.

What you ask of the Mercedes-Benz 450SL, it does for you in full measure. Without hesitation or unpleasant surprises. In every situation the Mercedes-Benz 450SL helps you to be the most assured driver you can be.

Legendary engineering ideas

The 450SL brings together in one superb machine an extraordinary array of the legendary engineering ideas from Mercedes-Benz. Consider:

The door opening probably is wider than the front doorway of your home (imagine!), so you can easily enter or leave the car.

The generous storage areas will accept luggage enough for a trip across the country—or load them up with your oddly shaped sports equipment…even your skis!

All four wheels of the 450SL have disc brakes. Most cars have no disc brakes, or only two at best. Think what a difference this can mean in an emergency stop.

Anatomically correct seats adjust not two or four, but *six* ways: forward and back, up and down, and in the tilt of the seat-back.

The seats work with the 450SL's remarkable four-wheel independent suspension system to keep you relaxed and comfortable through the longest drive.

Power steering with a sensitive "feel" makes backing up into a tight parking space refreshingly easy.

The 450SL's body is hand rubbed by craftsmen to a glowing finish; the sumptuous seats are painstakingly made, stitch by stitch, by artisans skilled in the upholstery craft.

You may have been first attracted to the 450SL because it is so fashionable. We hope this message has brought you the good and perhaps surprising news that the Mercedes-Benz 450SL is, first and foremost, a truly superb automobile —secure, serene, understated.

Drive the 450SL at your local Mercedes-Benz Dealer's. Learn for yourself that the Mercedes-Benz legend does, indeed, continue.

Mercedes-Benz
Engineered like no other car in the world.

© Mercedes-Benz, 1977

1977 450SL ad

Model	Body Type & Seating	Engine Type/CID	P.E. Price	Weight (lbs.)	Production Total
230					
230	4-dr Sedan-5P	I4/141	$12,509	3,070	**Note 1**
240D/300D (Diesel)					
240D	4-dr Sedan-5P	I4/147	$11,573	3,080	**Note 1**
300D	4-dr Sedan-5P	I5/183	$16,107	3,385	**Note 1**
280 SERIES					
280E	4-dr Sedan-5P	I6/168	$16,616	3,405	**Note 1**
280SE	4-dr Sedan-5P	I6/168	$19,411	3,750	**Note 1**
450SL					
450SL	2-dr Coupe/Roadster-2P	V8/276	$21,943	3,670	**Note 2**
450 SERIES					
450SEL	4-dr Sedan-5P	V8/276	$24,506	3,925	**Note 1**
450SLC	2-dr Coupe-4P	V8/276	$27,090	3,715	**Note 1**
6.9	4-dr Sedan-5P	V8/417	$39,377	4,235	**Note 1**

Note 1: A total of 401,250 Mercedes-Benz cars (all models) were produced during 1977, followed by 382,622 in 1978.

Note 2: A total of 66,298 450SL coupe/roadsters were produced during the full model run, 1971-80.

Price Note: Figures shown above were valid during 1977. Figure shown for 240D included manual transmission; automatic cost $12,379. Prices in 1978 ranged from $14,872 for the 240D sedan to $44,923 for the 6.9 sedan.

1978 Model Note: Three models were added during the 1978 model year. The 300CD coupe sold for $21,472; the 300SD turbodiesel sedan for $23,878; and the 280CE coupe sold for $22,141.

450SEL 6.9 — V-8 — A new, plush, and more expensive sedan joined the Mercedes lineup, carrying a 417 cid V-8 engine that developed 250 horsepower. Wheelbase was 116.5 inches and the 6.9 cost $15,000 more than the regular 450SEL sedan. The "450SEL" prefix was not always included in its model designation.

I.D. DATA: The Mercedes-Benz chassis serial number is atop the instrument panel (visible through the windshield), on the radiator cowl, or at the driver's door B-pillar; or for 450SE/SEL models, it may be at the center of the firewall in the engine compartment. The chassis serial number consists of 14 symbols. The first six symbols (all digits) indicate the model; the next two indicate standard (10) or automatic (12) transmission. The final six digits form the sequential production number. Starting serial number (1977 models): (230) 123.023-12-016749; (240D) 123.123-10-008892; (300D) 123.130-12-013872; (280E) 123.033-12-013707; (280SE) 116.024-12-072034; (450SEL) 116.033-12-059127; (450SL) 107.044-12-035387; (450SLC) 107.024-12-015075. Engine number is on left front or right rear of block.

ENGINES

Base Four (230): Inline, overhead-cam four-cylinder. Cast-iron block and aluminum head. Displacement: 140.8 cid (2,308 cc). Bore & stroke: 3.69 x 3.29 in. (94 x 83.6 mm). Compression ratio: 8.0:1. Brake horsepower: 86 at 4,800 rpm. Torque: 125 lbs.-ft. at 2,500 rpm. Five main bearings. Solid valve lifters. Single-barrel carburetor.

1977 230E

Diesel Four (240D): Inline, overhead-cam four-cylinder. Cast-iron block and head. Displacement: 146.7 cid (2,404 cc). Bore & stroke: 3.58 x 3.64 in. (91 x 92.4 mm). Compression ratio: 21.0:1. Brake horsepower: 62 at 4,000 rpm. Torque: 97 lbs.-ft. at 2,400 rpm. Five main bearings. Solid valve lifters. Fuel injection.

Diesel Five (300D): Inline, overhead-cam five-cylinder. Cast-iron block and head. Displacement: 183.4 cid (3,005 cc). Bore & stroke: 3.58 x 3.64 in. (91 x 92.4 mm). Compression ratio: 21.0:1. Brake horsepower: 77 at 4,000 rpm. Torque: 115 lbs.-ft. at 2,400 rpm. Six main bearings. Solid valve lifters. Fuel injection.

Base Six (280): Inline, dual-overhead-cam six-cylinder. Cast-iron block and aluminum head. Displacement: 167.6 cid (2,746 cc). Bore & stroke: 3.39 x 3.10 in. (86 x 78.8 mm). Compression ratio: 8.0:1. Brake horsepower: 142 at 5,750 rpm. Torque: 149 lbs.-ft. at 4,600 rpm. Seven main bearings. Solid valve lifters. Fuel injection.

Base V-8 (450 SERIES): 90-degree, overhead-cam, eight-cylinder. Cast-iron block and aluminum heads. Displacement: 275.8 cid (4,520 cc). Bore & stroke: 3.62 x 3.35 in. (92 x 85 mm). Compression ratio: 8.0:1. Brake horsepower: 180 at 4,750

rpm. Torque: 220 lbs.-ft. at 3,000 rpm. Five main bearings. Hydraulic valve lifters. Bosch fuel injection.

Base V-8 (6.9 sedan): 90-degree, overhead-cam, eight-cylinder. Cast-iron block and aluminum heads. Displacement: 417 cid (6,834 cc). Bore & stroke: 4.21 x 3.74 in. (107 x 95 mm). Compression ratio: 8.0:1. Brake horsepower: 250 at 4,000 rpm. Torque: 360 lbs.-ft. at 2,500 rpm. Five main bearings. Hydraulic valve lifters. Bosch K-Jetronic fuel injection.

CHASSIS

Wheelbase: (230/240D/280/300D) 110 in.; (280SE) 112.8 in.; (450SL) 96.9 in.; (450SLC) 111.0 in.; (450SEL) 116.7 in.; (6.9) 116.5 in. Overall length: (230/240D/280/300D) 190.9 in.; (280SE) 205.5 in. (450SL) 182.3 in.; (450SLC) 196.4 in.; (450SE) 205.5 in.; (450SEL) 209.4 in.; (6.9) 210 in. Height: (230/240D/280/300D) 56.6 in.; (280SE) 56.1 in.; (450SL) 50.8 in.; (450SLC) 52.4 in.; (450SEL) 56.3 in.; (6.9) 55.5 in. Width: (230/240D/280/300D) 70.3 in.; (280SE) 73.6 in.; (450SL/SLC) 70.5 in.; (450SEL) 73.6 in.; (6.9) 73.6 in. Front tread: (230/240D/280/300D) 58.6 in.; (280SE) 59.9 in.; (450SL/SLC) 57.2 in.; (450SE/SEL) 60.0 in.; (6.9) 59.5 in. Rear tread: (230/240D/280/300D) 56.9 in.; (280SE) 59.3 in.; (450SL/SLC) 56.7 in.; (450SEL) 59.3 in.; (6.9) 59.3 in. Standard tires: (230/240D) 175SR14; (300D) 195/70HR14; (280E) 195/70HR14; (280SE) 185HR14; (450 Series) 205/70HR14; (6.9) 215/70HR14.

TECHNICAL

Layout: front-engine, rear-drive. Transmission: (240D) four-speed manual, four-speed automatic optional; (230/280/300D) four-speed automatic standard; (450 Series) three-speed automatic standard. Steering: recirculating ball. Suspension (front): unequal-length A-arms, coil springs, and stabilizer bar. Suspension (rear): diagonal swing axles with coil springs and stabilizer bar. Brakes: front/rear disc. Body construction: steel unibody.

MAJOR OPTIONS: Air conditioning (230/240D). Automatic transmission (240D). AM/FM stereo. Alloy wheels. Sunroof. Leather seats.

PRODUCTION/SALES: A total of 48,872 Mercedes-Benz passenger cars were sold in the U.S. during 1977, plus about 4,946 cars delivered to tourists in Europe. A total of 46,695 passenger cars were sold in the U.S. during 1978, plus 3,569 cars delivered to tourists in Europe.

Manufacturer: Daimler-Benz AG, Stuttgart, West Germany.

Distributor: Mercedes-Benz of North America Inc., Montvale, New Jersey.

HISTORY

The 1977 models were introduced to the U.S. market in December 1976; the 1978 models in November 1977. *Consumer Guide's Auto '78* ranked the 300D as the top Mercedes, for its mix of "prestige, quality, and excellent fuel economy." Only its high price kept the 300D from being named one of the top cars in any class.

1979-1980

240D — DIESEL FOUR — Production of the four-cylinder diesel sedan continued with little change, powered by a 146.7 cid engine that developed 62 horsepower. The 230 sedan with four-cylinder gasoline engine was dropped.

300D/CD/TD — DIESEL FIVE — A five-cylinder diesel engine again powered the 300D sedan and 300CD coupe. During 1979, a 300TD station wagon was added, with the same 77-bhp engine and 110-inch wheelbase. An automatic rear load leveler on the wagon operated from a hydraulic pump at the engine. An optional rear-facing seat could be ordered (suitable for two children). Roof rails were standard, a roof rack optional. A manual sliding roof was standard on the wagon.

300SD — TURBODIESEL FIVE — Production of the turbodiesel sedan, introduced late in the 1978 model year, continued with little change.

280 SERIES — SIX — The 280CE coupe and 280E sedan continued with little change. The 280SE sedan rode a longer (112.8-inch) wheelbase. Under the hood of each model was a 168 cid six producing 142 horsepower.

Body Note: W123 was the Mercedes-Benz internal code for the shorter-wheelbase 240/280/300 body group. Some 280/300 models rode a longer wheelbase and were actually part of the larger S-Class category.

450SL — V-8 — Little change was evident in the two-seat coupe/roadster, which included a removable hardtop. As before, the 4.5-liter (276 cid) V-8 engine developed 180 bhp and an automatic transmission was standard.

450SEL/SLC — V-8 — Two additional 450 Series models remained, a coupe and sedan, again carrying the same 4.5-liter engine used in the 450SL coupe/roadster.

450SEL 6.9 — V-8 — The powerful and expensive sedan, introduced in 1978 with its 417 cid V-8 engine, lasted through 1979 before departing from the lineup of Mercedes models sold in the U.S.

Engine Note: Engine horsepower/torque ratings changed for the 1980 model year; see data below.

I.D. DATA: The Mercedes-Benz chassis serial number is atop the instrument panel (visible through the windshield), on the radiator cowl, or at the driver's door B-pillar; or for 450 SEL models, it may be at the center of the firewall in the engine compartment. The chassis serial number consists of 14 symbols. The first six symbols (all digits) indicate the model; the next two indicate standard (10) or automatic (12) transmission. The final six digits form the sequential production number. Starting serial number (1979 models): (240D) 123.123-10-085343; (300D) 123.130-12-107713; (300CD) 123.150-12-002879; (300SD) 116.120-12-001944; (300TD) 123.190-12-000001; (280E) 123.033-12-044014; (280CE) 123.053-12-010847; (450SEL) 116.033-12-083626; (450SL) 107.044-12-049156; (450SLC) 107.024-12-022921; (6.9) 116.036-12-004609.

ENGINES

Base Diesel Four (240D): Inline, overhead-cam four-cylinder. Cast-iron block and head. Displacement: 146.7 cid (2,404 cc). Bore & stroke: 3.58 x 3.64 in. (91 x 92.4 mm). Compression ratio: 21.0:1. Brake horsepower: 62 at 4,000 rpm (67 bhp in 1980). Torque: 97 lbs.-ft. at 2,400 rpm. Five main bearings. Solid valve lifters. Fuel injection.

Base Diesel Five (300D): Inline, overhead-cam five-cylinder. Cast-iron block and head. Displacement: 183.4 cid (3,005 cc). Bore & stroke: 3.58 x 3.64 in. (91 x 92.4 mm). Compression ratio: 21.0:1. Brake horsepower: 77 at 4,000 rpm (83 bhp at 4200 rpm in 1980). Torque: 115 lbs.-ft. at 2,400 rpm (120 lbs.-ft. in 1980). Six main bearings. Solid valve lifters. Fuel injection.

Base Turbodiesel Five (300SD): Same as 3,005 cc five above, but with a turbocharger Compression ratio: 21.5:1. Brake horsepower: 110 at 4,200 rpm (120 bhp at 4,350 rpm in 1980). Torque: 168 lbs.-ft. at 2,400 rpm (170 at 2,400 rpm in 1980).

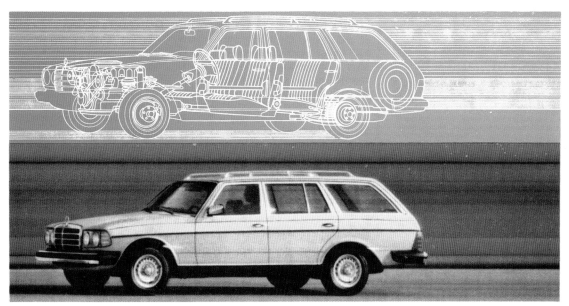

Mercedes-Benz didn't invent the station wagon-they just raised it up to Mercedes-Benz standards.

Mercedes-Benz waited 94 years to build a station wagon—and then built one like none before …"it is not only the best wagon we've tested," says **Car and Driver**, *"it ranks right up there as one of the all-time best cars in our experience."*

For instance, heavy loads cause the rear suspension to automatically adjust itself and keep the vehicle riding level. Part of the interior converts into a cargo hold almost 10 feet long. And one critic quips, "The only way to shake something loose would be to drive it off a cliff."

Grins of disbelief

With 50.8 percent of its weight over the front axle and 49.2 percent over the rear, the 300 TD is almost perfectly balanced. It flattens curves with a fully independent suspension similar to the exotic 450 SL Roadster.

Euphoria results. "The TD begins to amaze, to bring on grins of disbelief, to entertain, when it's up to speed and moving on down the road," *Car and Driver* reports.

And when it stops? *Car and Driver* found that it stopped "in a phenomenally short distance" —bested only by a 160-mph, $36,000 European sports coupe.

A workhorse that sprints

If any automobile engine is indestructible it is the workhorse Diesel. The 300 TD's Diesel engine is a responsive, 5-cylinder powerplant—beneficiary of a 44-year Mercedes-Benz Diesel Research & Development program.

And the 300 TD is miserly with fuel, generating an EPA estimated 23 mpg.* The EPA highway estimate is 28 mpg. Compare this to other cars. You may get different mileage, depending on speed, weather conditions, and trip length. Your actual highway mileage will probably be less than the highway estimates.

A wagon, Mercedes-Benz style

From the driver's seat, the 300 TD gives no inkling that it is anything but a Mercedes-Benz automobile. Civilization reigns, from a comprehensive bi-level climate control system to electric window lifts to AM/FM stereo radio.

Face rearward and the 300 TD is a wagon—a remarkable wagon.

"It is simply one of our finest cars when it comes to the all-important accommodation and transportation of its load," *Car and Driver* declares.

Why Mercedes-Benz owners are smiling

To duplicate this engineering and workmanship would require that you have a station wagon custom built. This may help put the 300 TD's $28,056** price in perspective.

And because it is a Mercedes-Benz, it stands a fine chance of retaining much of its value over time. Mercedes-Benz owners today are finding that cars they bought 3 years ago are now worth *80 percent* of their purchase price.

The 300 TD. It may haul cargo like a station wagon. Clearly, it does everything else like a Mercedes-Benz.

Engineered like no other car in the world

1980 300TD ad

Model	Body Type & Seating	Engine Type/CID	P.O.E. Price	Weight (lbs.)	Production Total
240D/300D (Diesel)					
240D	4-dr Sedan-5P	I4/147	$15,068	3,010	**Note 1**
300D	4-dr Sedan-5P	I5/183	$20,911	3,385	**Note 1**
300CD	2-dr Coupe-4/5P	I5/183	$23,619	N/A	**Note 1**
300TD	4-dr Station Wagon-5P	I5/183	$23,900	3,635	**Note 1**
300SD (Turbodiesel)					
300SD	4-dr Sedan-5P	I5/183	$26,265	3,705	**Note 1**
280 SERIES					
280E	4-dr Sedan-5P	I6/168	$22,318	3,415	**Note 1**
280CE	2-dr Coupe-5P	I6/168	$24,951	3,365	**Note 1**
280SE	4-dr Sedan-5P	I6/168	$26,177	3,670	**Note 1**
450 SERIES					
450SL	2-dr Coupe/Roadster-2P	V8/276	$30,729	3,595	**Note 2**
450SEL	4-dr Sedan-5P	V8/276	$32,858	3,860	**Note 1**
450SLC	2-dr Coupe-4P	V8/276	$36,519	3,650	**Note 1**
6.9	4-dr Sedan-5P	V8/417	$50,190	4,285	**Note 1**

Note 1: A total of 393,754 Mercedes-Benz cars (all models) were produced during 1979, followed by 401,848 in 1980.

Note 2: A total of 66,298 450SL coupe/roadsters were produced during the full model run, 1971-80.

Price Note: Figures shown above were valid during 1979. Figure shown for 240D included manual transmission; automatic cost $16,313. Prices in 1980 ranged from $17,533 for the 240D sedan to $42,592 for the 450SLC coupe.

Base Six (280): Inline, dual-overhead-cam six-cylinder. Cast-iron block and aluminum head. Displacement: 167.6 cid (2,746 cc). Bore & stroke: 3.39 x 3.10 in. (86 x 78.8 mm). Compression ratio: 8.0:1. Brake horsepower: 142 at 5,750 rpm (140 at 5,500 rpm in 1980). Torque: 149 lbs.-ft. at 4,600 rpm (145 at 4,500 rpm in 1980). Seven main bearings. Solid valve lifters. Fuel injection.

Base V-8 (450 SERIES): 90-degree, overhead-cam, eight-cylinder. Cast-iron block and aluminum heads. Displacement: 275.8 cid (4,520 cc). Bore & stroke: 3.62 x 3.35 in. (92 x 85 mm). Compression ratio: 8.0:1. Brake horsepower: 180 at 4,750 rpm (160 at 4,200 rpm in 1980). Torque: 220 lbs.-ft. at 3000 rpm (230 at 2,500 rpm in 1980). Five main bearings. Hydraulic valve lifters. Bosch fuel injection.

Base V-8 (6.9 sedan): 90-degree, overhead-cam, eight-cylinder. Cast-iron block and aluminum heads. Displacement: 417 cid (6,834 cc). Bore & stroke: 4.21 x 3.74 in. (107 x 95 mm). Compression ratio: 8.0:1. Brake horsepower: 250 at 4,000 rpm. Torque: 360 lbs.-ft. at 2,500 rpm. Five main bearings. Hydraulic valve lifters. Bosch K-Jetronic fuel injection.

CHASSIS

Wheelbase: (240D/280/300D) 110 in.; (280SE) 112.8 in.; (300CD) 106.7 in.; (300SD) 112.8 in.; (300TD) 110 in.; (450SL) 96.9 in.; (450SLC) 111.0 in.; (450SEL) 116.7 in.; (6.9) 116.5 in. Overall length: (240D/280/300D) 190.9 in.; (280SE) 205.5 in. (300CD) 187.5 in.; (300SD) 205.5 in.; (300TD) 190.9 in.; (450SL) 182.3 in.; (450SLC) 196.4 in.; (450SE) 205.5 in.; (450SEL) 209.4 in.; (6.9) 210 in. Height: (240D/280/300D) 56.6 in.; (280SE) 56.1 in.; (300CD) 54.9 in.; (300SD) 56.1 in.; (300TD) 57.9 in.; (450SL) 50.8 in.; (450SLC) 52.4 in.; (450SEL) 56.3 in.; (6.9) 55.5 in. Width: (240D/280/300D) 70.3 in.; (280SE) 73.6 in.; (300CD/TD) 70.3 in.; (300SD) 73.6 in.; (450SL/SLC) 70.5 in.; (450SEL) 73.6 in.; (6.9) 73.6 in. Front tread: (240D/280/300D) 58.6 in.; (280SE) 59.9 in.; (450SL/ SLC) 57.2 in.; (450SE/SEL) 60.0 in.; (6.9) 59.5 in. Rear tread: (240D/280/300D) 56.9 in.; (280SE) 59.3 in.; (450SL/SLC) 56.7 in.; (450SEL) 59.3 in.; (6.9) 59.3 in. Standard tires: (240D) 175SR14; (300D) 195/70HR14; (300CD/TD) 195/70HR14 or 195/70SR14; (280E) 195/70HR14; (280SE) 185HR14; (450 Series) 205/70HR14; (6.9) 215/70HR14.

TECHNICAL

Layout: front-engine, rear-drive. Transmission: (240D) four-speed manual, or optional automatic; (others) automatic standard. Steering: recirculating ball. Suspension (front): unequal-length A-arms, coil springs and stabilizer bar. Suspension (rear): diagonal swing axles with coil springs and stabilizer bar. Brakes: front/rear disc. Body construction: steel unibody.

MAJOR OPTIONS: Air conditioning (240D). Automatic transmission (240D). AM/FM stereo. AM/FM stereo with tape player. Alloy wheels. Sunroof. Leather or velour seats.

PRODUCTION/SALES: A total of 52,820 Mercedes-Benz passenger cars were sold in the U.S. during 1979, followed by 53,790 in 1980.

Manufacturer: Daimler-Benz AG, Stuttgart, West Germany.

Distributor: Mercedes-Benz of North America Inc., Montvale, New Jersey.

HISTORY

The 1979 models were introduced to the U.S. market in September 1978 (except station wagon, March 1979). Sales in the U.S. broke a record in 1979. Of the total sold, more than 70 percent had a diesel engine.

ABOUT THE ONLY THING AS VALUABLE AS TODAY'S MERCEDES-BENZ IS YESTERDAY'S MERCEDES-BENZ

The Mercedes-Benz philosophy precludes annual styling changes and the mass production of inexpensive cars. As a result, even a comparitively young Mercedes-Benz – a five-year-old sedan for example – usually commands over 70 percent of its original price. And some models actually get more valuable as they get older.

According to authoritative used car pricing guides, Mercedes-Benz cars retain their value better than any fine car built in North America. Which gives you one more reason to consider a Mercedes-Benz: Its investment value.

You can buy or lease a new Mercedes-Benz warmed by the knowledge that you'll get an excellent return on your investment.

Engineers, not stylists, are the heroes of Mercedes-Benz. And their aim is doggedly single-minded. It is to build safe, comfortable, high-performance cars with as few imperfections as possible.

Form follows function

Consequently, every new Mercedes-Benz is an exercise in self improvement. Form follows function. It does today – it will tomorrow.

A Mercedes-Benz is also a driver's car. You always feel in touch with the road. And as the road gets worse the ride gets more impressive.

Performance and safety

Some manufacturers boast four-wheel disc brakes as a recent innovation. They have been standard on every Mercedes-Benz for more than a decade.

It's small wonder that a Mercedes-Benz retains its value. Every model since 1886 has represented the state of the art in automotive technology. Perhaps this is because we have a unique legacy: our founders invented the automobile.

We've never stopped trying to perfect our invention.

A Mercedes-Benz is engineered like no other car in the world.

1980 450SL ad

1981-1982

240D — DIESEL FOUR — Production of the four-cylinder diesel sedan continued with little change. As before, a four-speed manual gearbox was standard; automatic transmission optional.

300 SERIES — DIESEL/TURBODIESEL FIVE — A quartet of models made up the five-cylinder diesel Series. Each sedan rode a 110-inch wheelbase except the 300SD sedan, which measured 115.6 inches (and was actually part of the larger S-Class Series). The 300CD coupe had a 106.7-inch wheelbase. The five-cylinder engine developed 120 horsepower under the 300SD/TD hoods, or 83 bhp for other models. For the 1982 model year, all diesel models were turbocharged, including the 300D and 300CD.

280E/CE — SIX — The 280 Series coupe and sedan lasted through the 1981 model year, powered by a 168 cid six-cylinder engine that developed 140 horsepower.

Note: W123 was the Mercedes-Benz internal code for the shorter-wheelbase 240/280/300 body group.

380SL/SEL/SLC — S-CLASS — V-8 — An all-aluminum 3.8-liter V-8 engine went under the hood of the Series of replacements for the 450 Series. Leading the list was the 380SL two-seater coupe/roadster (again coded R107), joined by a 380SEL sedan and 380SLC coupe. The 380SL and 380SLC rode the carryover R107 platform, whereas the sedan platform was now coded W126.

I.D. DATA: The 17-symbol Vehicle Identification Number is on the upper left of the instrument panel, visible through the windshield. Symbols 1-3 indicate country, make, and vehicle type. Symbols 4-7 indicate model. The next symbol identifies the restraint system. Symbol 10 indicates model year ('B' = 1981; 'C' = 1982). Symbol 11 identifies the assembly plant. The final six digits form the sequential production number. Starting serial number (1981 models): (240D)

WDBAB23A4BB213229; (300D) WDBAB30A6BB214778; (300CD) WDBAB50A6BB006797;(300TD-T) WDBAB93A6BN000094; (280E) WDBAA33A4BB081307; (380SEL) WDBCA33AXBB006202; (380SL) WDBBA45A6BB000654; (380SLC) WDBBA25A250BB000735.

ENGINES

Base Diesel Four (240D): Inline, overhead-cam four-cylinder. Cast-iron block and head. Displacement: 146.7 cid (2,404 cc). Bore & stroke: 3.58 x 3.64 in. (91 x 92.4 mm). Compression ratio: 21.0:1. Brake horsepower: 67 at 4,000 rpm. Torque: 97 lbs.-ft. at 2,400 rpm. Five main bearings. Solid valve lifters. Fuel injection.

Base Diesel Five (1981 300D/CD): Inline, overhead-cam five-cylinder. Cast-iron block and head. Displacement: 183.4 cid (3,005 cc). Bore & stroke: 3.58 x 3.64 in. (91 x 92.4 mm). Compression ratio: 21.0:1. Brake horsepower: 83 at 4,200 rpm. Torque: 120 lbs.-ft. at 2,400 rpm. Six main bearings. Solid valve lifters. Fuel injection.

Base Turbodiesel Five (300SD/TD): Same as 3,005 cc five above, but with turbocharger. Compression ratio: 21.5:1. Brake horsepower: 120 at 4,350 rpm. Torque: 170 lbs.-ft. at 2,400 rpm.

Base Six (280 SERIES): Inline, dual-overhead-cam six-cylinder. Cast-iron block and aluminum head. Displacement: 167.6 cid (2,746 cc). Bore & stroke: 3.39 x 3.10 in. (86 x 78.8 mm). Compression ratio: 8.0:1. Brake horsepower: 140 at 5,500 rpm. Torque: 145 lbs.-ft. at 4,500 rpm. Seven main bearings. Fuel injection.

Base V-8 (380 SERIES): 90-degree, overhead-valve eight-cylinder. Aluminum block and heads. Displacement: 234

MODEL	BODY TYPE & SEATING	ENGINE TYPE/CID	P.E. PRICE	WEIGHT (LBS.)	PRODUCTION TOTAL
240D (Diesel)					
240D	4-dr Sedan-5P	I4/147	$19,312	3,020	**Note 1**
300 SERIES (Diesel/Turbodiesel)					
300D	4-dr Sedan-5P	I5/183	$25,640	3,295	**Note 1**
300CD	2-dr Coupe-4/5P	I5/183	$29,231	3,285	**Note 1**
300SD	4-dr Sedan-5P	I5/183	$34,185	3,625	**Note 1**
300TD	4-dr Station Wagon-5P	I5/183	$31,373	3,615	**Note 1**
280 SERIES (1981 models)					
280E	4-dr Sedan-5P	I6/168	$26,848	3,330	**Note 1**
280CE	2-dr Coupe-4/5P	I6/168	$30,314	3,320	**Note 1**
380 SERIES					
380SL	2-dr Roadster-2P	V8/234	$38,993	3,460	**Note 1**
380SEL	4-dr Sedan-5P	V8/234	$44,298	3,570	**Note 1**
380SLC	2-dr Coupe-4/5P	V8/234	$46,638	3,440	**Note 1**

Note 1: A total of 414,527 Mercedes-Benz passenger cars (all models) were produced during 1981, followed by 428,725 in 1982.

Model Note: A 380SEC coupe was added in 1982.

Price Note: Figures shown were valid in 1981. Figure shown for 240D included manual gearbox; a 240D with automatic cost $20,558 in 1981.

cid (3,839 cc). Bore & stroke: 3.46 x 3.11 in. (88 x 79 mm). Compression ratio: 8.3:1. Brake horsepower: 155 at 4,750 rpm. Torque: 196 lbs.-ft. at 2,750 rpm. Five main bearings. Hydraulic valve lifters. Fuel injection.

CHASSIS

Wheelbase: (240D/300D/300TD) 110.0 in.; (300CD coupe) 106.7 in.; (300SD) 115.6 in.; (280E) 110.0 in.; (280CE coupe) 106.7 in.; (380SL) 96.9 in.; (380SEC) 112.2 in.; (380SLC) 111 in.; (380SEL) 121.1 in. Overall length: (240D/300D/ 300TD) 190.9 in.; (300CD coupe) 187.5 in.; (280E) 190.9 in.; (280CE coupe) 187.5 in.; (380SL) 182.3 in.; (380SEC) 199.2 in.; (300SD) 202.6 in.; (380SLC) 196.4 in.; (380SEL) 208.1 in. Height: (240D/300D) 56.6 in.; (300CD coupe) 54.9 in.; (300TD wag) 57.9 in.; (300SD) 56.3 in.; (280E) 56.6 in.; (280CE coupe) 54.9 in.; (380SL) 50.8 in.; (380SEC) 55.4 in.; (380SLC) 52.4 in.; (380SEL) 56.7 in. Width: (240D/ 300D/300TD/300CD) 70.3 in.; (300SD) 71.7 in.; (280) 70.3 in.; (380SL/SLC) 70.5 in.; (380SEC) 72.0 in.; (380SEL) 71.7 in. Front tread: (240D/300D/300CD/300TD) 58.6 in.; (300SD) 60.8 in.; (380SL/SLC) 57.2 in.; (380SEL) 60.8 in. Rear tread: (240D/300D) 56.9 in.; (300SD) 59.7 in.; (300TD wag) 57.2 in.; (380SL/SLC) 56.7 in.; (380SEL) 59.7 in.

TECHNICAL

Layout: front-engine, rear-drive. Transmission: (240D) four-speed manual, or optional four-speed automatic; (others) automatic standard. Steering: power recirculating ball. Suspension (front): upper/lower A-arms with coil springs and anti-roll bar. Suspension (rear): independent, semi-trailing arms with coil springs and anti-roll bar. Brakes: front/rear disc. Body Construction: steel unibody.

PRODUCTION/SALES: A total of 63,059 Mercedes-Benz passenger cars were sold in the U.S. during 1981, and 65,963 in 1982.

Manufacturer: Daimler-Benz AG, Stuttgart, West Germany.

Distributor: Mercedes-Benz of North America Inc., Montvale, New Jersey.

HISTORY

European versions of the 380SL carried a 5.0-liter version of the V-8 engine, consequently offering swifter performance. That difference created a demand for the bigger engines in the U.S., which was satisfied in some cases by "gray market" importation.

1982 300CE 6.3 AMG

1983

240D — DIESEL FOUR — Powered by a diesel four-cylinder (non-turbo) engine, the 240D four-door sedan changed little this year. A remote-controlled passenger door mirror was now standard and the speedometer now displayed readings above 85 mph Either a four-speed manual or four-speed automatic transmission was available.

300 SERIES — TURBODIESEL FIVE — Changes to the 300D turbodiesel sedan were similar to the 240D, and all three of these models got the revised speedometer and remote mirror. The 3.0-liter (183 cid) five-cylinder inline engine produced 120 horsepower and came only with four-speed automatic.

Note: W123 was the Mercedes-Benz internal code for the shorter-wheelbase 240/300 body group. The 300SD sedan rode a longer wheelbase and was part of the larger S-Class category.

300/380 SERIES — S-CLASS –TURBODIESEL FIVE/V-8 — The Mercedes senior S-Class lineup changed little for 1983. Models included the 300SD sedan with five-cylinder turbodiesel engine, and three 380S models with V-8 power: the four-passenger 380SEC coupe, two-seat 380SL roadster, and 380SEL sedan on a long (121-inch) wheelbase. The all-aluminum 3.8-liter V-8, introduced in 1981, produced 155 horsepower. The 380SL roadster rode the old R107 platform, but the others used the W126 platform that debuted in 1981. This year, the V-8 engine got some modest modifications in the ignition system and electronic idle-speed control, and the dashboard displayed a different speedometer (unlike the 85-mph unit installed formerly). A power remote passenger mirror was now standard. The only transmission choice was a four-speed automatic.

I.D. DATA: The 17-symbol Vehicle Identification Number is on the upper left of the instrument panel, visible through the windshield. Symbols 1-3 indicate country, make and vehicle type. Symbols 4-7 indicate model. The next symbol identifies the restraint system. Symbol 10 indicates model year ('D' = 1983). Symbol 11 identifies the assembly plant. The final six digits form the sequential production number.

ENGINES

Base Diesel Four (240D): Inline, overhead-cam four-cylinder. Cast-iron block and head. Displacement: 146.7 cid (2,404 cc). Bore & stroke: 3.58 x 3.64 in. (91 x 92.4 mm). Compression ratio: 21.0:1. Brake horsepower: 67 at 4,000 rpm. Torque: 97 lbs.-ft. at 2,400 rpm. Five main bearings. Solid valve lifters. Fuel injection.

Base Turbodiesel Five (300 SERIES): Inline, overhead-cam five-cylinder, with turbocharger. Cast-iron block and head. Displacement: 183 cid (2,998 cc). Bore & stroke: 3.58 x 3.64 in. (91 x 92.4 mm). Compression ratio: 21.5:1. Brake horsepower: 120 at 4,350 rpm. Torque: 170 lbs.-ft. at 2,400 rpm. Six main bearings. Solid valve lifters. Fuel injection.

Base V-8 (380 SERIES): 90-degree, overhead-cam, eight-cylinder. Light alloy block and heads. Displacement: 234 cid (3,839 cc). Bore & stroke: 3.46 x 3.11 in. (88 x 79 mm). Compression ratio: 8.3:1. Brake horsepower: 155 at 4,750 rpm. Torque: 196 lbs.-ft. at 2,750 rpm. Five main bearings. Fuel injection.

CHASSIS

Wheelbase: (240D) 110.0 in.; (300 coupe) 106.7 in.; (300 sedan/wagon) 110.0 in.; (380SL) 96.9 in.; (380SEC) 112.2 in.; (300SD) 115.6 in.; (380SEL) 121.1 in. Overall length: (240D) 190.9 in.; (300 coupe) 187.5 in.; (300 sedan/wag) 190.9 in.; (380SL) 182.3 in.; (380SEC) 199.2 in.; (300SD) 202.6 in.; (380SEL) 208.1 in. Height: (240D) 56.6 in.; (300 coupe) 54.9 in.; (300 sedan) 56.6 in.; (300 wag) 58.7 in.; (380SL) 50.8 in.; (380SEC) 55.4 in.; (300SD) 56.3 in.; (380SEL) 56.7 in. Width: (240D) 70.3 in.; (300) 70.3 in.; (380SL) 70.5 in.; (380SEC) 72.0 in.; (300SD) 71.7 in.; (380SEL) 71.7 in. Front tread: (240D) 58.6 in.; (300) 58.6 in.; (380SL) 57.2 in.; (380SEC) 60.8 in.; (300SD) 60.8 in.; (380SEL) 60.8 in. Rear tread: (240D) 56.9 in.; (300 coupe/sedan) 56.9 in.; (300 wag) 57.2 in.; (380SL) 56.7 in.; (380SEC) 59.7 in.; (300SD) 59.7 in.; (380SEL) 59.7 in.

TECHNICAL

Layout: front-engine, rear-drive. Transmission: (240D) four-speed manual, or optional four-speed automatic; (others) four-speed automatic. Steering: power recirculating ball. Suspension (front): upper/lower A-arms with coil springs and anti-roll bar Suspension (rear): independent, semi-trailing arms with coil springs and anti-roll bar. Brakes: front/rear disc. Body Construction: steel unibody.

PRODUCTION/SALES: A total of 73,692 Mercedes-Benz cars were sold in the U.S. during 1983.

Manufacturer: Daimler-Benz AG, Stuttgart, West Germany.

Distributor: Mercedes-Benz of North America Inc., Montvale, New Jersey.

Model	Body Type & Seating	Engine Type/CID	P.E. Price	Weight (lbs.)	Production Total
240D (Diesel)					
240D	4-dr Sedan-5P	I4/147	$22,470	3,155	**Note 1**
300 SERIES (Turbodiesel)					
300D	4-dr Sedan-5P	I5/183	$30,530	3,450	**Note 1**
300CD	2-dr Coupe-5P	I5/183	$33,750	3,450	**Note 1**
300SD	4-dr Sedan-5P	I5/183	$37,970	3,650	**Note 1**
300TD	4-dr Station Wagon-5P	I5/183	$33,850	3,660	**Note 1**
380 SERIES					
380SL	2-dr Roadster-2P	V8/234	$43,030	3,505	**Note 1**
380SEL	4-dr Sedan-5P	V8/234	$47,870	3,640	**Note 1**
380SEC	2-dr Coupe-4/5P	V8/234	$53,570	3,615	**Note 1**

Note 1: A total of 483,359 Mercedes-Benz passenger cars (all models) were produced during 1983.

1984 190E

1984-1985

190 SERIES — GAS/DIESEL FOUR — Both gasoline and diesel four-cylinder engines were available in the new Mercedes compact luxury sedan Series, driving either a five-speed manual or four-speed automatic transmission. The former 240 sedan was dropped, making the 190 the least costly model. The 190 four-door had fully independent suspension and front/rear disc brakes. Basic appearance and details were typical Mercedes, led by the familiar grille shape. A revised camshaft and intake manifold gave the 2.3-liter gasoline engine a horsepower boost for 1985 (from 113 to 120).

300 SERIES — TURBODIESEL FIVE — Little was new on the turbodiesel Series, except for a slight change in engine horsepower (due to a revised method of measurement, not mechanical modifications). A revised four-speed automatic became standard for 1985, with a different torque converter that was intended to help overcome turbo lag and boost low-speed acceleration.

300/380 SERIES — S-CLASS — TURBODIESEL FIVE/V-8 — Only two models made up the 380 Series for 1984: the two-seat 380SL roadster and 380SE four-door sedan. A larger V-8 engine went into the SEL sedan and SEC coupe, to create a new 500 Series. The 380SE was essentially a gasoline-powered version of the 300SD diesel sedan (also a member of the S-Class), with larger tires. All S-Class models now included an anti-theft alarm and outside temperature sensor. Power seats included a two-position memory. A driver's airbag was now optional. For 1985, anti-lock braking became standard.

500 SERIES — S-CLASS — V-8 — A new, all-aluminum 5.0-liter overhead-cam V-8 powered the 500SEC coupe and long-wheelbase 500SEL sedan, which formerly carried the smaller (3.8-liter) engine. An anti-theft alarm and outside temperature sensor were standard. Anti-lock braking became standard on the 1985 models, along with the driver's airbag,

electrically adjustable headrests, and heated outside mirrors.

I.D. DATA: The 17-symbol Vehicle Identification Number is on the upper left of the instrument panel, visible through the windshield. Symbols 1-3 indicate country, make, and vehicle type. Symbols 4-7 indicate model. The next symbol identifies the restraint system. Symbol 10 indicates model year ('E' = 1984; 'F' = 1985). Symbol 11 identifies the assembly plant. The final six digits form the sequential production number.

ENGINES

Base Four (190E): Inline, overhead-cam four-cylinder. Cast-iron block and light alloy head. Displacement: 140.3 cid (2,300 cc). Bore & stroke: 3.76 x 3.16 in. (95.5 x 80.2 mm). Compression ratio: 8.0:1. Brake horsepower: (1984) 113 at 5,000 rpm; (1985) 120 at 5,000 rpm. Torque: (1984) 133 lbs.-ft. at 3,500 rpm; (1985) 136 lbs.-ft. at 3,500 rpm. Five main bearings. Multi-point fuel injection.

Base Diesel Four (190D): Inline, overhead-cam four-cylinder. Displacement: 134 cid (2,197 cc). Bore & stroke: 3.43 x 3.64 in. (87 x 92.4 mm). Compression ratio: 22.0:1. Brake horsepower: 72 at 4,200 rpm. Torque: 96 lbs.-ft. at 2,800 rpm. Five main bearings. Fuel injection.

Base Turbodiesel Five (300 SERIES): Inline, overhead-cam five-cylinder, with turbocharger. Cast-iron block and head. Displacement: 183 cid (2,998 cc). Bore & stroke: 3.58 x 3.64 in. (91 x 92.4 mm). Compression ratio: 21.5:1. Brake horsepower: 123 at 4,350 rpm. Torque: 184 lbs.-ft. at 2,400 rpm. Six main bearings. Solid valve lifters. Fuel injection.

Base V-8 (380 SERIES): 90-degree, overhead-cam, eight-cylinder. Light alloy block and heads. Displacement: 234 cid (3,839 cc). Bore & stroke: 3.46 x 3.11 in. (88 x 79 mm). Compression ratio: 8.3:1. Brake horsepower: 155 at 4,750 rpm.

1985 300SC Turbodiesel

1985 300CD Turbodiesel

MODEL	BODY TYPE & SEATING	ENGINE TYPE/CID	P.E. PRICE	WEIGHT (LBS.)	PRODUCTION TOTAL
190 SERIES					
190E	4-dr Sedan-5P	I4/140	$22,850	2,575	**Note 1**
190D (Diesel)	4-dr Sedan-5P	I4/134	$22,930	2,555	**Note 1**
300 SERIES (Turbodiesel)					
300D	4-dr Sedan-5P	I5/183	$31,490	3,360	**Note 1**
300CD	2-dr Coupe-5P	I5/183	$35,220	3,360	**Note 1**
300SD	4-dr Sedan-5P	I5/183	$39,500	3,605	**Note 1**
300TD	4-dr Station Wagon-5P	I5/183	$35,310	3,630	**Note 1**
380 SERIES					
380SL	2-dr Roadster-2P	V8/234	$43,820	3,505	**Note 1**
380SE	4-dr Sedan-5P	V8/234	$42,730	3,540	**Note 1**
500 SERIES					
500SEL	4-dr Sedan-5P	V8/303	$51,200	3,730	**Note 1**
500SEC	2-dr Coupe-5P	V8/303	$56,800	3,605	**Note 1**

Note 1: A total of 469,385 Mercedes-Benz passenger cars (all models) were produced during 1984, and 537,909 in 1985.

Price Note: Figures shown were valid in 1984 and 1985.

Torque: 196 lbs.-ft. at 2,750 rpm. Five main bearings. Multi-point fuel injection.

Base V-8 (500 SERIES): 90-degree, overhead-cam, eight-cylinder. Light alloy block and heads. Displacement: 303 cid (4,973 cc). Bore & stroke: 3.80 x 3.35 in. (96.5 x 85 mm). Compression ratio: 8.0:1. Brake horsepower: 184 at 4,500 rpm. Torque: 247 lbs.- ft. at 2,000 rpm. Five main bearings. Multi-point fuel injection.

CHASSIS

Wheelbase: (190) 104.9 in.; (300 coupe) 106.7 in.; (300 sedan/wag) 110.0 in.; (380SL) 96.9 in.; (500SEC) 112.0 in.; (300SD/380SE) 115.6 in.; (500SEL) 120.9 in. Overall length: (190) 175.0 in.; (300 coupe) 187.5 in.; (300 sedan/wag) 190.9 in.; (380SL) 180.3 in.; (500SEC) 199.2 in.; (300SD/380SE) 202.6 in.; (500SEL) 208.1 in. Height: (190) 54.4 in.; (300 coupe) 54.9 in.; (300 sedan) 56.6 in.; (300 wag) 58.7 in.; (380SL) 50.8 in.; (500SEC) 55.4 in.; (300SD) 56.3 in.; (380SE) 56.5 in.; (500SEL) 55.5 in. Width: (190) 66.1 in.; (300) 70.3 in.; (380SL) 70.5 in.; (500SEC) 72.0 in.; (300SD, 380SE) 71.7 in.; (500SEL) 71.7 in. Front tread: (190) 56.2 in.; (300) 58.6 in.; (380SL) 57.2 in.; (500SEC) 60.8 in.; (300SD, 380SE) 60.8 in.; (500SEL) 60.8 in. Rear tread: (190) 55.7 in.; (300 coupe/sedan) 56.9 in.; (300 wag) 57.2 in.; (380SL) 56.7 in.; (500SEC) 59.7 in.; (300SD, 380SE) 59.7 in.; (500SEL) 59.7 in.

TECHNICAL

Layout: front-engine, rear-drive. Transmission: (190) five-speed manual, or optional four-speed automatic; (others) four-speed automatic. Steering: power recirculating ball. Suspension (front): upper/lower A-arms with coil springs and anti-roll bar except (190) modified MacPherson struts with coil springs and anti-roll bar. Suspension (rear): independent, semi-trailing arms with coil springs and anti-roll bar except (190) five-link independent with coil springs and anti-roll bar. Brakes: front/rear disc. Body Construction: steel unibody.

PRODUCTION/SALES: A total of 79,222 Mercedes-Benz cars were sold in the U.S. during 1984 and 86,903 in 1985.

Manufacturer: Daimler-Benz AG, Stuttgart, West Germany.

Distributor: Mercedes-Benz of North America Inc., Montvale, New Jersey.

1985 300D Turbodiesel

Eagle NCT. Sticky when wet.

It's a *total* performance tire. Not just a fair-weather friend.

Eagle NCT's tread pattern is derived from our World Champion racing rain tire. For outstanding wet traction.

And its tread *compound* is the result of what we've learned in *all* types of road racing — from Formula One to Indy. For outstanding dry-weather performance.

We've done our homework. So you can do some serious roadwork — with Eagle NCT. It's in the Eagles' Nest at your nearby Goodyear retailer.

GOOD YEAR
QUALITY AND INNOVATION

FLY WITH THE EAGLES

1984 ad

1986

190 SERIES — GAS FOUR/DIESEL FIVE — A new 2.5-liter five-cylinder engine now was installed in diesel versions of the 190 sedan. Besides that, a more potent 16-valve variant of the 2.3-liter four went into a new sports model, known as the 190E 2.3-16 (or 16V). Exhausting through tubular headers, the dual-overhead-cam sport engine developed 167 horsepower, versus 121 bhp for the regular four. Standard equipment on the sport version included anti-lock braking, a limited-slip differential, 205/55VR15 tires (on wider wheels), thicker stabilizer bars, and a hydraulic rear-leveling system. Aero add-on components on the outside, including a front air dam, made the sport edition easier to spot. Passenger capacity diminished by one, however, as the sport model's back seat was shaped to hold only two people.

300E/300D — GAS/TURBODIESEL SIX — Mercedes-Benz introduced a new mid-size sedan for 1986, powered by an inline gasoline six-cylinder engine that developed 177 horsepower. The gasoline-powered sedan was joined by a turbodiesel version, with slightly larger engine displacement and rated 148 bhp These two replaced the W123 Series. Only slightly taller than its predecessor, and a tad longer in wheelbase, the new sedan was shorter and narrower overall, and lost some 200 lbs. Styling followed the wedge profile introduced with the 190 Series. The windshield had a steeper angle than before, with a lower nose and taller trunk lid. Standard equipment included a driver's airbag, anti-lock braking, headlamp wiper/washers, central locking, and an anti-theft alarm system.

300SDL/420SEL — S-CLASS — TURBODIESEL SIX/GAS V-8 — A new 420 Series sedan joined the Mercedes-Benz lineup in 1986, powered by an enlarged (4.2-liter) V-8 engine that developed 201 horsepower. Its turbodiesel counterpart was the 300SDL, with a 3.0-liter six under its hood. Wheelbases were longer than predecessors, measuring 121.1 inches.

560 SERIES — S-CLASS — V-8 — A 5.6-liter V-8 engine went into the new 560 Series, which included the two-seat 560SL coupe/roadster, as well as a 560SEL sedan and 560SEC coupe. A four-speed automatic transmission was standard. Appearance and dimensions were similar to the prior 380 Series. The new 560SL had larger brakes, wheels and tires, as well as a recalibrated suspension.

I.D. DATA: The 17-symbol Vehicle Identification Number is on the upper left of the instrument panel, visible through the windshield. Symbols 1-3 indicate country, make, and vehicle type. Symbols 4-7 indicate model. The next symbol identifies the restraint system. Symbol 10 indicates model year ('G' = 1986). Symbol 11 identifies the assembly plant. The final six digits form the sequential production number.

ENGINES

Base Four (190E): Inline, overhead-cam four-cylinder. Cast-iron block and light alloy head. Displacement: 140.3 cid (2,300 cc). Bore & stroke: 3.76 x 3.16 in. (95.5 x 80.2 mm). Compression ratio: 8.0:1. Brake horsepower: 121 at 5,000 rpm. Torque: 136 lbs.-ft. at 3,500 rpm. Five main bearings. Hydraulic valve lifters. Multi-point fuel injection.

Base Four (190E 2.3-16): Same as above, except dual-overhead-cam (16-valve) cylinder head. Brake horsepower: 167 at 5,800 rpm. Torque: 162 lbs.-ft. at 4,750 rpm.

Base Diesel Five (190D): Inline, overhead-cam five-cylinder. Displacement: 152 cid (2,492 cc). Bore & stroke: 3.43 x 3.31 in. (87 x 84 mm). Compression ratio: 22.0:1. Brake horsepower: 93 at 4,600 rpm. Torque: 122 lbs.-ft. at 2,800 rpm. Five main bearings. Fuel injection.

Base Six (300E): Inline, overhead-cam six-cylinder. Displacement: 180.8 cid (2,964 cc). Bore & stroke: 3.48 x 3.16 in. (88 x 80 mm). Compression ratio: 9.2:1. Brake horsepower: 177 at 5,700 rpm. Torque: 188 lbs.-ft. at 4,400 rpm. Hydraulic valve lifters. Multi-point fuel injection.

Base Turbodiesel Six (300D, 300SDL): Inline, overhead-cam six-cylinder, with turbocharger. Cast-iron block and head. Displacement: 183 cid (2,998 cc). Bore & stroke: 3.43 x 3.31 in. (87 x 84 mm). Compression ratio: 22.0:1. Brake horsepower: 148 at 4,600 rpm. Torque: 201 lbs.-ft. at 2,400 rpm. Fuel injection.

Base V-8 (420SEL): 90-degree, overhead-cam, eight-cylinder. Light alloy block and heads. Displacement: 256 cid (4,197 cc). Bore & stroke: 3.62 x 3.11 in. (92 x 79 mm). Compression ratio: 9.0:1. Brake horsepower: 201 at 5,200 rpm. Torque: 228 lbs.-ft. at 3,600 rpm. Five main bearings. Hydraulic valve lifters. Multi-point fuel injection.

Base V-8 (560 SERIES): 90-degree, overhead-cam, eight-cylinder. Light alloy block and heads. Displacement: 338.5 cid (5,549 cc). Bore & stroke: 3.80 x 3.73 in. (96.5 x 94.7 mm). Compression ratio: 9.0:1. Brake horsepower: 238 at 5,200 rpm. Torque: 287 lbs.-ft. at 3,500 rpm. Five main bearings. Hydraulic valve lifters. Multi-point fuel injection.

1986 560SEC

1986 560SEL

CHASSIS

Wheelbase: (190) 104.9 in.; (300D/E) 110.2 in.; (300SDL/420SEL) 121.1 in.; (560SL) 96.7 in.; (560SEC) 112.0 in.; (560SEL) 120.9 in. Overall length: (190) 175.0 in.; (300D/E) 187.2 in.; (300SDL/420SEL) 208.1 in.; (560SL) 180.3 in.; (560SEC) 199.2 in.; (560SEL) 208.1 in. Height: (190) 54.4 in.; (300D/E) 56.9 in.; (300SDL/420SEL) 56.7 in.; (560SL) 50.8 in.; (560SEC) 55.6 in.; (560SEL) 55.7 in. Width: (190) 66.1 in.; (300D/E) 68.5 in.; (300SDL/420SEL) 71.7 in.; (560SL) 70.5 in.; (560SEC) 72.0 in.; (560SEL) 71.7 in. Front tread: (190) 56.2 in.; (190E 2.3-16) 56.9 in.; (300D/E) 58.9 in.; (300SDL/420SEL) 61.2 in.; (560SL) 57.6 in.; (560SEC/SEL) 61.2 in. Rear tread: (190) 55.7 in.; (190E 2.3-16) 56.3 in.; (300D/E) 58.6 in.; (300SDL/420SEL) 60.1 in.; (560SL) 57.7 in.; (560SEC/SEL) 60.1 in.

TECHNICAL

Layout: front-engine, rear-drive. Transmission: (190) five-speed manual, or optional four-speed automatic; (others) four-speed automatic standard. Steering: power recirculating ball. Suspension (front): upper/lower A-arms with coil springs and anti-roll bar except (190) modified MacPherson struts with coil springs and anti-roll bar; (300) gas-pressurized struts with coil springs and anti-roll bar. Suspension (rear): independent, semi-trailing arms with coil springs and anti-roll bar except (190/300) five-link independent with coil springs and anti-roll bar. Brakes: front/rear disc. Body construction: steel unibody.

PRODUCTION/SALES: A total of 99,314 Mercedes-Benz cars were sold in the U.S. during 1986.

Manufacturer: Daimler-Benz AG, Stuttgart, West Germany.

Distributor: Mercedes-Benz of North America Inc., Montvale, New Jersey.

MODEL	BODY TYPE & SEATING	ENGINE TYPE/CID	P.E. PRICE	WEIGHT (LBS.)	PRODUCTION TOTAL
190 SERIES					
190E	4-dr Sedan-5P	I4/140	$23,700	2,660	**Note 1**
190E 2.3-16	4-dr Sedan-4P	I4/140	$34,800	2,930	**Note 1**
190D (Diesel)	4-dr Sedan-5P	I5/152	$23,700	2,765	**Note 1**
300 SERIES (Gasoline)					
300E	4-dr Sedan-5P	I6/181	$33,900	3,190	**Note 1**
300 SERIES (Diesel)					
300D	4-dr Sedan-5P	I6/183	N/A	3,255	**Note 1**
300SDL	4-dr Sedan-5P	I6/183	$43,800	3,680	**Note 1**
420 SERIES					
420SEL	4-dr Sedan-5P	V8/256	$45,100	3,705	**Note 1**
560 SERIES					
560SEL	4-dr Sedan-5P	V8/338	$58,300	3,980	**Note 1**
560SEC	2-dr Coupe-4P	V8/338	$58,700	3,815	**Note 1**
560SL	2-dr Roadster-2P	V8/338	$48200	3,650	**Note 1**

Note 1: A total of 591,916 Mercedes-Benz passenger cars (all models) were produced during 1986.

DRESSED TO THRILL

AMG owners are self-confessed lovers of the best. They zealously pursue the highest standards of excellence and style. That's why they start with a Mercedes where transcending the best creates a new, more personalized interpretation of the fine art of engineering.

Every AMG motorcar represents a singular aesthetic phenomenon born from the union of taste and tradition. The 100-year old tradition of Daimler-Benz engineering achievement. AMG's uncompromised technological taste artfully translated from their many racing successes. Sensitively orchestrated by the AMG owner. You.

AMG owners are their own architects of car design. Their AMG motorcars are born equal in the Mercedes family. But they aim for more. Style, power, aerodynamics, roadholding, interior comfort and luxury. That's why they dress their Mercedes with AMG enhancements. Each AMG motorcar is created to thrill you and the world. Today and every tomorrow.

With aerodynamics. Where form is another word for function. Fluid. Smooth. Where wind tunnel proven AMG body kits minimize lift and make drag virtually nonexistent. And driving confidence means mastery of the laws of physics.

With performance. Where the thrill of perfection is measured in seconds and road-holding tenacity. Where race-bred AMG engine tuning increases horsepower and torque. Where AMG Sport Exhaust and Limited Slip Differential further slash acceleration times. Where spirited driving is a symphony for the senses derived from a precise marriage of suspension tuning, alloy wheels and high performance tires.

With elegance. Where the thrill of luxury is evident in individualized interiors. Your choice of AMG leather steering wheels, and hand-finished wood panelling of burl walnut or zebrano, not to mention a television, video cassette player and refrigerator-freezer unit.

Owning an AMG equipped motorcar is a personalized statement of excellence and tradition. A tradition reminiscent of coach-built quality. In automotive engineering and performance. In design and elegance. A thrill uniquely Mercedes. Get complete information including the name of the AMG dealer near you.

Find out how AMG enhancements can add new thrills to your present Mercedes or the one you plan to acquire. Call toll-free today: 1-800-652-2366. You can order the American AMG color catalog for $5.00 or a giant size European AMG catalog (forgive the quaint flavor of this continental translation, still it is quite comprehensive) for $20.00. Supplies are limited so order today.

AMG

233 West Ogden Avenue • Westmont, Illinois 60559
To order catalogs Toll Free: 1-800-652-2366. IL: 1-312-971-2066
Visa, MasterCard, American Express Accepted

BEVERLY HILLS   CHICAGO   DALLAS   FORT LAUDERDALE   NEW YORK

1986 AMG ad

1987

190 SERIES — GAS FOUR/SIX, DIESEL FIVE — The 190 Series grew considerably more complex for 1987, with five different engines and two new models added later in the season. A new 190E 2.6 adopted the 2.6-liter six-cylinder engine installed in the larger 260E sedan. A turbocharged version of the five-cylinder diesel engine went into a new 190D 2.5 Turbo sedan. Each of the new models included a special front air dam, intended to boost engine cooling. All 190 Series sedans gained new aero halogen headlamps. The 190E's gasoline four-cylinder engine got a boost in compression and horsepower this year. Headlamp washers became standard on the high-performance 190E 2.3-16, which continued with its dual-overhead-cam version of the four-cylinder engine.

260E/300 SERIES — GAS/TURBODIESEL SIX — The mid-size Mercedes lineup expanded its model offerings for 1987 with a new 260E sedan, powered by a new 2.6-liter six-cylinder engine. In addition to that, a 300D Turbo sedan and 300TD Turbo station wagon were available. The wagon included a hydropneumatic self-leveling rear suspension.

300SDL/420SEL — S-CLASS — TURBODIESEL SIX/ GAS V-8 — Little was new in the two long-wheelbase sedans, powered by a six-cylinder turbodiesel or a 4.2-liter gasoline V-8 engine.

560 SERIES — S-CLASS — V-8 — Each of the three 560 Series models was carried over with little change.

I.D. DATA: The 17-symbol Vehicle Identification Number is on the upper left of the instrument panel, visible through the windshield. Symbols 1-3 indicate country, make and vehicle type. Symbols 4-7 indicate model. The next symbol identifies the restraint system. Symbol 10 indicates model year ('H' = 1987). Symbol 11 identifies the assembly plant. The final six digits form the sequential production number.

ENGINES

Base Four (190E): Inline, overhead-cam four-cylinder. Cast-iron block and light alloy head. Displacement: 140.3 cid (2,300 cc). Bore & stroke: 3.76 x 3.16 in. (95.5 x 80.2 mm). Compression ratio: 9.0:1. Brake horsepower: 130 at 5,100 rpm. Torque: 146 lbs.-ft. at 3,500 rpm. Five main bearings. Hydraulic valve lifters. Multi-point fuel injection.

Base Four (190E 2.3-16): Same as above, except dual-overhead-cam (16-valve) cylinder head. Brake horsepower: 167 at 5,800 rpm. Torque: 162 lbs.-ft. at 4,750 rpm.

Base Diesel Five (190D): Inline, overhead-cam five-cylinder. Displacement: 152 cid (2,492 cc). Bore & stroke: 3.43 x 3.31 in. (87 x 84 mm). Compression ratio: 22.0:1. Brake horsepower: 93 at 4,600 rpm. Torque: 122 lbs.-ft. at 2,800 rpm. Five main bearings. Fuel injection.

Base Turbodiesel Five (190D Turbo): Same as diesel five above, but with turbocharger Brake horsepower: 123 at 4,600 rpm. Torque: 168 lbs.-ft. at 2,400 rpm.

Base Six (190E 2.6, 260E): Inline, overhead-cam six-cylinder. Displacement: 158.6 cid (2,600 cc). Bore & stroke: 3.26 x 3.16 in. (83 x 80 mm). Compression ratio: 9.2:1. Brake horsepower: 158 at 5,800 rpm. Torque: 162 lbs.-ft. at 4,600 rpm. Multi-point fuel injection.

MODEL	BODY TYPE & SEATING	ENGINE TYPE/CID	P.E. PRICE	WEIGHT (LBS.)	PRODUCTION TOTAL
190 SERIES (Gasoline)					
190E 2.3	4-dr Sedan-5P	I4/140	$26,400	2,780	**Note 1**
190E 2.3-16	4-dr Sedan-4P	I4/140	$39,600	2,900	**Note 1**
190E 2.6	4-dr Sedan-5P	I6/159	$30,300	2,750	**Note 1**
190 SERIES (Diesel)					
190D 2.5	4-dr Sedan-5P	I5/152	$26,400	2,750	**Note 1**
190D 2.5 Turbo	4-dr Sedan-4P	I5/152	$29,800	2,920	**Note 1**
260 SERIES					
260E	4-dr Sedan-5P	I6/159	$33,700	3,100	**Note 1**
300 SERIES (Gasoline)					
300E	4-dr Sedan-5P	I6/181	$38,600	3,110	**Note 1**
300 SERIES (Turbodiesel)					
300D	4-dr Sedan-5P	I6/183	$39,500	3,255	**Note 1**
300TD	4-dr Station Wagon-5P	I6/183	$42,500	3,550	**Note 1**
300SDL	4-dr Sedan-5P	I6/183	$47,000	3,680	**Note 1**
420 SERIES					
420SEL	4-dr Sedan-5P	V8/256	$52,000	3,695	**Note 1**
560 SERIES					
560SEL	4-dr Sedan-5P	V8/338	$61,500	3,925	**Note 1**
560SEC	2-dr Coupe-4P	V8/338	$68,000	3,750	**Note 1**
560SL	2-dr Roadster-2P	V8/338	$55,300	3,570	**Note 1**

Note 1: A total of 595,765 Mercedes-Benz passenger cars (all models) were produced during 1987.

Base Six (300E): Inline, overhead-cam six-cylinder. Displacement: 180.8 cid (2,964 cc). Bore & stroke: 3.48 x 3.16 in. (88 x 80 mm). Compression ratio: 9.2:1. Brake horsepower: 177 at 5,700 rpm. Torque: 188 lbs.-ft. at 4,400 rpm. Hydraulic valve lifters. Multi-point fuel injection.

Base Turbodiesel Six (300D SERIES): Inline, overhead-cam six-cylinder, with turbocharger. Cast-iron block and head. Displacement: 183 cid (2,998 cc). Bore & stroke: 3.43 x 3.31 in. (87 x 84 mm). Compression ratio: 22.0:1. Brake horsepower: 143 at 4,600 rpm. Torque: 195 lbs.-ft. at 2,400 rpm. Fuel injection.

Base V-8 (420SEL): 90-degree, overhead-cam, eight-cylinder. Light alloy block and heads. Displacement: 256 cid (4,197 cc). Bore & stroke: 3.62 x 3.11 in. (92 x 79 mm). Compression ratio: 9.0:1. Brake horsepower: 201 at 5,200 rpm. Torque: 228 lbs.-ft. at 3,600 rpm. Five main bearings. Hydraulic valve lifters. Multi-point fuel injection.

Base V-8 (560 SERIES): 90-degree, overhead-cam, eight-cylinder. Light alloy block and heads. Displacement: 338.5 cid (5,549 cc). Bore & stroke: 3.80 x 3.73 in. (96.5 x 94.7 mm). Compression ratio: 9.0:1. Brake horsepower: 238 at 4,800 rpm (227 at 4,750 rpm in 560SL). Torque: 287 lbs.-ft. at 3,500 rpm (279 at 3,250 rpm in 560SL). Five main bearings. Hydraulic valve lifters. Multi-point fuel injection.

CHASSIS

Wheelbase: (190) 104.9 in.; (260E, 300D/E) 110.2 in.; (300SDL/420SEL) 121.1 in.; (560SL) 96.7 in.; (560SEC) 112.0 in.; (560SEL) 120.9 in. Overall length: (190E) 175.1 in.; (190E 2.3-16) 174.4 in.; (190D) 175.0 in.; (260E, 300D/E) 187.2 in.; (300SDL/420SEL) 208.1 in.; (560SL) 180.3 in.;

(560SEC) 199.2 in.; (560SEL) 208.1 in. Height: (190D/E) 54.7 in.; (190E 2.3-16) 53.6 in.; (260E, 300D/E) 56.9 in.; (300SDL/420SEL) 56.7 in.; (560SL) 51.5 in.; (560SEC) 55.0 in.; (560SEL) 56.3 in. Width: (190D/E) 66.1 in.; (190E 2.3-16) 67.2 in.; (260E, 300D/E) 68.5 in.; (300SDL/420SEL) 71.7 in.; (560SL) 70.5 in.; (560SEC) 72.0 in.; (560SEL) 71.7 in. Front tread: (190D/E) 56.6 in.; (190E 2.3-16) 56.9 in.; (260E, 300D/E) 58.9 in.; (300SDL/420SEL) 61.2 in.; (560SL) 57.7 in.; (560SEC/SEL) 61.2 in. Rear tread: (190D/E) 55.8 in.; (190E 2.3-16) 56.3 in.; (260E, 300D/E) 58.6 in.; (300SDL/420SEL) 60.1 in.; (560SL) 57.7 in.; (560SEC/SEL) 60.1 in.

TECHNICAL

Layout: front-engine, rear-drive. Transmission: (190E 2.3) five-speed manual, or optional four-speed automatic; (others) four-speed automatic standard. Steering: power recirculating ball. Suspension (front): upper/lower A-arms with coil springs and anti-roll bar except (190) modified MacPherson struts with coil springs and anti-roll bar; (260/300) gas-pressurized struts with coil springs and anti-roll bar. Suspension (rear): independent, semi-trailing arms with coil springs and anti-roll bar except (190/260/300) five-link independent with coil springs and anti-roll bar. Brakes: front/rear disc. Body construction: steel unibody.

PRODUCTION/SALES: A total of 89,918 Mercedes-Benz cars were sold in the U.S. during 1987.

Manufacturer: Daimler-Benz AG, Stuttgart, West Germany.

Distributor: Mercedes-Benz of North America Inc., Montvale, New Jersey.

1988

190 SERIES — GAS FOUR/SIX, DIESEL FIVE — The sporty, high-performance 190E 2.3-16 model dropped out this year, as did the turbodiesel five. Thus, only one diesel model was offered. A five-speed manual gearbox was standard on all gasoline models, including the 2.6-liter engine (formerly offered only with the four-speed automatic).

260/300 SERIES — SIX — A four-seat 300CE coupe joined the former sedan and station wagon this year, but the turbodiesel six-cylinder engine faded away so all models had gasoline engines. Wheelbase of the new coupe was shorter than the sedan, and it displayed a steeper windshield as well as frameless window glass. Leather upholstery was standard on the coupe, with velour optional. A five-speed manual gearbox was now standard in the 260E and 300E, with four-speed automatic optional (standard in other models).

300SE/300SEL/420SEL — S-CLASS — SIX/V-8 — Because the six-cylinder turbodiesel engine was dropped this year, the 300SDL sedan faded away; but it was replaced by a 300SEL with gasoline six. Otherwise, change was minimal

in the long-wheelbase sedans. A 300SE on 115.6-inch wheelbase was added later in the model year.

560 SERIES — S-CLASS — V-8 — Little change was evident in the 5.6-liter versions of the upper Mercedes lineup.

I.D. DATA: The 17-symbol Vehicle Identification Number is on the upper left of the instrument panel, visible through the windshield. Symbols 1-3 indicate country, mak,e and vehicle type. Symbols 4-7 indicate model. The next symbol identifies the restraint system. Symbol 10 indicates model year ('J' = 1988). Symbol 11 identifies the assembly plant. The final six digits form the sequential production number.

ENGINES

Base Four (190E): Inline, overhead-cam four-cylinder. Cast-iron block and light alloy head. Displacement: 140.3 cid (2,300 cc). Bore & stroke: 3.76 x 3.16 in. (95.5 x 80.2 mm). Compression ratio: 9.0:1. Brake horsepower: 130 at 5,100

MODEL	BODY TYPE & SEATING	ENGINE TYPE/CID	P.E. PRICE	WEIGHT (LBS.)	PRODUCTION TOTAL
190 SERIES					
190E 2.3	4-dr Sedan-5P	I4/140	$29,190	2,705	**Note 1**
190E 2.6	4-dr Sedan-5P	I6/159	$33,500	2,795	**Note 1**
190D (Diesel)	4-dr Sedan-5P	I5/152	$29,960	2,795	**Note 1**
260 SERIES					
260E	4-dr Sedan-5P	I6/159	$37,250	3,065	**Note 1**
300 SERIES					
300E	4-dr Sedan-5P	I6/181	$42,680	3,090	**Note 1**
300TE	4-dr Station Wagon-5P	I6/181	$46,980	3,360	**Note 1**
300CE	2-dr Coupe-4P	I6/181	$52,500	3,200	**Note 1**
300SE	4-dr Sedan-5P	I6/181	$49,900	N/A	**Note 1**
300SEL	4-dr Sedan-5P	I6/181	$52,650	3,630	**Note 1**
420 SERIES					
420SEL	4-dr Sedan-5P	V8/256	$58,150	3,740	**Note 1**
560 SERIES					
560SEL	4-dr Sedan-5P	V8/338	$68,660	3,940	**Note 1**
560SEC	2-dr Coupe-4P	V8/338	$75,850	3,775	**Note 1**
560SL	2-dr Roadster-2P	V8/338	$61,130	3,570	**Note 1**

Note 1: A total of 553,772 Mercedes-Benz passenger cars (all models) were produced during 1988.

rpm. Torque: 146 lbs.-ft. at 3,500 rpm. Five main bearings. Hydraulic valve lifters. Multi-point fuel injection.

Base Diesel Five (190D): Inline, overhead-cam five-cylinder. Displacement: 152 cid (2,492 cc). Bore & stroke: 3.43 x 3.31 in. (87 x 84 mm). Compression ratio: 22.0:1. Brake horsepower: 93 at 4,600 rpm. Torque: 122 lbs.-ft. at 2,800 rpm. Five main bearings. Fuel injection.

Base Six (190E 2.6, 260E): Inline, overhead-cam six-cylinder. Displacement: 158.6 cid (2,600 cc). Bore & stroke: 3.26 x 3.16 in. (83 x 80 mm). Compression ratio: 9.2:1. Brake horsepower: 158 at 5,800 rpm. Torque: 162 lbs.-ft. at 4,600 rpm. Multi-point fuel injection.

Base Six (300): Inline, overhead-cam six-cylinder. Displacement: 180.8 cid (2,964 cc). Bore & stroke: 3.48 x 3.16 in. (88 x 80 mm). Compression ratio: 9.2:1. Brake horsepower: 177 at 5,700 rpm. Torque: 188 lbs.-ft. at 4,400 rpm. Hydraulic valve lifters. Multi-point fuel injection.

Base V-8 (420SEL): 90-degree, overhead-cam, eight-cylinder. Light alloy block and heads. Displacement: 256 cid (4,197 cc). Bore & stroke: 3.62 x 3.11 in. (92 x 79 mm). Compression ratio: 9.0:1. Brake horsepower: 201 at 5,200 rpm. Torque: 228 lbs.-ft. at 3,600 rpm. Five main bearings. Hydraulic valve lifters. Multi-point fuel injection.

Base V-8 (560 SERIES): 90-degree, overhead-cam, eight-cylinder. Light alloy block and heads. Displacement: 338.5 cid (5,549 cc). Bore & stroke: 3.80 x 3.73 in. (96.5 x 94.7 mm). Compression ratio: 9.0:1. Brake horsepower: 238 at 4,800 rpm (227 at 4,750 rpm in 560SL). Torque: 287 lbs.-ft. at 3,500 rpm (279 at 3,250 rpm in 560SL). Five main bearings. Hydraulic valve lifters. Multi-point fuel injection.

CHASSIS

Wheelbase: (190) 104.9 in.; (260E, 300E/TE) 110.2 in.; (300CE) 106.9 in.; (300SE) 115.6 in.; (300SEL/420SEL/560SEL) 121 in.; (560SL) 96.7 in.; (560SEC) 112.0 in. Overall length: (190E) 175.1 in.; (190D) 175.0 in.; (260E/300E)

187.2 in.; (300CE) 183.9 in.; (300TE) 188.2 in.; (300SE) 202.6 in.; (300SEL/420SEL) 208.1 in.; (560SL) 180.3 in.; (560SEC) 199.2 in.; (560SEL) 208.1 in. Height: (190) 54.7 in.; (260E, 300E/TE) 56.9 in.; (300CE) 55.5 in.; (300SE/300SEL/420SEL) 56.7 in.; (560SL) 51.1 in.; (560SEC) 55.0 in.; (560SEL) 56.3 in. Width: (190D/E) 66.1 in.; (260E/300) 68.5 in.; (300SE/300SEL/420SEL) 71.7 in.; (560SL) 70.5 in.; (560SEC) 72.0 in.; (560SEL) 71.7 in. Front tread: (190D/E) 56.6 in.; (260E/300) 58.9 in.; (300SE/300SEL/420SEL) 61.2 in.; (560SL) 57.7 in.; (560SEC/SEL) 61.2 in. Rear tread: (190D/E) 55.8 in.; (260E/300) 58.6 in.; (300SE/300SEL/420SEL) 60.1 in.; (560SL) 57.7 in.; (560SEC/SEL) 60.1 in.

TECHNICAL

Layout: front-engine, rear-drive. Transmission: (190/260E/300E) five-speed manual, or optional four-speed automatic; (others) four-speed automatic standard. Steering: power recirculating ball. Suspension (front): upper/lower A-arms with coil springs and anti-roll bar except (190) modified MacPherson struts with coil springs and anti-roll bar; (260/300) gas-pressurized struts with coil springs and anti-roll bar. Suspension (rear): independent, semi-trailing arms with coil springs and anti-roll bar except (190/260/300) five-link independent with coil springs and anti-roll bar. Brakes: front/rear disc. Body construction: steel unibody.

PRODUCTION/SALES: A total of 83,727 Mercedes-Benz cars were sold in the U.S. during 1988.

Manufacturer: Daimler-Benz AG, Stuttgart, West Germany.

Distributor: Mercedes-Benz of North America Inc., Montvale, New Jersey.

HISTORY

Although the prospect of a replacement for the aging 560SL coupe/roadster was rumored through the late 1980s, it would not arrive until the 1990 model year (as the 300SL/500SL).

1989

190 SERIES — GAS SIX/DIESEL FIVE — Only the six-cylinder gasoline engine and five-cylinder diesel remained for 1989, as four-cylinder power faded away. Diesel popularity had waned sharply in the late 1980s and no other Mercedes model offered a diesel engine (which was unavailable in California). Anti-lock brakes were now standard on all models. Otherwise, apart from a modest facelift that included the addition of wide body-side moldings, restyled bumpers, and a deeper front air dam, little was changed for 1989.

260/300 SERIES — SIX — The Mercedes mid-size lineup was carried over with little change, except for the addition of a passenger airbag to the option list. Power again came from one of two six-cylinder engines, offered only with an automatic transmission; the five-speed manual gearbox was dropped.

300SE/300SEL/420SEL — S-CLASS — SIX/V-8 — Except for the addition of a passenger's airbag as an option, and new soft leather upholstery as standard equipment, little was new among the long-wheelbase models, available with a 3.0-liter six or 4.2-liter V-8 engine.

560 SERIES — S-CLASS — V-8 — Little change was evident in the biggest-engined Series, except for an optional passenger's airbag on the 560SEL sedan and 560SEC coupe.

I.D. DATA: The 17-symbol Vehicle Identification Number is on the upper left of the instrument panel, visible through the windshield. Symbols 1-3 indicate country, make and vehicle type. Symbols 4-7 indicate model. The next symbol identifies the restraint system. Symbol 10 indicates model year ('K' = 1989). Symbol 11 identifies the assembly plant. The final six digits form the sequential production number.

ENGINES

Base Diesel Five (190D): Inline, overhead-cam five-cylinder. Displacement: 152 cid (2,492 cc). Bore & stroke: 3.43 x 3.31 in. (87 x 84 mm). Compression ratio: 22.0:1. Brake horsepower: 90 at 4,600 rpm. Torque: 117 lbs.-ft. at 2,800 rpm. Five main bearings. Fuel injection.

Base Six (190E 2.6, 260E): Inline, overhead-cam six-cylinder. Displacement: 158.6 cid (2,600 cc). Bore & stroke: 3.26 x 3.16 in. (83 x 80 mm). Compression ratio: 9.2:1. Brake horsepower: 158 at 5,800 rpm. Torque: 162 lbs.-ft. at 4,600 rpm. Multi-point fuel injection.

Base Six (300): Inline, overhead-cam six-cylinder. Displacement: 180.8 cid (2,964 cc). Bore & stroke: 3.48 x 3.16 in. (88 x 80 mm). Compression ratio: 9.2:1. Brake horsepower: 177 at 5,700 rpm. Torque: 188 lbs.-ft. at 4,400 rpm. Hydraulic valve lifters. Multi-point fuel injection.

Base V-8 (420SEL): 90-degree, overhead-cam, eight-cylinder. Light alloy block and heads. Displacement: 256 cid (4,197 cc). Bore & stroke: 3.62 x 3.11 in. (92 x 79 mm). Compression ratio: 9.0:1. Brake horsepower: 201 at 5,200 rpm. Torque: 228 lbs.-ft. at 3,600 rpm. Five main bearings. Hydraulic valve lifters. Multi-point fuel injection.

Base V-8 (560 SERIES): 90-degree, overhead-cam, eight-cylinder. Light alloy block and heads. Displacement: 338.5 cid (5,549 cc). Bore & stroke: 3.80 x 3.73 in. (96.5 x 94.7 mm). Compression ratio: 9.0:1. Brake horsepower: 238 at 4,800 rpm (227 at 4,750 rpm in 560SL). Torque: 287 lbs.-ft. at 3,500 rpm (279 at 3,250 rpm in 560SL). Five main bearings. Hydraulic valve lifters. Multi-point fuel injection.

Model	Body Type & Seating	Engine Type/CID	P.E. Price	Weight (lbs.)	Production Total
190 SERIES					
190E 2.6	4-dr Sedan-5P	I6/159	$31,590	2,870	**Note 1**
190D (Diesel)	4-dr Sedan-5P	I5/152	$30,980	2,860	**Note 1**
260 SERIES					
260E	4-dr Sedan-5P	I6/159	$39,200	N/A	**Note 1**
300 SERIES					
300E	4-dr Sedan-5P	I6/181	$44,850	3,155	**Note 1**
300TE	4-dr Station Wagon-5P	I6/181	$48,210	3,415	**Note 1**
300SE	4-dr Sedan-5P	I6/181	$51,400	3,585	**Note 1**
300CE	2-dr Coupe-4P	I6/181	$53,800	3,200	**Note 1**
300SEL	4-dr Sedan-5P	I6/181	$55,100	3,630	**Note 1**
420 SERIES					
420SEL	4-dr Sedan-5P	V8/256	$61,210	3,740	**Note 1**
560 SERIES					
560SEL	4-dr Sedan-5P	V8/338	$72,280	3,940	**Note 1**
560SEC	2-dr Coupe-4P	V8/338	$79,840	3,775	**Note 1**
560SL	2-dr Roadster-2P	V8/338	$64,230	3,570	**Note 1**

Note 1: A total of 75,714 Mercedes-Benz cars were sold in the U.S. during 1989.

CHASSIS

Wheelbase: (190) 104.9 in.; (260E, 300E/TE) 110.2 in.; (300CE) 106.9 in.; (300SE) 115.6 in.; (300SEL/420SEL/560SEL) 121.1 in.; (560SL) 96.7 in.; (560SEC) 112.2 in. Overall length: (190) 175.1 in.; (260E/300E) 187.2 in.; (300CE) 183.9 in.; (300TE) 188.2 in.; (300SE) 202.6 in.; (300SEL/420SEL) 208.1 in.; (560SL) 180.3 in.; (560SEC) 199.2 in.; (560SEL) 208.1 in. Height: (190) 54.7 in.; (260E/300) 56.9 in.; (300CE) 55.5 in.; (300TE) 59.8 in.; (300SE) 56.6 in.; (300SEL/420SEL) 56.7 in.; (560SL) 51.1 in.; (560SEC) 55.0 in.; (560SEL) 56.3 in. Width: (190D/E) 66.5 in.; (260E/300) 68.5 in.; (300SE/300SEL/420SEL) 71.7 in.; (560SL) 70.5 in.; (560SEC) 72.0 in.; (560SEL) 71.7 in. Front tread: (190D/E) 56.6 in.; (260E/300) 58.9 in.; (300SE/300SEL/420SEL) 61.5 in.; (560SL) 57.7 in.; (560SEC/SEL) 61.5 in. Rear tread: (190D/E) 55.8 in.; (260E/300) 58.6 in.; (300SE/300SEL/420SEL) 60.4 in.; (560SL) 57.7 in.; (560SEC/SEL) 60.4 in.

TECHNICAL

Layout: front-engine, rear-drive. Transmission: (190E 2.6) five-speed manual, or optional four-speed automatic; (others) four-speed automatic standard. Steering: power recirculating ball. Suspension (front): upper/lower A-arms with coil springs and anti-roll bar except (190) modified MacPherson struts with coil springs and anti-roll bar; (260/300) gas-pressurized struts with coil springs and anti-roll bar. Suspension (rear): independent, semi-trailing arms with coil springs and anti-roll bar except (190/260/300) five-link independent with coil springs and anti-roll bar. Brakes: front/rear disc. Body construction: steel unibody.

Manufacturer: Daimler-Benz AG, Stuttgart, West Germany.

Distributor: Mercedes-Benz of North America Inc., Montvale, New Jersey.

1990 E320 coupe

1990

190E 2.6 — SIX — Only a single version of the 190 Series remained this year, powered by the 2.6-liter gasoline engine. Diesel power departed from the entry-level Mercedes line. Either a five-speed manual gearbox or four-speed automatic was available.

260/300 SERIES — SIX — Automatic 4Matic four-wheel-drive became available this year on both the 300E sedan and 300TE station wagon, again powered by a 3.0-liter six-cylinder engine. The 300CE coupe added 40 extra horsepower by virtue of a new dual-overhead-cam version of the 3.0-liter six (a detuned version of the engine used in the new 300SL roadster). The 260E with its smaller 2.6-liter engine adopted the designation 300E 2.6. Later in the season, a 300D 2.5-liter turbodiesel sedan joined the series, with a 2.5-liter five-cylinder engine.

300SE/300SEL/420SEL — S-CLASS — SIX/V-8 — Except for a new fuel-injection system, little was new in the smaller-engined members of the S-Class. A passenger airbag was optional.

350SDL — TURBODIESEL SIX — Late in the model year, a 350SDL sedan was added, powered by a 3.5-liter turbodiesel six (the first Mercedes turbodiesel since 1987).

560 SERIES — S-CLASS — V-8 — A new fuel-injection system was the only significant change for the S-Class coupe and sedan, again powered by a 5.6-liter V-8 engine.

300SL/500SL — SIX/V-8 — At last, the long-awaited replacement for the aged 560SL coupe/ roadster was ready for the marketplace, on an all-new platform. The former design had been around for some 18 years, so a new version was much needed. Again rear-drive, the two-seaters rode a 99-inch wheelbase with a far rounder, smoother and more aerodynamic appearance than their predecessors. The customary Mercedes-Benz tri-star emblem again sat in the center of the grille, which had a new angled profile rather than the former upright look. Aero-shaped, flush-style headlamps stood alongside wraparound parking lights. Small air-extractor vents ahead of the doors served as reminders of the original 300SL gullwing coupe. Among the new technical features was a rollbar that normally sat flush with the tonneau cover, but was designed to rise in three-tenths of a second if sensors detected an imminent rollover accident. The bar could also be raised into place at any time, by pushing a button. Each roadster came with both a folding soft-top and removable aluminum hardtop.

Two dual-overhead-cam engines were available: a 3.0-liter (24-valve) six in the 300SL, and a 5.0-liter (32-valve) V-8 in the 500SL, the latter rated 322 horsepower. An electro-hydraulic mechanism automatically adjusted the engine's valve timing, for higher torque at midrange and more power at higher engine speeds. A five-speed manual gearbox was standard in the 300SL, with five-speed automatic (overdrive fifth gear) optional. The 500SL came only with a four-speed automatic. Airbags were installed for both the driver and passenger.

I.D. DATA: The 17-symbol Vehicle Identification Number is on the upper left of the instrument panel, visible through the windshield. Symbols 1-3 indicate country, make, and vehicle type. Symbols 4-7 indicate model. The next symbol identifies the restraint system. Symbol 10 indicates model year ('L' = 1990). Symbol 11 identifies the assembly plant. The final six digits form the sequential production number.

ENGINES

Base Six (190E 2.6, 300E 2.6): Inline, overhead-cam six-cylinder. Displacement: 158.6 cid (2,600 cc). Bore & stroke: 3.26 x 3.16 in. (83 x 80 mm). Compression ratio: 9.2:1. Brake horsepower: 158 at 5,800 rpm. Torque: 162 lbs.-ft. at 4,600 rpm. Multi-point fuel injection.

Base Six (300): Inline, overhead-cam six-cylinder. Displacement: 180.8 cid (2,964 cc). Bore & stroke: 3.48 x 3.16 in. (88.5 x 80.2 mm). Compression ratio: 9.2:1. Brake horsepower: 177 at 5,700 rpm. Torque: 188 lbs.-ft. at 4,400 rpm. Hydraulic valve lifters. Multi-point fuel injection.

Base Six (300CE): Inline, dual-overhead-cam six-cylinder. Displacement: 180.8 cid (2,964 cc). Bore & stroke: 3.48 x 3.16 in. (88.5 x 80.2 mm). Compression ratio: 10.0:1. Brake horsepower: 217 at 6,400 rpm. Torque: 195 lbs.-ft. at 4,600 rpm.

Base Six (300SL): Inline, dual-overhead-cam six-cylinder (24-valve). Aluminum crossflow head. Displacement: 180.8 cid (2,964 cc). Bore & stroke: 3.48 x 3.16 in. (88.5 x 80.2 mm). Compression ratio: 10.0:1. Brake horsepower: 228 at 6,300 rpm. Torque: 201 lbs.-ft. at 4,600 rpm. 300SL Engine Note: Outside North America, a variant of the 300SL with a 12-valve six-cylinder engine was also marketed.

Base Turbodiesel Five (300D 2.5): Inline, overhead-cam five-cylinder, with turbocharger. Displacement: 152 cid (2,492 cc). Bore & stroke: 3.43 x 3.31 in. (87 x 84 mm). Compression ratio: 22.0:1. Brake horsepower: 121 at 4,600 rpm. Torque: 165 lbs.-ft. at 2,400 rpm. Fuel injection.

Base Turbodiesel Six (350SDL): Inline, overhead-cam six-cylinder, with turbocharger. Displacement: 208 cid (3,407 cc). Bore & stroke: 3.50 x 3.60 in. (89 x 91 mm). Compression ratio: 22.0:1. Brake horsepower: 121 at 4,600 rpm. Torque: 165 lbs.-ft. at 2,400 rpm. Fuel injection.

Base V-8 (420SEL): 90-degree, overhead-cam, eight-cylinder. Light alloy block and heads. Displacement: 256 cid (4,197 cc). Bore & stroke: 3.62 x 3.11 in. (92 x 79 mm). Compression ratio: 9.0:1. Brake horsepower: 201 at 5,200 rpm. Torque: 228 lbs.-ft. at 3,600 rpm. Five main bearings. Hydraulic valve lifters. Multi-point fuel injection.

Base V-8 (500SL): 90-degree, dual-overhead-cam, eight-cylinder (32-valve). Aluminum alloy block. Displacement: 304 cid (4,983 cc). Bore & stroke: 3.80 x 3.35 in. (96.5 x 85 mm). Compression ratio: 10.0:1. Brake horsepower: 322 at 5,500 rpm. Torque: 332 lbs.-ft. at 4,000 rpm. Bosch KE 5 CIS multi-point fuel injection.

Base V-8 (560 SERIES): 90-degree, overhead-cam, eight-cylinder. Light alloy block and heads. Displacement: 338.5 cid (5,549 cc). Bore & stroke: 3.80 x 3.73 in. (96.5 x 94.7 mm). Compression ratio: 9.0:1. Brake horsepower: 238 at 4,800 rpm. Torque: 287 lbs.-ft. at 3,500 rpm. Five main bearings. Hydraulic valve lifters. Multi-point fuel injection.

1990 E320 coupe

Model	Body Type & Seating	Engine Type/CID	P.E. Price	Weight (lbs.)	Production Total
190E					
190E	4-dr Sedan-5P	I6/159	$31,600	2,870	**Note 1**
300 SERIES					
300E 2.6	4-dr Sedan-5P	I6/159	$39,950	3,155	**Note 1**
300E	4-dr Sedan-5P	I6/181	$45,950	3,210	**Note 1**
300E 4Matic	4-dr Sedan-5P	I6/181	$52,550	3,505	**Note 1**
300TE	4-dr Station Wagon-5P	I6/181	$49,650	3,450	**Note 1**
300TE 4Matic	4-dr Station Wagon-5P	I6/181	$56,250	3,725	**Note 1**
300CE	2-dr Coupe-4P	I6/181	$55,700	3,395	**Note 1**
300SE	4-dr Sedan-5P	I6/181	$52,950	3,595	**Note 1**
300SEL	4-dr Sedan-5P	I6/181	$56,800	3,640	**Note 1**
300/350 SERIES (Turbodiesel)					
300D 2.5	4-dr Sedan-5P	I5/152	$39,700	N/A	**Note 1**
350SDL	4-dr Sedan-5P	I6/208	$56,800	N/A	**Note 1**
420SEL					
420SEL	4-dr Sedan-5P	V8/256	$62,500	3,770	**Note 1**
300/500SL					
300SL	2-dr Coupe/Roadster-2P	I6/181	$72,500	3,850	
500SL	2-dr Coupe/Roadster-2P	V8/304	$83,500	4,025	
560 SERIES					
560SEL	4-dr Sedan-5P	V8/338	$73,800	3,960	**Note 1**
560SEC	2-dr Coupe-4P	V8/338	$81500	3,770	**Note 1**

Note 1: A total of 78,375 Mercedes-Benz cars were sold in the U.S. during 1990.

CHASSIS

Wheelbase: (190) 104.9 in.; (300E/TE) 110.2 in.; (300CE) 106.9 in.; (300SE) 115.6 in.; (300SEL/420SEL/560SEL) 121.1 in.; (300/500SL) 99.0 in.; (560SEC) 112.2 in. Overall length: (190) 175.1 in.; (300E) 187.2 in.; (300CE) 183.9 in.; (300TE) 188.2 in.; (300SE) 202.6 in.; (300SEL/420SEL) 208.1 in.; (300/500SL) 176.0 in.; (560SEC) 199.2 in.; (560SEL) 208.1 in. Height: (190) 54.1 in.; (300) 56.3 in.; (300E 4WD) 57.1 in.; (300CE) 54.9 in.; (300TE) 59.8 in.; (300SE) 56.6 in.; (300SEL/420SEL) 56.7 in.; (300/500SL) 50.7 in.; (560SEC) 55.0 in.; (560SEL) 56.3 in. Width: (190) 66.5 in.; (300) 68.5 in.; (300SE/300SEL/420SEL) 71.7 in.; (300/500SL) 71.3 in.; (560SEC) 72.0 in.; (560SEL) 71.7 in. Front tread: (190) 56.7 in.; (300) 59.1 in.; (300TE, 300E 4WD) 58.9 in.; (300SE/300SEL/420SEL) 61.5 in.; (300/500SL) 60.4 in.; (560SEC/SEL) 61.5 in. Rear tread: (190) 55.9 in.; (300) 58.7 in.; (300TE, 300E 4WD) 58.5 in.; (300SE/300SEL/420SEL) 60.4 in.; (300/500SL) 60.0 in.; (560SEC/SEL) 60.4 in.

TECHNICAL

Layout: front-engine, rear-drive. Transmission: (190E 2.6) five-speed manual, or optional four-speed automatic; (300SL) five-speed manual or five-speed automatic; (others) four-speed automatic standard. Steering: power recirculating ball. Suspension (front): upper/lower A-arms with coil springs and anti-roll bar except (190) modified MacPherson struts with coil springs and anti-roll bar; (300) gas-pressurized struts with coil springs and anti-roll bar; (300/500SL) struts with coil springs on A-arms and torsion bar stabilizer. Suspension (rear): independent, semi-trailing arms with coil springs and anti-roll bar except (190/300) five-link independent with coil springs and anti-roll bar; (300/500SL) multi-link independent with coil springs, torsion-bar stabilizer, and level control. Brakes: front/rear disc. Body construction: steel unibody.

PERFORMANCE

Top Speed: (300SL) 143 mph claimed; (500SL) 155 mph claimed. Acceleration (0-60 mph): (300SL) about 8.3 sec. claimed; (500SL) about 6.3 sec. claimed.

Manufacturer: Daimler-Benz AG, Stuttgart, Germany.

Distributor: Mercedes-Benz of North America Inc., Montvale, New Jersey.

1991

190E 2.3/190E 2.6 — FOUR/SIX — The first Mercedes in two years offered for under $30,000 debuted as the four-cylinder 190E 2.3. Both the 190E 2.3 and the 190E 2.6 were available with acceleration slip control (ASR).

260/300 SERIES — GAS SIX/TURBODIESEL FIVE — The turbocharged 2.5-liter, five-cylinder diesel engine received an improved prechamber design, resulting in lower emissions and quieter operation. ASR traction control was available.

300SE/300SEL/420SEL — S-CLASS — SIX/V-8 — With seven models to choose from, S-Class aficionados had the widest selection ever offered.

350SD/350SDL — TURBODIESEL SIX — The 350SDL was joined by a standard wheelbase 350SD. Both diesel models were available with the ASD version of traction control.

560 SERIES — S-CLASS — V-8 — No change for 1991.

300SL/500SL — V-8 — The flagship sportscars were available with Adaptive Damping System (ADS.) This allowed for a smooth highway ride, yet could also provide firm control on bad roads and improved responsiveness in emergency situations.

I.D. DATA: Same as 1990.

ENGINES

Base Four (190E 2.3): Inline, overhead-cam four-cylinder. Displacement: 140.3 cid (2,300 cc). Brake horsepower: 130 at 5,100 rpm. Torque 146 lbs.-ft at 3,500 rpm. Multi-point fuel injection.

Base Six (190E 2.6, 300E 2.6): Inline, overhead-cam six-cylinder. Displacement: 158.6 cid (2,600 cc). Bore & stroke: 3.26 x 3.16 in. (83 x 80 mm). Compression ratio: 9.2:1. Brake horsepower: 158 at 5,800 rpm. Torque: 162 lbs.-ft. at 4,600 rpm. Multi-point fuel injection.

Base Six (300): Inline, overhead-cam six-cylinder. Displacement: 180.8 cid (2,964 cc). Bore & stroke: 3.48 x 3.16 in. (88.5 x 80.2 mm). Compression ratio: 9.2:1. Brake horsepower: 177 at 5,700 rpm. Torque: 188 lbs.-ft. at 4,400 rpm. Hydraulic valve lifters. Multi-point fuel injection.

Base Six (300CE): Inline, dual-overhead-cam six-cylinder. Displacement: 180.8 cid (2,964 cc). Bore & stroke: 3.48 x 3.16 in. (88.5 x 80.2 mm). Compression ratio: 10.0:1. Brake horsepower: 217 at 6,400 rpm. Torque: 195 lbs.-ft. at 4,600 rpm.

Base Six (300SL): Inline, dual-overhead-cam six-cylinder (24-valve). Aluminum cross-flow head. Displacement: 180.8 cid (2,964 cc). Bore & stroke: 3.48 x 3.16 in. (88.5 x 80.2 mm). Compression ratio: 10.0:1. Brake horsepower: 228 at 6,300 rpm. Torque: 201 lbs.-ft. at 4,600 rpm. 300SL Engine Note:

Model	Body Type & Seating	Engine Type/CID	P.E. Price	Weight (lbs.)	Production Total
190E					
190E 2.3	4-dr Sedan-5P	I4/140	$28,350	6,213	
190E 2.6	4-dr Sedan-5P	I6/159	$32,870	7,536	
300 SERIES					
300E 2.6	4-dr Sedan-5P	I6/159	$41,000	3,155	3,891
300E	4-dr Sedan-5P	I6/181	$47,200	3,210	9,317
300E 4Matic	4-dr Sedan-5P	I6/181	$54,150	3,505	608
300TE	4-dr Station Wagon-5P	I6/181	$51,150	3,450	1,181
300TE 4Matic	4-dr Station Wagon-5P	I6/181	$57,900	3,725	751
300CE	2-dr Coupe-4P	I6/181	$57,350	3,395	1,302
300SE	4-dr Sedan-5P	I6/181	N/A	3,595	4,221
300SEL	4-dr Sedan-5P	I6/181	N/A	3,640	996
300/350 SERIES (Turbodiesel)					
300D 2.5	4-dr Sedan-5P	I5/152	$41,400	1,776	
350SD	4-dr Sedan-5P	I6/208	$53,900	1,372	
350SDL	4-dr Sedan-5P	I6/208	$57,800	1,199	
420SEL					
420SEL	4-dr Sedan-5P	V8/256	N/A	3,770	4,219
300/500SL					
300SL	2-dr Coupe/Roadster-2P	I6/181	N/A	3,850	2,308
500SL	2-dr Coupe/Roadster-2P	V8/304	N/A	4,025	5,137
560 SERIES					
560SEL	4-dr Sedan-5P	V8/338	N/A	3,960	2,779
560SEC	2-dr Coupe-4P	V8/338	N/A	3,770	671

Outside North America, a variant of the 300SL with a 12-valve six-cylinder engine was also marketed.

Base Turbodiesel Five (300D 2.5): Inline, overhead-cam five-cylinder, with turbocharger. Displacement: 152 cid (2,492 cc). Bore & stroke: 3.43 x 3.31 in. (87 x 84 mm). Compression ratio: 22.0:1. Brake horsepower: 121 at 4,600 rpm. Torque: 165 lbs.-ft. at 2,400 rpm. Fuel injection.

Base Turbodiesel Six (350SDL): Inline, overhead-cam six-cylinder, with turbocharger. Displacement: 208 cid (3,407 cc). Bore & stroke: 3.50 x 3.60 in. (89 x 91 mm). Compression ratio: 22.0:1. Brake horsepower: 121 at 4,600 rpm. Torque: 165 lbs.-ft. at 2,400 rpm. Fuel injection.

Base V-8 (420SEL): 90-degree, overhead-cam, eight-cylinder. Light alloy block and heads. Displacement: 256 cid (4,197 cc). Bore & stroke: 3.62 x 3.11 in. (92 x 79 mm). Compression ratio: 9.0:1. Brake horsepower: 201 at 5,200 rpm. Torque: 228 lbs.-ft. at 3,600 rpm. Five main bearings. Hydraulic valve lifters. Multi-point fuel injection.

Base V-8 (500SL): 90-degree, dual-overhead-cam, eight-cylinder (32-valve). Aluminum alloy block. Displacement: 304 cid (4,983 cc). Bore & stroke: 3.80 x 3.35 in. (96.5 x 85 mm). Compression ratio: 10.0:1. Brake horsepower: 322 at 5,500 rpm. Torque: 332 lbs.-ft. at 4,000 rpm. Bosch KE 5 CIS multi-point fuel injection.

Base V-8 (560 SERIES): 90-degree, overhead-cam, eight-cylinder. Light alloy block and heads. Displacement: 338.5 cid (5,549 cc). Bore & stroke: 3.80 x 3.73 in. (96.5 x 94.7 mm). Compression ratio: 9.0:1. Brake horsepower: 238 at 4,800 rpm. Torque: 287 lbs.-ft. at 3,500 rpm. Five main bearings. Hydraulic valve lifters. Multi-point fuel injection.

CHASSIS

Wheelbase: (190) 104.9 in.; (300E/TE) 110.2 in.; (300CE) 106.9 in.; (300SE) 115.6 in.; (300SEL/420SEL/560SEL) 121.1 in.; (300/500SL) 99.0 in.; (560SEC) 112.2 in. Overall length: (190) 175.1 in.; (300E) 187.2 in.; (300CE) 183.9 in.; (300TE) 188.2 in.; (300SE) 202.6 in.; (300SEL/420SEL) 208.1 in.; (300/500SL) 176.0 in.; (560SEC) 199.2 in.; (560SEL) 208.1 in. Height: (190) 54.1 in.; (300) 56.3 in.; (300E 4WD) 57.1 in.; (300CE) 54.9 in.; (300TE) 59.8 in.; (300SE) 56.6 in.; (300SEL/420SEL) 56.7 in.; (300/500SL) 50.7 in.; (560SEC) 55.0 in.; (560SEL) 56.3 in. Width: (190) 66.5 in.; (300) 68.5 in.; (300SE/ 300SEL/420SEL) 71.7 in.; (300/500SL) 71.3 in.; (560SEC) 72.0 in.; (560SEL) 71.7 in. Front tread: (190) 56.7 in.; (300) 59.1 in.; (300TE, 300E 4WD) 58.9 in.; (300SE/300SEL/ 420SEL) 61.5 in.; (300/500SL) 60.4 in.; (560SEC/SEL) 61.5 in. Rear tread: (190) 55.9 in.; (300) 58.7 in.; (300TE, 300E 4WD) 58.5 in.; (300SE/300SEL/420SEL) 60.4 in.; (300/ 500SL) 60.0 in.; (560SEC/SEL) 60.4 in.

TECHNICAL

Layout: front-engine, rear-drive. Transmission: (190E 2.6) five-speed manual, or optional four-speed automatic; (300SL) five-speed manual or five-speed automatic; (others) four-speed automatic standard. Steering: power recirculating ball. Brakes: front/rear disc. Body construction: steel unibody.

PERFORMANCE

Acceleration (0-60 mph): (300E 4Matic) 9.2 sec.; (300SE) 9.2 sec.; (300SL) 9.1 sec.; (500SL) 6.1 sec. Acceleration (quarter mile): (300E 4Matic) 17.0 sec.; (300SE) 17.0 sec.; (300SL) 17.0 sec.; (500SL) 14.4 sec. EPA fuel economy City/highway miles per gallon: (300E 4Matic) 17/21; (300SE) 17/21; (300SL) 16/22; (500SL) 14/18. Performance Figures by *Motor Trend*.

Manufacturer: Daimler-Benz AG, Stuttgart, Germany.

Distributor: Mercedes-Benz of North America Inc., Montvale, New Jersey.

1992

190E 2.3/190E 2.6 — FOUR/SIX — The 190E was available in a Sportline version for 1992. The package included a sport-tuned suspension, quicker-ratio, power-assisted steering, wider tires and wheels, and a discreet "Sportline" emblem on each front fender. The package was also available on the 300E and 300CE.

260/300/400/500 SERIES — TURBODIESEL SIX/ GAS SIX/V-8 — While there were many cars that wore the label, "sport sedan" manufactured before 1992, Mercedes-Benz set a new standard with the 400E and limited edition, 500E. With an emphasis on "cultivation, smoothness and quietness," the 268-hp 400E gave purchasers of mid-size Mercedes-Benz sedans their first V-8s. Unique eight-hole alloy wheels and 195/65x15 tires visually separated the V-8 from its lesser siblings. Front fender flares highlighted the 322-hp 500E. Assembled by fellow Stuttgart neighbor, Porsche, the 500E could rip to 60 mph in a mere 5.8 seconds. The suspension also received a major upgrade and 225/55X16 tires delivered the power to the pavement.

S-CLASS — SIX/V-8/V-12 — A new generation of S-Class sedans was launched. While the styling left no one confused as to its lineage, innovations abounded beneath the gleaming steel. Dual-pane side glass improved sound insulation and aided the charcoal-filtered climate control in maintaining a consistent temperature. The front seatbelt upper anchor points automatically adjusted as the seat moved fore and aft. This was the beginning of dual-zone climate controls with separate thermostats; the 600SEL even had a third and fourth system for rear-seat passengers. The attentive S-Class even raised "positioning rods" from its rear flanks when reverse gear was selected, the better to tell where the long car ended.

300SL/500SL — V-8 — While basically unchanged from its 1990 debut, the SL family still offered "the first fully automatic convertible top in the auto industry." With the touch of a button, 15 hydraulic servos, 11 solenoids, and 17 proximity switches raised and lowered the top.

I.D. DATA: Same as 1990.

ENGINES

Base Four (190E 2.3): Inline, overhead-cam four-cylinder. Displacement: 140.3 cid (2,300 cc). Brake horsepower: 130 at 5,100 rpm. Torque 146 lbs.-ft. at 3,500 rpm. Multi-point fuel injection.

Base Turbodiesel Five (300D 2.5): Inline, overhead-cam five-cylinder, with turbocharger. Displacement: 152 cid (2,492 cc). Bore & stroke: 3.43 x 3.31 in. (87 x 84 mm). Compression ratio: 22.0:1. Brake horsepower: 121 at 4,600 rpm. Torque: 165 lbs.-ft. at 2,400 rpm. Fuel injection.

Base Six (190E 2.6, 300E 2.6): Inline, overhead-cam six-cylinder. Displacement: 158.6 cid (2,600 cc). Bore & stroke: 3.26 x 3.16 in. (83 x 80 mm). Compression ratio: 9.2:1. Brake horsepower: 158 at 5,800 rpm. Torque: 162 lbs.-ft. at 4,600 rpm. Multi-point fuel injection.

Base Six (300): Inline, overhead-cam six-cylinder. Displacement: 180.8 cid (2,964 cc). Bore & stroke: 3.48 x 3.16 in. (88.5 x 80.2 mm). Compression ratio: 9.2:1. Brake horsepower: 177 at 5,700 rpm. Torque: 188 lbs.-ft. at 4,400 rpm. Hydraulic valve lifters. Multi-point fuel injection.

Base Six (300CE): Inline, dual-overhead-cam six-cylinder. Displacement: 180.8 cid (2,964 cc). Bore & stroke: 3.48 x 3.16 in. (88.5 x 80.2 mm). Compression ratio: 10.0:1. Brake horsepower: 217 at 6,400 rpm. Torque: 195 lbs.-ft. at 4,600 rpm.

MODEL	BODY TYPE & SEATING	ENGINE TYPE/CID	P.E. PRICE	WEIGHT (LBS.)	PRODUCTION TOTAL
190E					
190E 2.3	4-dr Sedan-5P	I4/140	$28,350	6,882	
190E 2.6	4-dr Sedan-5P	I6/159		2,870	9,084
300 SERIES					
300E 2.6	4-dr Sedan-5P	I6/159	$42,950	3,155	2,876
300E	4-dr Sedan-5P	I6/181		3,210	6,340
300E 4Matic	4-dr Sedan-5P	I6/181		3,505	1,008
300TE	4-dr Station Wagon-5P	I6/181		3,450	1,186
300TE 4Matic	4-dr Station Wagon-5P	I6/181		3,725	660
300CE	2-dr Coupe-4P	I6/181		3,395	1,770
300SE	4-dr Sedan-5P	I6/195	$69,400	3,595	5,528
400E	4-dr Sedan-5P	V8/244		3,640	5,274
500E	4-dr Sedan-5P	V8/304		3,640	554
300/350 SERIES (Turbodiesel)					
300D 2.5	4-dr Sedan-5P	I5/152	$42,950	2,490	
300SD	4-dr Sedan-5P	I6/214		1,324	
400 SERIES					
400SE	4-dr Sedan-5P	V8/256		2,784	
300/500SL					
300SL	2-dr Coupe/Roadster-2P	I6/181		3,850	1,226
500SL	2-dr Coupe/Roadster-2P	V8/304		4,025	3,486
500 SERIES					
500SEL	4-dr Sedan-5P	V8/305		3,960	4,375
560 SERIES					
560SEC	2-dr Coupe-4P	V8/338		3,770	557
(Only 1991 models available)					
600 SERIES					
600SEL	4-dr Sedan-5P	V12/366			874

Base Six (300SL): Inline, dual-overhead-cam six-cylinder (24-valve). Aluminum crossflow head. Displacement: 180.8 cid (2,964 cc). Bore & stroke: 3.48 x 3.16 in. (88.5 x 80.2 mm). Compression ratio: 10.0:1. Brake horsepower: 228 at 6,300 rpm. Torque: 201 lbs.-ft. at 4,600 rpm. 300SL Engine Note: Outside North America, a variant of the 300SL with a 12-valve six-cylinder engine was also marketed.

Base V-8 (420SEL): 90-degree, overhead-cam, eight-cylinder. Light alloy block and heads. Displacement: 256 cid (4,197 cc). Bore & stroke: 3.62 x 3.11 in. (92 x 79 mm). Compression ratio: 9.0:1. Brake horsepower: 201 at 5,200 rpm. Torque: 228 lbs.-ft. at 3,600 rpm. Five main bearings. Hydraulic valve lifters. Multi-point fuel injection.

Base V-8 (500SL, 500SEL): 90-degree, dual-overhead-cam, eight-cylinder (32-valve). Aluminum alloy block. Displacement: 304 cid (4,983 cc). Bore & stroke: 3.80 x 3.35 in. (96.5 x 85 mm). Compression ratio: 10.0:1. Brake horsepower: 322 at 5,500 rpm. Torque: 332 lbs.-ft. at 4,000 rpm. Bosch KE 5 CIS multi-point fuel injection.

Base V-12 (600 SERIES): 60-degree, dual-overhead-cam, 12-cylinder (48-valve). Aluminum alloy block and heads. Displacement: 365.4 cid (5,987 cc). Bore & stoke: 3.50 x 3.16 in. (89.0 x 80.2 mm). Compression ratio: 10.0:1. Brake horsepower: 389 at 5,200 rpm. Torque: 420 lbs.-ft. at 3,800 rpm. Multi-point fuel injection.

CHASSIS

Wheelbase: (190) 104.9 in.; (300E/TE) 110.2 in.; (300CE) 106.9 in.; (300SE) 115.6 in.; (300/500SL) 99.0 in. Overall length: (190) 175.1 in.; (300E) 187.2 in.; (300CE) 183.9 in.; (300TE) 188.2 in.; (300SE) 202.6 in.; (300/500SL) 176.0 in.; Height: (190) 54.1 in.; (300) 56.3 in.; (300E 4WD) 57.1 in.; (300CE) 54.9 in.; (300TE) 59.8 in.; (300SE) 56.6 in.; (300/500SL) 50.7 in. Width: (190) 66.5 in.; (300) 68.5 in.; (300/500SL) 71.3 in. Front tread: (190) 56.7 in.; (300) 59.1 in.; (300TE, 300E 4WD) 58.9 in.; (300/500SL) 60.4 in. Rear tread: (190) 55.9 in.; (300) 58.7 in.; (300TE, 300E 4WD) 58.5 in.; (300/500SL) 60.0 in.

TECHNICAL

Layout: front-engine, rear-drive. Transmission: (190E 2.6) five-speed manual, or optional four-speed automatic; (300SL) five-speed manual or five-speed automatic; (others) four-speed automatic standard. Steering: power recirculating ball. Brakes: front/rear disc. Body construction: steel unibody.

PERFORMANCE

Acceleration (0-60 mph): (300E 4Matic) 9.2 sec.; (300SE) 9.2 sec.; (300SL) 9.1 sec.; (400E) 7.6 sec.; (500SL) 6.1 sec.; (500SEL) 7.4 sec. Acceleration (quarter mile): (300E 4Matic) 17.0 sec.; (300SE) 17.0 sec.; (300SL) 17.0 sec.; (400E) 15.8 sec.; (500SL) 14.4 sec.; (500SEL) 15.7 sec. EPA fuel economy City/highway miles per gallon: (300E 4Matic) 17/21; (300SE) 17/21; (300SL) 16/22; (400E) 15/20; (500SL) 14/18; (500SEL) 13/16. Performance Figures by *Motor Trend*.

Manufacturer: Daimler-Benz AG, Stuttgart, Germany.

Distributor: Mercedes-Benz of North America Inc., Montvale, New Jersey.

1993

190E 2.3 — FOUR — Unchanged for its final year.

190E 2.6 — SIX — Unchanged for its final year.

300/400/500 SERIES — SIX/V-8 — After a 21-year hiatus, a four-seat Mercedes-Benz convertible returned to the model line. The 300CE Cabriolet added even greater diversity to the already varied mid-size Mercedes-Benz models. This would prove to be a much sought-after model. The new 3.2-liter 24-valve, DOHC, variable intake valve timing, six-cylinder model introduced in the 1992 300SE sedan, showed up in the 300E, 300TE, 300CE, and the new 300CE Cabriolet. 4Matic sedan and station wagons still had the older two-valve-per-cylinder engine. Passenger side airbags became standard equipment. The 300E 2.6 became the 300E 2.8 thanks to an increase in displacement.

300SE/400SEL — S-CLASS — SIX/V-8 — The 400SEL long-wheelbase sedan replaced the 400SE standard wheelbase. Power in the 4.2-liter V-8 was boosted to 275 hp thanks to a jump in compression ratio to 11.0:1.

300SD — TURBODIESEL SIX — No changes.

S-CLASS — V-8/V-12 — Two brand new coupes, the 500SEC and the 600SEC joined the recently introduced S-Class sedans. The standard wheelbase cars were available with either a gasoline six- or five-cylinder diesel engine. The long-wheelbase cars were available with two V-8s and a V-12.

300SL/500SL/600SL — SIX/V-8/V-12 — The glorious 6.0-liter V-12, that made its appearance in the 600SEL last year, was shoehorned into the two-seat 600SL.

I.D. DATA: Same as 1990.

ENGINES

Base Four (190E 2.3): Inline, overhead-cam four-cylinder. Displacement: 140.3 cid (2,300 cc). Brake horsepower: 130 at 5,100 rpm. Torque 146 lbs.-ft. at 3,500 rpm. Multi-point fuel injection.

Base Six (190E 2.6): Inline, overhead-cam six-cylinder. Displacement: 158.6 cid (2,600 cc). Bore & stroke: 3.26 x 3.16 in. (83 x 80 mm). Compression ratio: 9.2:1. Brake horsepower: 158 at 5,800 rpm. Torque: 162 lbs.-ft. at 4,600 rpm. Multi-point fuel injection.

Base Six (300E 2.8): Inline, overhead-cam six-cylinder. Displacement: 170.8 cid (2,800 cc). Compression ratio: 9.2:1. Brake horsepower: 194 at 5,500 rpm. Torque: 191 lbs.-ft. at 3,750 rpm. Multi-point fuel injection.

MODEL	BODY TYPE & SEATING	ENGINE TYPE/CID	P.E. PRICE	WEIGHT (LBS.)	PRODUCTION TOTAL
190E					
190E 2.3	4-dr Sedan-5P	I4/140	$28,350	5,431	
190E 2.6	4-dr Sedan-5P	I6/159		2,870	5,809
300 SERIES					
300E 2.8	4-dr Sedan-5P	I6/171	$42,950	3,155	6,682
300E	4-dr Sedan-5P	I6/195		3,210	4,639
300E 4Matic	4-dr Sedan-5P	I6/181		3,505	336
300TE	4-dr Station Wagon-5P	I6/195		3,450	637
300TE 4Matic	4-dr Station Wagon-5P	I6/181		3,725	260
300CE	2-dr Coupe-4P	I6/195		3,395	891
300CE	2-dr Conv-4P	I6/195		4,025	593
300SE	4-dr Sedan-5P	I6/195	$69,400	3,595	3,393
400E	4-dr Sedan-5P	V8/244		3,640	2,882
500E	4-dr Sedan-5P	V8/304		3,640	540
300/350 SERIES (Turbodiesel)					
300D 2.5	4-dr Sedan-5P	I5/152	$42,950	1,808	
300SD	4-dr Sedan-5P	I6/214			649
400 SERIES					
400SEL	4-dr Sedan-5P	V8/256		3,279	
300/500SL/600SL					
300SL	2-dr Coupe/Roadster-2P	$I6/181		3,850	629
500SL	2-dr Coupe/Roadster-2P	V8/304		4,025	1,394
600SL	2-dr Coupe/Roadster-2P	V12/366			501
500 SERIES					
500SEL	4-dr Sedan-5P	V8/305		3,960	2,265
500SEC	2-dr Coupe-4P	V8/338		3,770	169
600 SERIES					
600SEL	4-dr Sedan-5P	V12/366			517
600SEC	2-dr Coupe-4P	V12/366			134

Base Six (300E 4Matic): Inline, overhead-cam six-cylinder. Displacement: 180.8 cid (2,964 cc). Bore & stroke: 3.48 x 3.16 in. (88.5 x 80.2 mm). Compression ratio: 9.2:1. Brake horsepower: 177 at 5,700 rpm. Torque: 188 lbs.-ft. at 4,400 rpm. Hydraulic valve lifters. Multi-point fuel injection.

Base Six (300CE): Inline, dual-overhead-cam (24-valve) variable intake valve timing six-cylinder. Displacement: 195.2 cid (3,199 cc). Bore & stroke: 3.54 x 3.30 in. (89.9 x 84.0 mm).

Compression ratio: 10.0:1. Brake horsepower: 217 at 5,500 rpm. Torque: 229 lbs.-ft. at 3,750 rpm.

Base Six (300SL): Inline, dual-overhead-cam six-cylinder (24-valve). Aluminum crossflow head. Displacement: 180.8 cid (2,964 cc). Bore & stroke: 3.48 x 3.16 in. (88.5 x 80.2 mm). Compression ratio: 10.0:1. Brake horsepower: 228 at 6,300 rpm. Torque: 201 lbs.-ft. at 4,600 rpm.

1993 AMG 300E

1993 190E Limited Edition 2.6

1993 190E Limited Edition 2.6 interior

Base V-8 (400SEL): 90-degree, overhead-cam, eight-cylinder. Light alloy block and heads. Displacement: 256 cid (4,197 cc). Bore & stroke: 3.62 x 3.11 in. (92 x 79 mm). Compression ratio: 11.0:1. Brake horsepower: 275 at 5,700 rpm. Torque: 295 lbs.-ft. at 3,900 rpm. Five main bearings. Hydraulic valve lifters. Multi-point fuel injection.

Base V-8 (500E, 500SL, 500SEL): 90-degree, dual-overhead-cam, eight-cylinder (32-valve). Aluminum alloy block. Displacement: 304 cid (4,983 cc). Bore & stroke: 3.80 x 3.35 in. (96.5 x 85 mm). Compression ratio: 10.0:1. Brake horsepower: 315 at 5,600 rpm. Torque: 347 lbs.-ft. at 3,900 rpm. Bosch KE 5 CIS multi-point fuel injection.

Base V-12 (600SL, 600SEL, 600SEC): 60-degree, dual-overhead-cam, 12-cylinder (48-valve). Aluminum alloy block and heads. Displacement: 365.4 cid (5,987 cc). Bore & stoke: 3.50 x 3.16 in. (89.0 x 80.2 mm). Compression ratio: 10.0:1. Brake horsepower: 389 at 5,200 rpm. Torque: 420 lbs.-ft. at 3,800 rpm. Multi-point fuel injection.

CHASSIS

Wheelbase: (190) 104.9 in.; (300E/TE) 110.2 in.; (300CE) 106.9 in.; (300SE) 115.6 in.; (300/500SL) 99.0 in. Overall length: (190) 175.1 in.; (300E) 187.2 in.; (300CE) 183.9 in.; (300TE) 188.2 in.; (300SE) 202.6 in.; (300/500SL) 176.0 in. Height: (190) 54.1 in.; (300) 56.3 in.; (300E 4WD) 57.1 in.; (300CE) 54.9 in.; (300CE Cab) 55.2 in.; (300TE) 59.8 in.; (300SE) 56.6 in.; (300/500SL) 50.7 in. Width: (190) 66.5 in.; (300) 68.5 in.; (300/500SL) 71.3 in. Front tread: (190) 56.7 in.; (300) 59.1 in.; (300TE, 300E 4WD) 58.9 in.; (300/500SL) 60.4 in. Rear tread: (190) 55.9 in.; (300) 58.7 in.; (300TE, 300E 4WD) 58.5 in.; (300/500SL) 60.0 in.

TECHNICAL

Layout: front-engine, rear-drive. Transmission: (190E 2.6) five-speed manual, or optional four-speed automatic; (300SL) five-speed manual or five-speed automatic; (others) four-speed automatic standard. Steering: power recirculating ball. Suspension (front): upper/lower A-arms with coil springs and anti-roll bar except (190) modified MacPherson struts with coil springs and anti-roll bar; (300) gas-pressurized struts with coil springs and anti-roll bar; (300/500SL) struts with coil springs on A-arms and torsion bar stabilizer. Suspension (rear): independent, semi-trailing arms with coil springs and anti-roll bar; (190/300) five-link independent with coil springs and anti-roll bar; (300/500SL) multi-link independent with coil springs, torsion bar stabilizer, and level control. Brakes: front/rear disc. Body construction: steel unibody.

PERFORMANCE

Acceleration (0-60 mph): (300E 4Matic) 9.2 sec.; (300SE) 9.2 sec.; (300SL) 9.1 sec.; (400E) 7.6 sec.; (500SL) 6.1 sec.; (500SEL) 7.4 sec. Acceleration (quarter mile): (300E 4Matic) 17.0 sec.; (300SE) 17.0 sec.; (300SL) 17.0 sec.; (400E) 15.8 sec.; (500SL) 14.4 sec.; (500SEL) 15.7 sec. EPA fuel economy City/highway miles per gallon: (300E 4Matic) 17/21; (300SE) 17/21; (300SL) 16/22; (400E) 15/20; (500SL) 14/18; (500SEL) 13/16. Top Speed: (Factory figures) (300SL) 143 mph claimed; (500SL) 155 mph claimed. Performance Figures by *Motor Trend*.

Manufacturer: Daimler-Benz AG, Stuttgart, Germany.

Distributor: Mercedes-Benz of North America Inc., Montvale, New Jersey.

1993 300CE cabriolet

1994

1994 represented a major change for Mercedes-Benz. The biggest news was a much-easier series of designations. The 190 Series was replaced by the C-Class. All mid-size models were E-Class, and the top-of-the-line sedans were called S-Class. The numbers following the letter, in most cases, would designate the engine size in liters.

C-CLASS — FOUR/SIX — The C-Class were designed to be "more car without more cost." Mercedes-Benz succeeded by offering more interior room, greater safety, higher fuel efficiency, and even improved performance. The C220 had a 2.2-liter engine, and was the lowest price Mercedes-Benz model at $29,900. You could also step up to the $34,900 C280 that added a 194-hp 2.8-liter six to the classy sedan. Overall, the C-Class represented a big step forward.

E-CLASS — FIVE/SIX/V-8 — The E-Class received a new front end and trunk lid to go along with the new model designations. The 4Matic models were dropped, as Mercedes-Benz felt their traction control was adequate in slippery situations.

S-CLASS — SIX/V-8/V-12 — By increasing the efficiency of the S320 engine, gas mileage improved by 18.8 percent. This resulted in a $1,700 savings in Gas Guzzler tax.

SL-CLASS — SIX/V-8/V-12 — The replacement of the 300SL engine with the SL320's efficient 3.2-liter six meant a decrease in the Gas Guzzler tax.

I.D. DATA: Same as 1990.

ENGINES

Base Four (C220): Inline, overhead-cam four-cylinder. Displacement: 134.2 cid (2,199 cc). Bore & stroke: 3.54 x 3.41 in. (89.9 x 86.6 mm). Compression ratio: 9.8:1. Brake horsepower: 148 at 5,500 rpm. Torque: 155 lbs.-ft. at 4,000 rpm. Multi-point fuel injection.

Base Six (C280): Inline, overhead-cam six-cylinder. Displacement: 170.8 cid (2,799 cc). Bore & stroke: 3.54 x 2.89 in. (89.9 x 73.5 mm). Compression ratio: 10.0:1. Brake horsepower: 194 at 5,500 rpm. Torque: 199 lbs.-ft. at 3,750 rpm. Multi-point fuel injection.

Base Six (E320, S320, SL320): Inline, dual-overhead-cam (24-valve) variable intake valve timing six-cylinder. Displacement: 195.2 cid (3,199 cc). Bore & stroke: 3.54 x 3.30 in. (89.9 x 84.0 mm). Compression ratio: 10.0:1. Brake horsepower: 217 at 5,500 rpm. Torque: 229 lbs.-ft. at 3,750 rpm.

Base Turbodiesel Six (E300 D): Inline, overhead-cam six-cylinder. Displacement: 182.8 cid (2,996 cc). Bore & stroke: 3.43 x 3.31 in. (87 x 84 mm). Compression ratio: 22.0:1. Brake horsepower: 134 at 5,000 rpm. Torque: 155 lbs.-ft. at 2,600 rpm. Mechanical fuel injection.

Base Turbodiesel Six (S350 D): Inline, overhead-cam six-cylinder, with turbocharger. Displacement: 210.5 cid (3,449 cc). Bore & stroke: 3.5 x 3.6 in. (89 x 92.4 mm). Compression ratio: 22.0:1. Brake horsepower: 148 at 4,000 rpm. Torque: 232 lbs.-ft. at 2,000 rpm. Fuel injection.

Model	Body Type & Seating	Engine Type/CID	P.E. Price	Weight (lbs.)	Production Total
C-CLASS					
C220	4-dr Sedan-5P	I4/134	$29,900	3,150	10,322
C280	4-dr Sedan-5P	I6/171	$34,900	3,350	16,802
E-CLASS					
E300 Diesel	4-dr Sedan-5P	I6/183	$40,000	3,495	2,837
E320	4-dr Sedan-5P	I6/195	$42,500	3,525	16,301
E420	4-dr Sedan-5P	V8/256	$51,000	3,745	3,518
E500	4-dr Sedan-5P	V8/304	$80,800	3,855	293
E320	4-dr Station Wagon-5P	I6/195	$46,200	3,750	2,837
E320	2-dr Coupe-4P	I6/195	$61,600	3,525	1,530
E320	2-dr Conv-4P	I6/195	$77,300	4,025	595
S-CLASS					
S350 D	4-dr Sedan-5P	I6/210	$70,600	4,610	592
S320	4-dr Sedan-5P	I6/195	$70,600	4,630	5,869
S420	4-dr Sedan-5P	V8/256	$79,500	4,760	4,586
S500	4-dr Sedan-5P	V8/304	$95,300	4,830	3,165
S600	4-dr Sedan-5P	V12/366	$95,300	5,095	345
S500	2-dr Coupe-4P	V8/304	$99,800	4,785	955
S600	2-dr Coupe-4P	V12/366	$133,300	5,075	319
SL-CLASS					
SL320	2-dr Coupe/Roadster-2P	I6/195	$85,200	4,090	1,725
SL500	2-dr Coupe/Roadster-2P	V8/304	$99,500	4,165	3,165

Base V-8 (E420, S420): 90-degree, overhead-cam, eight-cylinder. Light alloy block and heads. Displacement: 256 cid (4,197 cc). Bore & stroke: 3.62 x 3.11 in. (92 x 79 mm). Compression ratio: 11.0:1. Brake horsepower: 275 at 5,700 rpm. Torque: 295 lbs.-ft. at 3,900 rpm. Five main bearings. Hydraulic valve lifters. Multi-point fuel injection.

Base V-8 (S500, SL500, S500 C): 90-degree, dual-overhead-cam, eight-cylinder (32-valve). Aluminum alloy block. Displacement: 303.5 cid (4,973 cc). Bore & stroke: 3.80 x 3.35 in. (96.5 x 85 mm). Compression ratio: 10.0:1. Brake horsepower: 315 at 5,600 rpm. Torque: 345 lbs.-ft. at 3,900 rpm. Bosch KE 5 CIS multi-point fuel injection.

Base V-12 (S600, SL600, S600 C): 60-degree, dual-overhead-cam, 12-cylinder (48-valve). Aluminum alloy block and heads. Displacement: 365.4 cid (5,987 cc). Bore & stoke: 3.50 x 3.16 in. (89.0 x 80.2 mm). Compression ratio: 10.0:1. Brake horsepower: 389 at 5,200 rpm. Torque: 420 lbs.-ft. at 3,800 rpm. Multi-point fuel injection.

CHASSIS

Wheelbase: (C-Class) 105.9 in.; (E300, E420, E320 sedan, wagon) 110.2 in.; (E320 coupe, cab) 106.9 in; (S-Class) 123.6 in.; (except SWB S320, S350) 119.7 in.; (SL 300/500) 99.0 in.; (S500/600 C) 115.9 in. Overall length: (C-Class) 177.4 in.; (E300D, E320 sedan, E420) 187.2 in.; (E300 wagon) 188.2 in.; (E320 coupe, cab) 183.9 in.; (S-Class) 205.2 in.; (except SWB S320, S350) 201.3 in.; (SL320/500) 176.0 in.; (S500/600 C) 199.4 in. Height: (C220, C280) 56.1 in.; (C36) 55.6 in.; (E300, E420, E320 sedan) 56.3 in.; (E320 wagon) 59.8 in.; (E300 coupe) 54.9 in.; (E300 cab) 54.8 in.; (S-Class) 58.3 in.; (SL300/500) 51.3 in.; (S500/600 C) 56.7 in. Width: (C-Class) 67.7 in.; (E-Class) 68.5 in.; (S-Class) 74.3 in.; (SL320/500) 71.3 in.; (S-Class) 74.3 in.; (S500/600 C) 74.6 in. Front tread: (C220, C280) 58.8 in.; (C36) 58.9 in.; (E-Class) 59.1 in.; (except E320 wagon) 58.9 in.; (S-Class) 63.2 in.; (SL320/500) 60.4 in.; (S500/600 coupe) 63.2 in. Rear tread: (C220) 57.6 in.; (C280) 58.8 in.; (C36) 58.2 in.; (E-Class) 58.5 in.; (except E320 wagon) 58.7 in.; (S-Class) 62.2 in.; (SL320/500) 60.0 in.; (S500/600 coupe) 62.2 in.

TECHNICAL

Layout: front-engine, rear-drive. Transmission: (C220) five-speed manual, or optional four-speed automatic; (SL320) five-speed manual or five-speed automatic; (others) four-speed automatic standard. Steering: power recirculating ball. Brakes: front/rear disc. Body construction: steel unibody.

PERFORMANCE

Acceleration (0-60 mph): (C220) 8.7 sec.; (E320 Wag) 8.1 sec.; (S600 C) 6.5 sec. Acceleration (quarter mile): (C220) 16.9 sec.; (E320 Wag) 16.2 sec.; (S600 C) 14.8 sec. EPA fuel economy City/highway miles per gallon: (C220) 21/28; (E320 Wag) 18/24; (S600 C) 12/16. Performance Figures by *Motor Trend*.

Manufacturer: Daimler-Benz AG, Stuttgart, Germany.

Distributor: Mercedes-Benz of North America Inc., Montvale, New Jersey.

1995

C-CLASS — FOUR/SIX — The addition of the C36 to the Mercedes-Benz lineup marked the beginning of a beautiful partnership. The German tuning firm, AMG, had been modifying Mercedes-Benz cars for many years. Mercedes-Benz liked what AMG did enough to buy a share in the company, and the C36 was the first fruits of this union. Exterior changes were limited to tasteful rocker panel extensions, a discrete front spoiler, and distinctive AMG wheels shod with low-profile tires. The AMG-massaged 3.6-liter engine produced a satisfying 268 hp, making this car a joy to drive.

E-CLASS — The Über-sedan, the E500, left the lineup. A Special Edition was offered to celebrate 10 years of this successful model. It could be identified by unique alloy wheels and two special paint colors. The E300 Diesel was the first production car to use four-valve technology in a diesel engine.

S-CLASS — A revised exterior included a modified grille, redesigned lights, restyled bumpers, and a more rounded trunk lid. Electronic traction control was standard on all S-Class vehicles.

SL-CLASS — Unchanged for 1995.

I.D. DATA: Same as 1990.

ENGINES

Base Four (C220): Inline, overhead-cam four-cylinder. Displacement: 134.2 cid (2,199 cc). Bore & stroke: 3.54 x 3.41 in. (89.9 x 86.6 mm). Compression ratio: 9.8:1. Brake horsepower: 148 at 5,500 rpm. Torque 155 lbs.-ft. at 4,000 rpm. Multi-point fuel injection.

Base Six (C280): Inline, overhead-cam six-cylinder. Displacement: 170.8 cid (2,799 cc). Bore & stroke: 3.54 x 2.89 in. (89.9 x 73.5 mm). Compression ratio: 10.0:1. Brake horsepower: 194 at 5,500 rpm. Torque: 199 lbs.-ft. at 3,750 rpm. Multi-point fuel injection.

Base Six (E300 D): Inline, overhead-cam six-cylinder. Displacement: 182.8 cid (2,996 cc). Bore & stroke: 3.43 x 3.31 in. (87 x 84 mm). Compression ratio: 22.0:1. Brake horsepower:

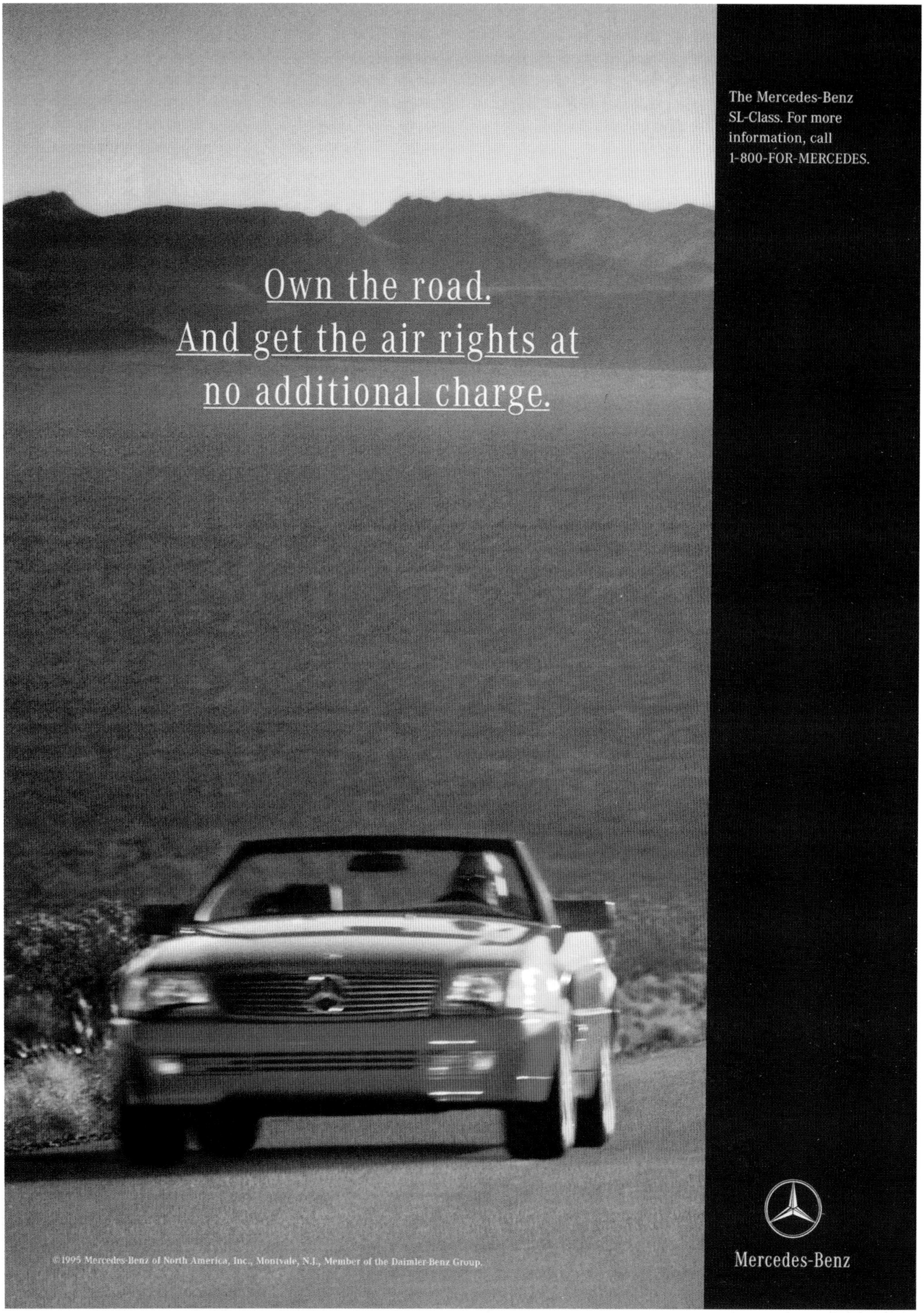
The Mercedes-Benz
SL-Class. For more
information, call
1-800-FOR-MERCEDES.
Own the road.
And get the air rights at
no additional charge.
©1995 Mercedes-Benz of North America, Inc., Montvale, N.J., Member of the Daimler-Benz Group.
Mercedes-Benz

1995 SL ad

1995 E Class sedan

134 at 5,000 rpm. Torque: 155 lbs.-ft. at 2,600 rpm. Mechanical fuel injection.

Base Six (E320, S320, SL320): Inline, dual-overhead-cam (24-valve) variable intake valve timing six-cylinder. Displacement: 195.2 cid (3,199 cc). Bore & stroke: 3.54 x

3.30 in. (89.9 x 84.0 mm). Compression ratio: 10.0:1. Brake horsepower: 217 at 5,500 rpm. Torque: 229 lbs.-ft. at 3,750 rpm. HFM Motronic fuel injection.

Base Six (C36): Inline, overhead-cam (24-valve) variable intake valve timing six-cylinder. Displacement: 220 cid (3,606

Model	Body Type & Seating	Engine Type/CID	P.E. Price	Weight (lbs.)	Production Total
C-CLASS					
C220	4-dr Sedan-5P	I4/134	$30,950	3,150	13,585
C280	4-dr Sedan-5P	I6/171	$36,300	3,350	12,821
C36	4-dr Sedan-5P	I6/220	$49,800	3,549	491
E-CLASS					
E300 Diesel	4-dr Sedan-5P	I6/183	$41,000	3,485	2,837
E320	4-dr Sedan-5P	I6/195	$43,500	3,525	12,548
E420	4-dr Sedan-5P	V8/256	$52,500	3,745	2,145
E320	4-dr Station Wagon-5P	I6/195	$47,500	3,750	2,647
E320	2-dr Coupe-4P	I6/195	$63,000	3,525	1,798
E320	2-dr Conv-4P	I6/195	$77,300	4,025	322
S-CLASS					
S350	4-dr Sedan-5P	I6/210	$65,900	4,610	188
S320	4-dr Sedan-5P	I6/195	$62,700	4,630	3,477
S320 LWB	4-dr Sedan-5P	I6/195	$65,900	4,720	3,781
S420	4-dr Sedan-5P	V8/256	$73,900	4,760	4,688
S500	4-dr Sedan-5P	V8/304	$87,500	4,830	3,911
S600	4-dr Sedan-5P	V12/366	$130,300	5,095	410
S500	2-dr Coupe-4P	V8/304	$91,900	4,695	888
S600	2-dr Coupe-4P	V12/366	$133,300	4,960	346
SL-CLASS					
SL320	2-dr Coupe/Roadster-2P	I6/195	$78,300	4,090	2,184
SL500	2-dr Coupe/Roadster-2P	V8/304	$89,900	4,165	4,139
SL600	2-dr Coupe/Roadster-2P	V12/366	$120,100	4,455	609

cc). Bore & stroke 3.58 x 3.64 in. (91.0 x 92.4 mm). Compression ratio: 10.5:1. Brake horsepower: 268 at 5,750 rpm. Torque: 280 lbs.-ft. at 4,000 rpm. Electronic fuel injection.

Base Turbodiesel Six (S350 D): Inline, overhead-cam six-cylinder, with turbocharger. Displacement: 210.5 cid (3,449 cc). Bore & stroke: 3.5 x 3.6 in. (89 x 92.4 mm). Compression ratio: 22.0:1. Brake horsepower: 148 at 4,000 rpm. Torque: 232 lbs.-ft. at 2,000 rpm. Fuel injection.

Base V-8 (E420, S420): 90-degree, overhead-cam, eight-cylinder. Light alloy block and heads. Displacement: 256 cid (4,197 cc). Bore & stroke: 3.62 x 3.11 in. (92 x 79 mm). Compression ratio: 11.0:1. Brake horsepower: 275 at 5,700 rpm. Torque: 295 lbs.-ft. at 3,900 rpm. Five main bearings. Hydraulic valve lifters. Multi-point fuel injection.

Base V-8 (S500, SL500, S500 C): 90-degree, dual-overhead-cam, eight-cylinder (32-valve). Aluminum alloy block. Displacement: 303.5 cid (4,973 cc). Bore & stroke: 3.80 x 3.35 in. (96.5 x 85 mm). Compression ratio: 10.0:1. Brake horsepower: 315 at 5,600 rpm. Torque: 345 lbs.-ft. at 3,900 rpm. Bosch KE 5 CIS multi-point fuel injection.

Base V-12 (S600, SL600, S600 C): 60-degree, dual-overhead-cam, 12-cylinder (48-valve). Aluminum alloy block and heads. Displacement: 365.4 cid (5,987 cc). Bore & stoke: 3.50 x 3.16 in. (89.0 x 80.2 mm). Compression ratio: 10.0:1. Brake horsepower: 389 at 5,200 rpm. Torque: 420 lbs.-ft. at 3,800 rpm. Multi-point fuel injection.

CHASSIS

Wheelbase: (C-Class) 105.9 in.; (E300 D, E420, E320 sedan, wagon) 110.2 in.; (E320 coupe, cab) 106.9 in; (S-Class) 123.6 in.; (except SWB S320, S350) 119.7 in.; (SL320/500) 99.0 in.; (S500/600 C) 115.9 in. Overall length: (C-Class) 177.4 in.; (E300 D, E320 sedan, E420) 187.2 in.; (E320 wagon) 188.2 in.; (E320 coupe, cab) 183.9 in.; (S-Class) 205.2 in.; (except SWB S320, S350) 201.3 in.; (SL320/500) 176.0 in.; (S500/600 C) 199.4 in. Height: (C220, C280) 56.1 in.; (C36) 55.6 in.; (E320, E420, E320 sedan) 56.3 in.; (E320 wagon) 59.8 in.; (E320 coupe) 54.9 in.; (E320 cab) 54.8 in.; (S-Class) 58.3 in.; (SL320/500) 51.3 in.; (S500/600 C) 56.7 in. Width: (C-Class) 67.7 in.; (E-Class) 68.5 in.; (S-Class) 74.3 in.; (SL 300/500) 71.3 in.; (S-Class) 74.3 in.; (S500/600 C) 74.6 in. Front tread: (C220, C280) 58.8 in.; (C36) 58.9 in.;

(E-Class) 59.1 in.; (except E320 wagon) 58.9 in.; (S-Class) 63.2 in.; (SL320/500) 60.4 in.; (S500/600 coupe) 63.2 in. Rear tread: (C220) 57.6 in.; (C280) 58.8 in.; (C36) 58.2 in.; (E-Class) 58.5 in.; (except E320 wagon) 58.7 in.; (S-Class) 62.2 in.; (SL320/500) 60.0 in.; (S500/600 coupe) 62.2 in.

TECHNICAL

Layout: front-engine, rear-drive. Transmission: (C-Class) five-speed manual, or optional four-speed automatic; (SL320) five-speed manual or five-speed automatic; (others) four-speed automatic standard. Steering: power-recirculating ball. Brakes: front/rear disc. Body construction: steel unibody.

PERFORMANCE

Acceleration (0-60 mph): (C220) 8.7 sec.; (E320 Wag) 8.1 sec.; (S600 C) 6.5 sec. Acceleration (quarter mile): (C220) 16.9 sec.; (E320 Wag) 16.2 sec.; (S600 C) 14.8 sec. EPA fuel economy city/highway miles per gallon: (C220) 21/28; (E320 Wag) 18/24; (S600 C) 12/16. Performance Figures by *Motor Trend.*

Manufacturer: Daimler-Benz AG, Stuttgart, Germany.

Distributor: Mercedes-Benz of North America Inc., Montvale, New Jersey.

1995 300CE coupe

1995 S500 coupe

1995 E320 cabriolet

1995 E320

1995 600SEL

1996

This was the year that a new, aggressive marketing plan could be better seen. The all-new E-Class debuted at prices lower by 5.7 percent to 9.7 percent. The standard C-Class cars dropped their prices by 1 percent and only the limited edition C36 received a 1.1 percent price increase. The rest of the models retained the same price.

C-CLASS — FOUR/SIX — The C-Class, along with all the other Mercedes-Benz models, featured a standard remote entry system that used an infrared light beam instead of a radio frequency. This was done to prevent "code grabbing" thieves.

E-CLASS — SIX/V-8 — A brand-new E-Class sedan debuted with a choice of 3.0 diesel, 3.2 gas, or a 4.2-liter V-8 engine. (The E420 was introduced in the spring of 1996.) The coupe, cabriolet, and wagon all were missing for this year. The new oval headlights initially drew criticism from some camps for being too avant-garde.

S-CLASS — SIX/V-8/V-12 — The S-Class was chosen to showcase Mercedes-Benz' new Electronic Stability Program (ESP). By using information from a variety of sensors, the S-Class could activate individual wheel brakes to stop a spin. A new ME 1 engine management system improved fuel economy on both the V-8 and V-12 models. The diesel S350 was dropped.

SL-CLASS — SIX/V-8/V-12 — Along with the new E-Class, the SL roadsters came standard with side airbags. They also received a facelift.

I.D. DATA: Same as 1990.

ENGINES

Base Four (C220): Inline, overhead-cam four-cylinder. Displacement: 134.2 cid (2,199 cc). Bore & stroke: 3.54 x 3.41 in. (89.9 x 86.6 mm). Compression ratio: 9.8:1. Brake horsepower: 148 at 5,500 rpm. Torque 155 lbs.-ft. at 4,000 rpm. Multi-point fuel injection.

Base Six (C280): Inline, overhead-cam six-cylinder. Displacement: 170.8 cid (2,799 cc). Bore & stroke: 3.54 x 2.89 in. (89.9 x 73.5 mm). Compression ratio: 10.0:1. Brake horsepower: 194 at 5,500 rpm. Torque: 199 lbs.-ft. at 3,750 rpm. Multi-point fuel injection.

Base Six (E320, S320, SL320): Inline, dual-overhead-cam (24-valve) variable intake valve timing six-cylinder. Displacement: 195.2 cid (3,199 cc). Bore & stroke: 3.54 x 3.30 in. (89.9 x 84.0 mm). Compression ratio: 10.0:1. Brake horsepower: 217 at 5,500 rpm. Torque: 229 lbs.-ft. at 3,750 rpm. HFM Motronic fuel injection.

Base Turbodiesel Six (E300 D): Inline, overhead-cam six-cylinder. Displacement: 182.8 cid (2,996 cc). Bore & stroke: 3.43 x 3.31 in. (87 x 84 mm). Compression ratio: 22.0:1. Brake horsepower: 134 at 5,000 rpm. Torque: 155 lbs.-ft. at 2,600 rpm. Mechanical fuel injection.

Base Six (C36): Inline, overhead-cam (24-valve) variable intake valve timing six-cylinder. Displacement: 220 cid (3,606 cc). Bore & stroke: 3.58 x 3.64 in. (91.0 x 92.4 mm). Compression ratio: 10.5:1. Brake horsepower: 268 at 5,750 rpm. Torque: 280 lbs.-ft. at 4,000 rpm. Electronic fuel injection.

MODEL	BODY TYPE & SEATING	ENGINE TYPE/CID	P.E. PRICE	WEIGHT (LBS.)	PRODUCTION TOTAL
C-CLASS					
C220	4-dr Sedan-5P	I4/134	$29,900	3,150	11,074
C280	4-dr Sedan-5P	I6/171	$35,250	3,350	12,316
C36	4-dr Sedan-5P	I6/220	$51,000	3,549	296
E-CLASS					
E300 Diesel	4-dr Sedan-5P	I6/183	$39,900	3,538	4,827
E320	4-dr Sedan-5P	I6/195	$43,500	3,605	22,680
E420	4-dr Sedan-5P	V8/256	$49,900	3,745	7,956
S-CLASS					
S320	4-dr Sedan-5P	I6/195	$62,700	4,480	4,215
S320 LWB	4-dr Sedan-5P	I6/195	$65,900	4,500	3,645
S420	4-dr Sedan-5P	V8/256	$73,900	4,650	4,345
S500	4-dr Sedan-5P	V8/304	$87,500	4,700	3,384
S600	4-dr Sedan-5P	V12/366	$130,300	4,960	517
S500	2-dr Coupe-4P	V8/304	$91,900	4,695	846
S600	2-dr Coupe-4P	V12/366	$133,300	4,960	285
SL-CLASS					
SL320	2-dr Coupe/Roadster-2P	I6/195	$78,300	4,010	2,648
SL500	2-dr Coupe/Roadster-2P	V8/304	$89,900	4,165	3,506
SL600	2-dr Coupe/Roadster-2P	V12/366	$120,100	4,455	680

Base V-8 (E420, S420): 90-degree, overhead-cam, eight-cylinder. Light alloy block and heads. Displacement: 256 cid (4,197 cc). Bore & stroke: 3.62 x 3.11 in. (92 x 79 mm). Compression ratio: 11.0:1. Brake horsepower: 275 at 5,700 rpm. Torque: 295 lbs.-ft. at 3,900 rpm. Five main bearings. Hydraulic valve lifters. Multi-point fuel injection.

Base V-8 (S500, SL500, S500 C): 90-degree, dual-overhead-cam, eight-cylinder (32-valve). Aluminum alloy block. Displacement: 303.5 cid (4,973 cc). Bore & stroke: 3.80 x 3.35 in. (96.5 x 85 mm). Compression ratio: 10.0:1. Brake horsepower: 315 at 5,600 rpm. Torque: 345 lbs.-ft. at 3,900 rpm. Bosch KE 5 CIS multi-point fuel injection.

Base V-12 (S600, SL600, S600 C): 60-degree, dual-overhead-cam, 12-cylinder (48-valve). Aluminum alloy block and heads. Displacement: 365.4 cid (5,987 cc). Bore & stoke: 3.50 x 3.16 in. (89.0 x 80.2 mm). Compression ratio: 10.0:1. Brake horsepower: 389 at 5,200 rpm. Torque: 420 lbs.-ft. at 3,800 rpm. Multi-point fuel injection.

1996 E CLASS wagon

CHASSIS

Wheelbase: (C-Class) 105.9 in.; (E-Class) 111.5 in.; (S-Class) 123.6 in.; (SWB S320, S350) 119.7 in.; (SL320/500) 99.0 in.; (S500/600 coupe) 115.9 in. Overall length: (C-Class) 177.4 in.; (E-Class) 189.4 in.; (S-Class) 205.2 in.; (except SWB S320, S350) 201.3 in.; (SL320/500) 176.0 in.; (S500/600 coupe) 199.4 in. Height: (C220, C280) 56.1 in.; (C36) 55.6 in.; (E-Class) 56.2 in.; (S-Class) 58.3 in.; (SL320/500) 51.3 in.; (S500/600 coupe) 56.7 in.; Width: (C-Class) 67.7 in.; (E-Class) 70.8 in.; (S-Class) 74.3 in.; (SL320/ 500) 71.3 in. Front tread: (C220, C280) 58.8 in.; (C36) 58.9 in.; (E-Class) 60.2 in.; (S-Class) 63.2 in.; (SL320/500) 60.4 in.; (S500/600 coupe) 63.2 in. Rear tread: (C220) 57.6 in.; (C280) 58.8 in.; (C36) 58.2 in.; (E-Class) 59.9 in.; (S-Class) 62.2 in.; (SL320/500) 60.0 in.; (S500/600 coupe) 62.2 in.

TECHNICAL

Layout: front-engine, rear-drive. Transmission: (C-Class) five-speed manual, or optional four-speed automatic; (SL320) five-speed manual or five-speed automatic; (others) four-speed automatic standard; (E420) five-speed automatic. Steering: power-recirculating ball; (E-Class) rack and pinion. Brakes: front/rear disc. Body construction: steel unibody.

PERFORMANCE

Acceleration (0-60 mph): (C220) 8.7 sec.; (C280) 7.3 sec.; (E320) 7.1 sec.; (S600 C) 6.5 sec. Acceleration (quarter mile): (C220) 16.9 sec.; (C280) 15.8 sec.; (E320) 15.4 sec.; (S600 C) 14.8 sec. EPA fuel economy city/highway miles per gallon: (C220) 21/28; (C280) 19/26; (E320) 19/26; (S600 C) 12/16. Performance Figures by *Motor Trend*.

Manufacturer: Daimler-Benz AG, Stuttgart, Germany.

Distributor: Mercedes-Benz of North America Inc., Montvale, New Jersey.

1997

All 1997 Mercedes-Benz models received the electronically controlled, driver-adaptive five-speed automatic transmission that debuted on the 1996 V-8 and V-12 S-Class and SL roadsters. A front seat occupancy detector stopped the passenger airbag from firing in a crash if it didn't sense a weight of 26 lbs. or more. A new transponder key made car theft with unauthorized keys impossible.

C-CLASS — FOUR/SIX — The C220 gave way to the C230. Now with a five-speed automatic transmission and a 2.3-liter engine, the C230 had more torque, better acceleration, and even increased fuel efficiency. The C36 entered its final year with slight horsepower and torque boosts.

E-CLASS — SIX/V-8 — With sales of the new 1996 E-Class running 60 percent over the previous year, Mercedes-Benz did little to change a winner. The five-speed automatic was added and the E300 diesel's price remained the same at $39,900.

S-CLASS — SIX/V-8/V-12 — Side airbags were added, along with a rain sensor that activated the windshield wipers. If you drove an S500 or S600 at night, you were very happy to have the Xenon high-intensity, gas-discharge headlights as standard equipment. The coupes received a new bumper design

that incorporated the Parktronic sonar parking system.

SL-CLASS — SIX/V-8/V-12 — If you couldn't decide whether your SL should wear its standard equipment aluminum hardtop or the well-insulated folding top, your decision became even more complicated because there was yet another choice: the optional Panorama glass hardtop allowed you to enjoy the view, regardless of the weather.

I.D. DATA: Same as 1990.

ENGINES

Base Four (C230): Inline, overhead-cam four-cylinder. Displacement: 140.0 cid (2,295 cc). Bore & stroke: 3.57 x 3.48 in. (90.9 x 88.4 mm). Compression ratio: 10.4:1. Brake horsepower: 148 at 5,500 rpm. Torque: 162 lbs.-ft. at 4,000 rpm. ME 2.1 fuel injection.

Base Six (C280): Inline, overhead-cam six-cylinder. Displacement: 170.8 cid (2,799 cc). Bore & stroke: 3.54 x 2.89 in. (89.9 x 73.5 mm). Compression ratio: 10.0:1. Brake horsepower: 194 at 5,500 rpm. Torque: 199 lbs.-ft. at 3,750 rpm. Multi-point fuel injection.

Model	Body Type & Seating	Engine Type/CID	P.E. Price	Weight (lbs.)	Production Total
C-CLASS					
C230	4-dr Sedan-5P	I4/140	$30,450	3,195	19,692
C280	4-dr Sedan-5P	I6/171	$35,400	3,360	12,600
C36	4-dr Sedan-5P	I6/220	$51,925	3,550	192
E-CLASS					
E300 Diesel	4-dr Sedan-5P	I6/183	$39,900	3,538	4,827
E320	4-dr Sedan-5P	I6/195	$43,500	3,605	22,680
E420	4-dr Sedan-5P	V8/256	$49,900	3,748	8,826
S-CLASS					
S320	4-dr Sedan-5P	I6/195	$63,300	4,480	3,497
S320 LWB	4-dr Sedan-5P	I6/195	$66,600	4,500	3,019
S420	4-dr Sedan-5P	V8/256	$73,900	4,650	4,414
S500	4-dr Sedan-5P	V8/304	$87,500	4,700	3,469
S600	4-dr Sedan-5P	V12/366	$130,300	4,960	478
S500	2-dr Coupe-4P	V8/304	$91,900	4,695	563
S600	2-dr Coupe-4P	V12/366	$133,300	4,960	256
SL-CLASS					
SL320	2-dr Coupe/Roadster-2P	I6/195	$79,600	4,010	1,648
SL500	2-dr Coupe/Roadster-2P	V8/304	$89,900	4,165	5,613
SL600	2-dr Coupe/Roadster-2P	V12/366	$123,200	4,455	738

1997 CLK

1997 C220

1997 SLK

Base Six (E320, S320, SL320): Inline, dual-overhead-cam (24-valve) variable intake valve timing six-cylinder. Displacement: 195.2 cid (3,199 cc). Bore & stroke: 3.54 x 3.30 in. (89.9 x 84.0 mm). Compression ratio: 10.0:1. Brake horsepower: 217 at 5,500 rpm. Torque: 229 lbs.-ft. at 3,750 rpm. HFM Motronic fuel injection.

Base Six (E300 D): Inline, overhead-cam six-cylinder. Displacement: 182.8 cid (2,996 cc). Bore & stroke: 3.43 x 3.31 in. (87 x 84 mm). Compression ratio: 22.0:1. Brake horsepower: 134 at 5,000 rpm. Torque: 155 lbs.-ft. at 2,600 rpm. Mechanical fuel injection.

Base Six (C36): Inline, overhead-cam (24-valve) variable intake valve timing six-cylinder. Displacement: 220 cid (3,606 cc). Bore & stroke: 3.58 x 3.64 in. (91.0 x 92.4 mm). Compression ratio: 10.5:1. Brake horsepower: 276 at 5,750 rpm. Torque: 284 lbs.-ft. at 4,000 rpm. Electronic fuel injection.

Base V-8 (E420, S420): 90-degree, overhead-cam, eight-cylinder. Light alloy block and heads. Displacement: 256 cid (4197 cc). Bore & stroke: 3.62 x 3.11 in. (92 x 79 mm). Compression ratio: 11.0:1. Brake horsepower: 275 at 5,700 rpm. Torque: 295 lbs.-ft. at 3,900 rpm. Five main bearings. Hydraulic valve lifters. Multi-point fuel injection.

Base V-8 (S500, SL500, S500 C): 90-degree, dual-overhead-cam, eight-cylinder (32-valve). Aluminum alloy block. Displacement: 303.5 cid (4,973 cc). Bore & stroke: 3.80 x 3.35 in. (96.5 x 85 mm). Compression ratio: 10.0:1. Brake horsepower: 315 at 5,600 rpm. Torque: 345 lbs.-ft. at 3,900 rpm. Bosch KE 5 CIS multi-point fuel injection.

Base V-12 (S600, SL600, S600 C): 60-degree, dual-overhead-cam, 12-cylinder (48-valve). Aluminum alloy block and heads. Displacement: 365.4 cid (5,987 cc). Bore & stoke: 3.50 x 3.16 in. (89.0 x 80.2 mm). Compression ratio: 10.0:1. Brake horsepower: 389 at 5,200 rpm. Torque: 420 lbs.-ft. at 3,800 rpm. Multi-point fuel injection.

CHASSIS

Wheelbase: (C-Class) 105.9 in.; (E-Class) 111.5 in.; (S-Class) 123.6 in.; (except SWB S320, S350) 119.7 in.; (SL320/500) 99.0 in.; (S500/600 coupe) 115.9 in. Overall length: (C-Class) 177.4 in.; (E-Class) 189.4 in.; (S-Class) 205.2 in.; (except SWB S320) 201.3 in.; (SL320/500) 176.0 in.; (S500/600 coupe) 199.4 in. Height: (C230, C280) 56.1 in.; (C36) 55.6 in.; (E-Class) 56.2 in.; (S-Class) 58.3 in.; (SL320/500) 51.3 in.; (S500/600 coupe) 56.7 in.; Width: (C-Class) 67.7 in.; (E-Class) 70.8 in.; (S-Class) 74.3 in.; (SL320/500) 71.3 in. Front tread: (C230, C280) 58.8 in.; (C36) 58.9 in.; (E-Class) 60.2 in.; (S-Class) 63.2 in.; (SL320/500) 60.4 in.; (S500/600 coupe) 63.2 in. Rear tread: (C230) 57.6 in.; (C280) 58.8 in.; (C36) 58.2 in.; (E-Class) 59.9 in.; (except E320 wagon) 58.7 in.; (S-Class) 62.2 in.; (SL320/500) 60.0 in.; (S500/600 coupe) 62.2 in.

TECHNICAL

Layout: front-engine, rear-drive. Transmission: driver-adaptive five-speed automatic transmission. Steering: power recirculating ball; (E-Class) rack and pinion. Brakes: front/rear disc. Body construction: steel unibody.

PERFORMANCE

Acceleration (0-60 mph): (C230) 8.7 sec.; (C280) 7.3 sec.; (C36) 5.9 sec.; (E320) 7.1 sec.; (S600 C) 6.5 sec. Acceleration (quarter mile): (C230) 16.9 sec.; (C280) 15.8 sec.; (C36) 14.4 sec.; (E320) 15.4 sec.; (S600 C) 14.8 sec. EPA fuel economy city/highway miles per gallon: (C280) 19/26; (E320) 19/26; (S600 C) 12/16. Performance Figures by *Motor Trend*.

Manufacturer: Daimler-Benz AG, Stuttgart, West Germany.

Distributor: Mercedes-Benz of North America Inc., Montvale, New Jersey.

1997 AMG C36 super sedan

1997 E420

1998 M Class all-activity vehicle

1998

This was a pivotal growth year for Mercedes-Benz in terms of U.S. sales. 1997 was the first year that Mercedes-Benz U.S. sales totaled more than 100,000 cars in a single year. To celebrate, they gave away the 100,000th vehicle to the woman who had placed the order. New models included the SLK, CLK and M-Class SUV.

C-CLASS — FOUR/SIX — The C36 may have left the lineup, but its influence lived on. Changes were made from the grille to the taillights, with the C36's aggressive stance as the model. Gone was the long-lived, inline six for the C280. It was replaced by a new generation, 3-valve, 2-plug per cylinder V-6. The principal advantage was greater torque, but fuel efficiency and acceleration also improved.

CLK-CLASS — SIX — With the launch of the CLK320, another class of affordable Mercedes-Benz cars was born. Priced at only $39,850, the CLK coupe promised the heady combination of fabulous style, excellent performance, and Mercedes quality. The last time Mercedes-Benz offered a coupe in this category was 1995. The 1995 E320 coupe had cost $23,000 more than the 1998 CLK320.

E-CLASS — SIX/V-8 — The station wagon returned to the E-Class, this time with standard 7-passenger seating. The E320 got the new 3-valve, 2-sparkplug per cylinder V-6 engine. The E300 diesel was upgraded to the E300 turbodiesel. The E320 wagon and sedan could both be ordered with a sophisticated electronic four-wheel traction control known as 4Matic.

S-CLASS — SIX/V-8/V-12 — Unchanged for 1998.

CL-CLASS — V-8/V-12 — While the cars were unchanged, the model designation was new. Just as the roadster models now consisted of the SL and SLK, the coupe could be had as CL or CLK. The CLs were still based on the S-Class sedans.

SLK-CLASS — FOUR — The value story continued here. In the previous year, a SL320 roadster would have cost you $79,600. Now a more modern engine could be had in a lighter body for half the price. The supercharged four-cylinder was known as the Kompressor. The car's most unique feature was its folding steel top. You no longer had to choose between the security of a solid roof and the joy of true open-air motoring. You could now have both in one vehicle.

Model	Body Type & Seating	Engine Type/CID	P.E. Price	Weigh (lbs.)	Production Total
C-CLASS					
C230	4-dr Sedan-5P	I4/140	$30,450	3,195	23,134
C280	4-dr Sedan-5P	V6/171	$35,400	3,360	10,325
CLK-CLASS					
CLK320	2-dr Coupe-4P	V6/195	$39,850	3,240	2,384
E-CLASS					
E300 Diesel	4-dr Sedan-5P	I6/183	$41,800	3,538	2,862
E320	4-dr Sedan-5P	V6/195	$45,500	3,605	26,727
E320 4Matic	4-dr Sedan-5P	V6/195	$48,250	3,605	2,291
E320	4-dr Station Wagon-7P	V6/195	$46,500	3,605	2,680
E320 4Matic	4-dr Station Wagon-5P	V6/195	$49,250	3,605	2,973
E420	4-dr Sedan-5P	V8/256	$49,900	3,748	996
S-CLASS					
S320	4-dr Sedan-5P	I6/195	$64,000	4,480	3,375
S320 LWB	4-dr Sedan-5P	I6/195	$67,300	4,500	2,968
S420	4-dr Sedan-5P	V8/256	$73,900	4,650	4,027
S500	4-dr Sedan-5P	V8/304	$87,500	4,700	2,595
S600	4-dr Sedan-5P	V12/366	$132,250	4,960	329
CL-CLASS					
CL500	2-dr Coupe-4P	V8/304	$91,900	4,695	837
CL600	2-dr Coupe-4P	V12/366	$135,300	4,960	231
SLK-CLASS					
SLK230	2-dr Roadster-2P	I4/140	$39,700	3,036	16,389
SL-CLASS					
SL500	2-dr Coupe/Roadster-2P	V8/304	$79,900	4,165	7,173
SL600	2-dr Coupe/Roadster-2P	V12/366	$123,200	4,455	574

1998 SLK roadster

1998 SLK

SL-CLASS — V-8/V-12 — The price of the 1998 SL500 was equal to the discontinued SL320 — it dropped by a full $10,000. An available Sport package added larger wheels, tires, and aerodynamic enhancements.

I.D. DATA: Same as 1990.

ENGINES

Base Four (C230): Inline, overhead-cam four-cylinder. Displacement: 140.0 cid (2,295 cc). Bore & stroke: 3.57 x 3.48 in. (90.9 x 88.4 mm). Compression ratio: 10.4:1. Brake horsepower: 148 at 5,500 rpm. Torque 162 lbs.-ft. at 4,000 rpm. ME 2.1 fuel injection.

Base Four (SLK): Inline, overhead-cam supercharged four-cylinder. Displacement: 140.0 cid (2,295 cc). Bore & stroke: 3.58 x 3.48 in. (90.9 x 88.4 mm). Compression ratio: 8.8:1. Brake horsepower: 185 at 5,300 rpm. Torque: 200 lbs.-ft. at 2,500-4,000 rpm. ME 2.1 fuel injection.

Base Six (C280): Overhead-cam, six-cylinder. Displacement:

1998 SLK230

1998 SLK coupe

170.8 cid (2,799 cc). Bore & stroke: 3.54 x 2.89 in. (89.9 x 73.5 mm). Compression ratio: 10.0:1. Brake horsepower: 194 at 5,800 rpm. Torque: 195 lbs.-ft. at 3,000-4,600 rpm. Sequential fuel injection.

Base Six (S320): Inline, dual-overhead-cam (24-valve) variable intake valve timing six-cylinder. Displacement: 195.2 cid (3,199 cc). Bore & stroke: 3.54 x 3.30 in. (89.9 x 84.0 mm). Compression ratio: 10.0:1. Brake horsepower: 217 at 5,500 rpm. Torque: 229 lbs.-ft. at 3,750 rpm. HFM Motronic fuel injection.

Base Six (E320, CLK320): 90-degree, dual-overhead-cam (18-valve) six-cylinder. Aluminum alloy block and head. s Displacement: 195.2 cid (3,199 cc). Bore & stroke: 3.54 x 3.30 in. (89.9 x 84.0 mm). Compression ratio: 10.0:1. Brake horsepower: 221 at 5,500 rpm. Torque: 232 lbs.-ft. at 3,000-4,800 rpm. Sequential fuel injection.

Base Turbodiesel Six (E300 D): Inline, overhead-cam six-cylinder. Cast-iron block and aluminum head. Displacement: 182.7 cid (2,996 cc). Bore & stroke: 3.43 x 3.31 in. (87 x 84 mm). Compression ratio: 22.0:1. Brake horsepower: 174 at 5,000 rpm. Torque: 244 lbs.-ft. at 1,600-3,000 rpm. Mechanical fuel injection.

1998 V-6

1998 CL500

Base V-8 (E420, S420): 90-degree, overhead-cam, eight-cylinder. Light alloy block and heads. Displacement: 256 cid (4,197 cc). Bore & stroke: 3.62 x 3.11 in. (92 x 79 mm). Compression ratio: 11.0:1. Brake horsepower: 275 at 5,700 rpm. Torque: 295 lbs.-ft. at 3,900 rpm. Five main bearings. Hydraulic valve lifters. Multi-point fuel injection.

Base V-8 (S500, SL500, CL500): 90-degree, dual-overhead-cam, eight-cylinder (32-valve). Aluminum alloy block. Displacement: 303.5 cid (4,973 cc). Bore & stroke: 3.80 x 3.35 in. (96.5 x 85 mm). Compression ratio: 10.0:1. Brake horsepower: 315 at 5,600 rpm. Torque: 345 lbs.-ft. at 3,900 rpm. Bosch KE 5 CIS multi-point fuel injection.

Base V-12 (S600, SL600, CL600): 60-degree, dual-overhead-cam, 12-cylinder (48-valve). Aluminum alloy block and heads. Displacement: 365.4 cid (5,987 cc). Bore & stroke: 3.50 x 3.16 in. (89.0 x 80.2 mm). Compression ratio: 10.0:1. Brake horsepower: 389 at 5,200 rpm. Torque: 420 lbs.-ft. at 3,800 rpm. Multi-point fuel injection.

CHASSIS

Wheelbase: (C-Class) 105.9 in.; (CLK) 105.9 in.; (E-Class) 111.5 in.; (S-Class) 123.6 in.; (SWB S320, S350) 119.7 in.; (CL) 115.9 in.; (SLK) 94.5 in.; (SL) 99.0 in. Overall length: (C-Class) 177.4 in.; (CLK) 180.2 in.; (E-Class) 189.4 in.; (S-Class) 205.2 in.; (SWB S320) 201.3 in.; (CL) 199.4 in.; (SLK) 157.3 in.; (SL) 176.0 in. Height: (C-Class) 56.1 in.; (CLK) 53.0 in.; (E-Class) 56.2 in.; (S-Class) 58.3 in.; (CL) 56.7 in.; (SLK) 50.7 in.; (SL320/ 500) 51.3 in. Width: (C-Class) 67.7 in.; (CLK) 67.8 in.; (E-Class) 70.8 in.; (S-Class) 74.3 in.; (CL) 74.3 in.; (SLK) 67.5 in.; (SL) 71.3 in. Front tread: (C-Class) 58.8 in.; (CLK) 59.3 in.; (E-Class) 60.2 in.; (S-Class) 63.2 in.; (CL) 63.2 in.; (SLK) 58.6 in.; (SL) 60.4 in. Rear tread: (C230) 57.6 in.; (C280) 58.8 in.; (CLK) 58.0 in.; (E-Class) 59.9 in.; (E320 wagon) 58.7 in.; (S-Class) 62.2 in.; (CL) 62.2 in.; (SLK) 58.1 in.; (SL) 60.0 in.

TECHNICAL

Layout: front-engine, rear-drive; (4Matic) four-wheel drive. Transmission: driver-adaptive five-speed automatic transmission; (SLK) five-speed manual standard. Steering: power recirculating ball; (E-Class) rack and pinion. Brakes: front/rear disc. Body construction: steel unibody.

PERFORMANCE

Acceleration (0-60 mph): (C230) 8.7 sec.; (C280) 7.3 sec.; (SLK230) 6.9 sec.; (E320) 7.1 sec. Acceleration (quarter mile): (C230) 16.9 sec.; (C280) 15.8 sec.; (SLK230) 16.8 sec.; (E320) 15.4 sec. EPA fuel economy city/highway miles per gallon: (C280) 19/26; (E320) 19/26. Performance Figures by *Motor Trend*.

Manufacturer: Daimler-Benz AG, Stuttgart, Germany.

Distributor: Mercedes-Benz of North America Inc., Montvale, New Jersey.

1998 SLK coupe

1999 CLK430 coupe

1999

The last time you could purchase a four-seat Mercedes-Benz convertible was 1995, and the E320 Cabriolet would have set you back $77,300. Granted the $39,850 CLK coupe was based on the smaller C-Class chassis, but for a little more than half the E Cabriolet's price you had a more modern, better equipped convertible that would seat four.

C-CLASS — FOUR/SIX/V-8 — With the introduction of the C43, Mercedes-Benz came back to the performance sedan business with a vengeance. The AMG-modified 4.3-liter V-8 throbbed with an output of 302 hp Even the basic four-cylinder C230 received a significant power boost in the form of the SLK's Kompressor engine. The engine change cut a full two seconds off the C230's 0-60 mph time. With available four-, six-, or eight-cylinder engines, a case could be made for the C-Class as the most versatile Mercedes-Benz chassis.

CLK-CLASS — SIX/V-8 — In a stunning glimpse of their new marketing plan, Mercedes-Benz did not rest on the laurels of their successful CLK320 coupe launch. They added a Cabriolet version of the six-cylinder coupe and also dropped the new-generation 275-hp 4.3-liter production V-8 into the sleek coupe. A standard AMG Sport Package added a purposeful look to the V-8 CLK.

E-CLASS — SIX/V-8 — The E420 becomes the E430 by installing the new-generation 3-valve, twin-plug-per-cylinder engine. Using the same architecture as the new 3.2-liter V-6 the all-aluminum engine made 275 hp and 295 lbs.-ft. of torque.

S-CLASS — SIX/V-8/V-12 — Unchanged for 1999.

CL-CLASS — V-8/V-12 — Unchanged for 1999.

SLK-CLASS — FOUR — The five-speed manual transmission became standard, and the five-speed automatic was a $900 option. Also new was the Sport Package, consisting of larger wheels and tires, rakishly styled side sills and new front and rear fascias.

SL-CLASS — V-8/V-12 — The SL500 got a new-generation 5.0-liter V-8. Like the new 3.2-liter V-6 and the new 4.3-liter V-8, the 5.0-liter had three valves per cylinder.

I.D. DATA: Same as 1990.

MODEL	BODY TYPE & SEATING	ENGINE TYPE/CID	P.E. PRICE	WEIGHT (LBS.)	PRODUCTION TOTAL
C-CLASS					
C230K	4-dr Sedan-5P	I4/140	$31,200	3,250	N/A
C280	4-dr Sedan-5P	V6/171	$35,600	3,316	N/A
C43	4-dr Sedan-5P	V8/260	$53,000	3,448	N/A
CLK-CLASS					
CLK320	2-dr Coupe-4P	V6/195	$40,600	3,316	N/A
CLK320	2-dr Conv.-4P	V6/195	$47,200	3,669	N/A
CLK430	2-dr Coupe-4P	V8/260	$47,900	3,426	N/A
E-CLASS					
E300 Diesel	4-dr Sedan-5P	I6/183	$42,400	3,690	N/A
E320	4-dr Sedan-5P	V6/195	$46,200	3,525	N/A
E320 4Matic	4-dr Sedan-5P	V6/195	$48,990	3,720	N/A
E320	4-dr Station Wagon-5P	V6/195	$47,200	3,757	N/A
E320 4Matic	4-dr Station Wagon-5P	V6/195	$49,990	3,952	N/A
E430	4-dr Sedan-5P	V8/260	$51,300	3,702	N/A
S-CLASS					
S320	4-dr Sedan-5P	I6/195	$64,750	4,506	N/A
S320 LWB	4-dr Sedan-5P	I6/195	$68,000	4,528	N/A
S420	4-dr Sedan-5P	V8/256	$73,900	4,705	N/A
S500	4-dr Sedan-5P	V8/304	$87,500	4,727	N/A
S600	4-dr Sedan-5P	V12/366	$132,250	4,969	N/A
CL-CLASS					
CL500	2-dr Coupe-4P	V8/304	$91,900	4,760	N/A
CL600	2-dr Coupe-4P	V12/366	$137,300	4,969	N/A
SLK-CLASS					
SLK230	2-dr Roadster-2P	I4/140	$40,000	2,992	N/A
SL-CLASS					
SL500	2-dr Coupe/Roadster-2P	V8/304	$81,100	4,121	N/A
SL600	2-dr Coupe/Roadster-2P	V12/366	$126,900	4,473	N/A

1999 C43 AMG

1999 E320

1999 E320 wagon

ENGINES

Base Four (SLK, C230): Inline, overhead-cam supercharged four-cylinder. Cast-iron block and aluminum head. Displacement: 140.0 cid (2,295 cc). Bore & stroke: 3.58 x 3.48 in. (90.9 x 88.4 mm). Compression ratio: 8.8:1. Brake horsepower: 185 at 5,300 rpm. Torque: 200 lbs.-ft. at 2,500-4,800 rpm. ME 2.1 fuel injection.

Base Six (C280): Inline, overhead-cam six-cylinder. Aluminum block and heads. Displacement: 170.8 cid (2,799 cc). Bore & stroke: 3.54 x 2.89 in. (89.9 x 73.5 mm). Compression

ratio: 10.0:1. Brake horsepower: 194 at 5,500 rpm. Torque: 199 lbs.-ft. at 3,750 rpm. Multi-point fuel injection.

Base Six (E320, CLK320): 90-degree, dual-overhead-cam (18-valve) variable intake valve timing six-cylinder. Aluminum block and heads. Displacement: 195.2 cid (3,199 cc). Bore & stroke: 3.54 x 3.30 in. (89.9 x 84.0 mm). Compression ratio: 10.0:1. Brake horsepower: 217 at 5,500 rpm. Torque: 229 lbs.-ft. at 3,750 rpm. HFM Motronic fuel injection.

Base Six (S320): Inline, dual-overhead-cam (24-valve)

variable intake valve timing six-cylinder. Displacement: 195.2 cid (3,199 cc). Bore & stroke: 3.54 x 3.30 in. (89.9 x 84.0 mm). Compression ratio: 10.0:1. Brake horsepower: 217 at 5,500 rpm. Torque: 229 lbs.-ft. at 3,750 rpm. HFM Motronic fuel injection.

Base Turbodiesel SIX (E300 D): Inline, overhead-cam six-cylinder. Cast-iron block and aluminum heads. Displacement: 182.8 cid (2,996 cc). Bore & stroke: 3.43 x 3.31 in. (87 x 84 mm). Compression ratio: 22.0:1. Brake horsepower: 134 at 5,000 rpm. Torque: 155 lbs.-ft. at 2,600 rpm. Mechanical fuel injection.

Base V-8 (S420): 90-degree, overhead-cam, eight-cylinder. Light alloy block and heads. Displacement: 256 cid (4,197 cc). Bore & stroke: 3.62 x 3.11 in. (92 x 79 mm). Compression ratio: 11.0:1. Brake horsepower: 275 at 5,700 rpm. Torque: 295 lbs.-ft. at 3,900 rpm. Five main bearings. Hydraulic valve lifters. Multi-point fuel injection.

Base V-8 (E430, CLK430, C43): 90-degree, overhead-cam, eight-cylinder. Aluminum alloy block and heads. Displacement: 260 cid (4,226 cc). Bore & stroke: 3.54 x 3.30 in. (89.9 x 84 mm). Compression ratio: 10.0:1. Brake horsepower: 275 at 5,750 rpm; (C43) 302 at 5,850 rpm. Torque: 295 lbs.-ft. 3,000-4,000 rpm; (C43) 302 lbs.-ft. at 3,250-5,000 rpm. Sequential fuel injection.

Base V-8 (S500, SL500, CL500): 90-degree, dual-overhead-cam, eight-cylinder (24-valve). Aluminum alloy block. Displacement: 303.5 cid (4,973 cc). Bore & stroke: 3.80 x 3.35 in. (96.5 x 85 mm). Compression ratio: 10.0:1. Brake horsepower: 315 at 5,600 rpm. Torque: 345 lbs.-ft. at 3,900 rpm. Bosch KE 5 CIS multi-point fuel injection.

Base V-12 (S600, SL600, CL600): 60-degree, dual-overhead-cam, 12-cylinder (48-valve). Aluminum alloy block and heads. Displacement: 365.4 cid (5,987 cc). Bore and stroke: 3.50 x 3.16 in. (89.0 x 80.2 mm). Compression ratio: 10.0:1. Brake horsepower: 389 at 5,200 rpm. Torque: 420 lbs.-ft. at 3,800 rpm. Multi-point fuel injection.

CHASSIS

Wheelbase: (C-Class) 105.9 in.; (CLK) 105.9 in.; (E-Class) 111.5 in.; (S-Class) 123.6 in.; (SWB S320, S350) 119.7 in.; (CL) 115.9 in.; (SLK) 94.5 in.; (SL) 99.0 in. Overall length: (C-Class) 177.4 in.; (CLK) 180.2 in.; (E-Class) 189.4 in.; (S-Class) 205.2 in.; (SWB S320) 201.3 in.; (CL) 199.4 in. (SLK) 157.3 in.; (SL) 176.0 in.; Height: (C-Class) 56.1 in.; (CLK coupe) 53.0 in.; (CLK Conv) 54.3 in.; (E-Class) 56.2 in.; (S-Class) 58.3 in.; (CL) 56.7 in. 56.3 in.; (SLK) 50.7 in.; (SL500) 51.3 in. Width: (C-Class) 67.7 in.; (CLK) 67.8 in.; (E-Class) 70.8 in.; (S-Class) 74.3 in.; (CL) 74.3 in.; (SLK) 67.5 in.; (SL) 71.3 in. Front tread: (C-Class) 58.8 in.; (CLK) 59.3 in.; (E-Class) 60.2 in.; (S-Class) 63.2 in.; (CL) 63.2 in.; (SLK) 58.6 in.; (SL) 60.4 in. Rear tread: (C230) 57.6 in.; (C280) 58.8 in.; (CLK) 58.0 in.; (E-Class) 59.9 in.; (E320 wagon) 58.7 in.; (S-Class) 62.2 in.; (CL) 62.2 in.; (SLK) 58.1 in.; (SL) 60.0 in.

TECHNICAL

Layout: front-engine, rear-drive; (4Matic) four-wheel drive. Transmission: driver-adaptive five-speed automatic transmission; (SLK), five-speed manual standard. Steering: power recirculating ball; (E-Class) rack and pinion. Brakes: front/rear disc. Body construction: steel unibody.

PERFORMANCE

Acceleration (0-60 mph): (C230K) 7.6 sec.; (C280) 7.3 sec.; (C43) 5.8 sec.; (CLK 430) 6.5 sec.; (SLK230) 6.9 sec.; (E320 Wag) 7.3 sec.; (CL600) 6.2 sec. Acceleration (quarter mile): (C230K) 15.7 sec.; (C280) 15.8 sec.; (C43) 14.4 sec.; (CLK430) 14.8 sec.; (SLK230) 16.8 sec.; (E320 Wag) 15.6 sec.; (CL600) 14.4 sec. EPA fuel economy City/highway miles per gallon: (C280) 19/26; (E320) 19/26. Performance Figures by *Motor Trend*.

Manufacturer: Daimler-Chrysler AG, Stuttgart, Germany.

Distributor: Mercedes-Benz of North America Inc., Montvale, New Jersey.

1999 E55

1999 SLK roadster

1999 ML430

1956, The 300Sc.
Created for a handful of the world's most discriminating enthusiasts. Only 200 were ever built.

1955, The 300SL Gullwing.
This legendary coupe proved itself at LeMans, the Nurburgring, and other venues on the world's racing circuits.

1935, The 500 K.
A supercharged Mercedes-Benz destined, as one critic put it, "to raise envy in the hearts of real motorists."

To be a Mercedes-Benz, you have to follow in some pretty impressive tire tracks.

1999 ad

2000

C-CLASS — FOUR/SIX/V-8 — Touch Shift meant that gears could be manually selected by pushing the shift lever to the left or to the right. It was standard equipment on all C-Class cars. A telescoping steering column was available for the first time.

CL-CLASS — V-8 — While the alphanumeric designation remained the same, the character of the 2000 CL500 moved further towards the sport side of the sport/luxury equation. There were even more touches of opulence, but the standard Active Body Control (ABC) transformed the CL into a sporting machine seemingly capable of defying the laws of physics. Thanks to advanced computers and extremely fast-acting hydraulic servos at each wheel, the CL500 was capable of virtually eliminating body roll and pitch during cornering, braking, and acceleration. Use of lightweight materials shaved over 600 lbs. off the CL.

CLK-CLASS — SIX/V-8 — With the addition of the CLK430 Cabriolet, CLK buyers had an even tougher time deciding between a six or a V-8, the coupe or the cabriolet. All CLKs gained new body-colored front and rear aprons, and the CLK320s received the sculptured rocker panels previously reserved for the 430 models.

E-CLASS — SIX/V-8 — The best news for performance enthusiast was the new E55. This powerful V-8 sedan leapt to the head of the class for V-8 sport sedans. While you may not know it to look at them, the 2000 E-Class received more than just a face-lift; over 1,600 individual changes were made according to Mercedes-Benz. Chief among them were the CLK-inspired front end and turn signal indicators in the mirrors. Rear sidebags were standard, as was ESP. The diesel was dropped.

S-CLASS — V-8 — A brand new flagship was launched. With an emphasis on luxury, this new sedan was easily recognized by new 1-piece headlights that resembled the oval units from the E-Class and CLKs. Only a 4.3- or 5.0-liter V-8 were initially available. The six and 12 cylinder cars were dropped.

SL-CLASS — V-8/V-12 — TeleAid allowed motorists to summon help or information with the push of a button and was standard on all SLs.

SLK-CLASS — FOUR — designo editions in Copper and Electric offered buyers additional choices to express their individuality.

I.D. DATA: Same as 1990.

Model	Body Type & Seating	Engine Type/CID	P.E. Price	Weight (lbs.)	Production Total
C CLASS					
C230K	4-dr Sedan-5P	I4/140	$31,750	3,250	N/A
C280	4-dr Sedan-5P	V-6/171	$35,950	3,316	N/A
C43	4-dr Sedan-5P	V-8/260	$53,000	3,448	N/A
CLK CLASS					
CLK320	2-dr Coupe-4P	V-6/195	$41,600	3,213	N/A
CLK320	2-dr Conv.-4P	I6/195	$49,100	3,566	N/A
CLK430	2-dr Coupe-4P	V-8/260	$48,100	3,323	N/A
CLK420	2-dr Conv.-4P	V-8/260	$55,600	3,665	N/A
E-CLASS					
E320	4-dr Sedan-5P	V-6/195	$47,100	3,691	N/A
E320 4Matic	4-dr Sedan-5P	V-6/195	$48,890	3,889	N/A
E320	4-dr Station Wagon-5P	V-6/195	$47,900	3,757	N/A
E320 4Matic	4-dr Station Wagon-5P	V-6/195	$50,690	3,955	N/A
E430	4-dr Sedan-5P	V-8/260	$52,450	3,702	N/A
E430 4Matic	4-dr Sedan-5P	V-8/260	$55,240	3,900	N/A
E55	4-dr Sedan-5P	V-8/332	$69,800	3,680	N/A
S-CLASS					
S430	4-dr Sedan-5P	V-8/256	$69,700	4,133	N/A
S500	4-dr Sedan-5P	V-8/304	$77,850	4,133	N/A
CL-CLASS					
CL500	2-dr Coupe-4P	V-8/304	$85,500	4,115	N/A
SLK-CLASS					
SLK230	2-dr Roadster-2P	I4/140	$41,000	2,992	N/A
SL-CLASS					
SL500	2-dr Coupe/Roadster-2P	V-8/304	$82,600	4,125	N/A
SL600	2-dr Coupe/Roadster-2P	V-12/366	$128,950	4,455	N/A

2000 SL500 Panorama

ENGINES

Base Four (SLK, C230): Inline, overhead-cam supercharged four-cylinder. Cast-iron block and aluminum head. Displacement: 140.0 cid (2,295 cc). Bore & stroke: 3.58 x 3.48 in. (90.9 x 88.4 mm). Compression ratio: 8.8:1. Brake horsepower: 185 at 5,300 rpm. Torque 200 lbs.-ft at 2,500-4,800 rpm. ME 2.1 fuel injection.

Base Six (C280): Inline, overhead-cam six-cylinder. Aluminum block and heads. Displacement: 170.8 cid (2,799 cc). Bore & stroke: 3.54 x 2.89 in. (89.9 x 73.5 mm). Compression ratio: 10.0:1. Brake horsepower: 194 at 5,500 rpm. Torque 199 lbs.-ft. at 3,750 rpm. Multi-point fuel injection.

Base Six (E320, S320, CLK320): Inline, dual-overhead-cam (24-valve) variable intake valve timing six-cylinder. Aluminum block and head Displacement: 195.2 cid (3,199 cc). Bore & stroke: 3.54 x 3.30 in. (89.9 x 84.0 mm). Compression ratio: 10.0:1. Brake horsepower: 217 at 5,500 rpm. Torque: 229 lbs.-ft. at 3,750 rpm. HFM Motronic fuel injection.

Base V-8 (E430, CLK430, S430, C43): 90-degree, overhead-cam, eight-cylinder. Aluminum alloy block and heads. Displacement: 260 cid (4,226 cc). Bore & stroke: 3.54 x 3.30 in.

2000 SLK Designo

(89.9 x 84 mm). Compression ratio: 10.0:1. Brake horsepower: 275 at 5,750 rpm; (C43) 302 at 5,850 rpm. Torque: 295 lbs.-ft. 3,000-4,000 rpm; (C43) 302 at 3,250-5,000 rpm. Sequential fuel injection.

Base V-8 (S500, SL500, CL500): 90-degree, dual-overhead-cam, eight-cylinder (24-valve). Aluminum alloy block. Displacement: 303.5 cid (4,973 cc). Bore & stroke: 3.80 x 3.35 in. (96.5 x 85 mm). Compression ratio: 10.0:1. Brake horsepower: 315 at 5,600 rpm. Torque: 345 lbs.-ft. at 3,900 rpm. Bosch KE 5 CIS multi-point fuel injection.

Base V-8 (E55): 90-degree, dual-overhead-cam, eight-cylinder (32-valve). Aluminum alloy block and heads. Displacement: 331.9 cid (5,439 cc). Bore & stroke: 3.82 x 3.62 in. (97 x 92 mm). Compression ratio: 10.5:1. Brake horsepower: 349 at 5,500 rpm. Torque: 391 lbs.-ft. at 3,000 rpm. Sequential fuel injection.

Base V-12 (SL600): 60-degree, dual-overhead-cam, 12-cylinder (48-valve). Aluminum alloy block and heads. Displacement: 365.4 cid (5,987 cc). Bore & stroke: 3.50 x 3.16 in. (89.0 x 80.2 mm). Compression ratio: 10.0:1. Brake horsepower: 389 at 5,200 rpm. Torque: 420 lbs.-ft at 3,800 rpm. Multi-point fuel injection.

CHASSIS

Wheelbase: (C-Class) 105.9 in.; (CLK) 105.9 in.; (E-Class) 111.5 in.; (S-Class) 123.6 in.; (CL) 113.6 in.; (SLK) 94.5 in.; (SL) 99.0 in. Overall length: (C-Class) 177.4 in.; (CLK) 180.2 in.; (E-Class) 189.4 in.; (S-Class) 205.2 in.; (CL) 196.6 in.; (SLK) 157.3 in.; (SL) 176.0 in. Height: (C-Class) 56.1 in.; (CLK Coupe) 53.0 in.; (CLK Conv) 54.3 in.; (E-Class) 56.2 in.; (S-Class) 58.3 in.; (CL) 55 in.; 56.3 in.; (SLK) 50.7 in.;

(SL500) 51.3 in. Width: (C-Class) 67.7 in.; (CLK) 67.8 in.; (E-Class) 70.8 in.; (S-Class) 74.3 in.; (CL) 73.1 in.; (SLK) 67.5 in.; (SL) 71.3 in. Front tread: (C-Class) 58.8 in.; (CLK) 59.3 in.; (E-Class) 60.2 in.; (S-Class) 63.2 in.; (CL) 62 in.; (SLK) 58.6 in.; (SL) 60.4 in. Rear tread: (C230) 57.6 in.; (C280) 58.8 in.; (CLK) 58.0 in.; (E-Class) 59.9 in.; (except E320 wagon) 58.7 in.; (S-Class) 62.2 in.; (CL) 62 in.; (SLK) 58.1 in.; (SL) 60.0 in.

TECHNICAL

Layout: front-engine, rear-drive; (4Matic) four-wheel drive. Transmission: driver-adaptive five-speed automatic transmission; (SLK) five-speed manual standard. Steering: power-ecirculating ball; S-Class, E-Class, CL-Class rack and pinion. Brakes: front/rear disc. Body construction: steel unibody.

PERFORMANCE

Acceleration (0-60 mph): (C230K) 7.6 sec.; (C280) 7.3 sec.; (C43) 5.8 sec.; (CLK430) 6.5 sec.; (SLK230) 6.9 sec.; (E430 Sport) 6.1 sec.; (E55) 6.1 sec.; (S500) 6.2 sec.; (CL500) 5.8 sec. Acceleration (quarter mile): (C230K) 15.7 sec.; (C280 S) 15.8 sec.; (C43) 14.4 sec.; (CLK430) 14.8 sec.; (SLK230) 16.8 sec.; (E430 Sport) 14.5 sec.; (E55) 14.8 sec.; (S500) 14.6 sec.; (CL500) 14.2 sec. EPA fuel economy city/highway miles per gallon: (C280) 19/26; (E320) 19/26. Performance Figures by *Motor Trend.*

Manufacturer: Daimler-Benz AG, Stuttgart, Germany.

Distributor: Mercedes-Benz USA, Montvale, New Jersey.

2001 CLK430 cabriolet

2001

C-CLASS — FOUR/SIX — An all-new C-Class raised the bar for the competition. Resembling its larger S-Class sibling more than its predecessor, the C-Class was available with a 2.4-liter four or the ubiquitous 3.2-liter V-6. A six-speed manual transmission was offered in the C240 only. This was the first time a manual transmission was available in a Mercedes-Benz sedan in over a decade.

CL-CLASS — V-8/V-12 — The CL-Class also received an AMG model (CL55) and a V-12 edition (CL600).

CLK-CLASS — V-8 — The big news here was the addition of the quickest-ever Mercedes-Benz, the CLK55. Take the powerful 5.5-liter AMG-massaged V-8, stuff it into the lighter CLK coupe body, and you have a car capable of screaming from 0-60 mph in 4.89 seconds on its way to its electronically limited 155 mph top speed.

E-CLASS — SIX/V-8 — A Sport Package was available for the E320 and E430 sedans.

S-CLASS — V-8/V-12 — Two new S-Class sedans joined the lineup. The new-generation V-12 debuted in the S600. The hand-assembled AMG 5.5-liter V-8 debuted in the S-Class in the S55. Both models received the ABC (Automatic Body Control) that debuted in last year's CL500.

SL-CLASS — Both the SL500 and the SL600 received AMG aerodynamic enhancements and the SL600 got a set of two-piece AMG wheels.

SLK-CLASS — FOUR — The SLK received the most changes since its 1997 debut. The ever-faithful 3.2-liter V-6 became available. The five-speed manual gearbox became a six-speed. All SLK models received new front and rear aprons, sculpted rocker panels, turn signal repeaters in the mirrors, and two-color taillight lenses. The interior also received revisions.

I.D. DATA: Same as 1990.

ENGINES

Base Four (SLK230): Inline, overhead-cam supercharged four-cylinder. Cast-iron block and aluminum head. Displacement: 140.0 cid (2,295 cc). Bore & stroke: 3.58 x 3.48 in. (90.9 x 88.4 mm). Compression ratio: 8.8:1. Brake horsepower: 185 at 5,300 rpm. Torque 200 lbs.-ft at 2,500-4,800 rpm. ME 2.1 fuel injection.

Base Four (C240): Inline, overhead-cam four-cylinder. Aluminum block and head. Displacement: 158.5 cid (2,597 cc). Bore & stroke: 3.54 x 2.69 in. (89.9 x 68.2 mm). Compression ratio: 10.5:1. Brake horsepower: 168 at 5,500 rpm. Torque: 177 lbs.-ft at 4,500 rpm. Sequential fuel injection.

Model	Body Type & Seating	Engine Type/CID	P.E. Price	Weight (lbs.)	Productiopn Total
C-CLASS					
C240	4-dr Sedan-5P	I4/156	$29,950	3,360	N/A
C280	4-dr Sedan-5P	V-6/171	$36,950	3,439	N/A
CLK-CLASS					
CLK320	2-dr Coupe-4P	V-6/195	$41,950	3,213	N/A
CLK320	2-dr Conv.-4P	I6/195	$48,900	3,566	N/A
CLK430	2-dr Coupe-4P	V-8/260	$49,650	3,323	N/A
CLK420	2-dr Conv.-4P	V-8/260	$56,500	3,665	N/A
CLK55	2-dr Conv.-4P	V-8/332	$67,400	3,665	N/A
E-CLASS					
E320	4-dr Sedan-5P	V-6/195	$47,850	3,491	N/A
E320 4Matic	4-dr Sedan-5P	V-6/195	$50,700	3,690	N/A
E320	4-dr Station Wagon-5P	V-6/195	$48,650	3,739	N/A
E320 4Matic	4-dr Station Wagon-5P	V-6/195	$51,500	3,926	N/A
E430	4-dr Sedan-5P	V-8/260	$53,200	3,624	N/A
E430 4Matic	4-dr Sedan-5P	V-8/260	$56,050	3,810	N/A
E55	4-dr Sedan-5P	V-8/332	$69,800	3,635	N/A
S-CLASS					
S430	4-dr Sedan-5P	V-8/256	$70,800	4,133	N/A
S500	4-dr Sedan-5P	V-8/304	$78,950	4,133	N/A
S600	4-dr Sedan-5P	V-12/353	$114,000	4,488	N/A
S55	4-dr Sedan-5P	V-8/332	$98,000	4,186	N/A
CL-CLASS					
CL500	2-dr Coupe-4P	V-8/304	$87,500	4,115	N/A
CL600	2-dr Coupe-4P	V-12/353	$117,200	4,115	N/A
CL55	2-dr Coupe-4P	V-8/332	$99,500	4,312	N/A
SLK-CLASS					
SLK230	2-dr Roadster-2P	I4/140	$38,900	2,909	N/A
SLK320	2-dr Roadster-2P	V-6/195	$43,900	3,018	N/A
SL-CLASS					
SL500	2-dr Coupe/Roadster-2P	V-8/304	$82,600	4,125	N/A
SL600	2-dr Coupe/Roadster-2P	V-12/366	$128,950	4,455	N/A

2001 C240

2001 E430

Base Six (C320, S320, CLK320, SLK320): Inline, dual-overhead-cam (18-valve) variable intake valve timing six-cylinder. Aluminum block and head. Displacement: 195.2 cid (3,199 cc). Bore & stroke: 3.54 x 3.30 in. (89.9 x 84.0 mm). Compression ratio: 10.0:1. Brake horsepower: 217 at 5,500 rpm. Torque: 229 lbs.-ft. at 3,750 rpm. HFM Motronic fuel injection.

Base V-8 (E430, CLK430, S430, C43): 90-degree, overhead-cam, eight-cylinder. Aluminum alloy block and heads. Displacement: 260 cid (4,226 cc). Bore & stroke: 3.54 x 3.30 in. (89.9 x 84 mm). Compression ratio: 10.0:1. Brake horsepower: 275 at 5750 rpm; (C43) 302 at 5,850 rpm. Torque: 295 lbs.-ft. 3,000-4,000 rpm; (C43) 302 at 3,250-5,000 rpm. Sequential fuel injection.

Base V-8 (S500, SL500, CL500): 90-degree, dual-overhead-cam, eight-cylinder (24-valve). Aluminum alloy block. Displacement: 303.5 cid (4,973 cc). Bore & stroke: 3.80 x 3.35 in. (96.5 x 85 mm). Compression ratio: 10.0:1. Brake horsepower: 315 at 5,600 rpm. Torque: 345 lbs.-ft. at 3,900 rpm. Bosch KE 5 CIS multi-point fuel injection.

Base V-8 (E55, CLK55, S55): 90-degree, dual-overhead-cam, eight-cylinder (32-valve). Aluminum alloy block and heads. Displacement: 331.9 cid (5,439 cc). Bore & stroke: 3.82 x 3.62 in. (97 x 92 mm). Compression ratio: 10.5:1. Brake horsepower: 349 at 5,500 rpm; (CLK55) 342 at 5,500 rpm; (S55) 354 at 5,500 rpm. Torque: 391 lbs.-ft. at 3,000 rpm; (CLK55) 376 at 3,000 rpm. Sequential fuel injection.

Base V-12 (SL600): 60-degree, dual-overhead-cam, 12-cylinder (48-valve). Aluminum alloy block and heads. Displacement: 365.4 cid (5,987 cc). Bore & stroke: 3.50 x 3.16 in. (89.0 x 80.2 mm). Compression ratio: 10.0:1. Brake horsepower: 389 at 5,200 rpm. Torque: 420 lbs.-ft. at 3,800 rpm. Multi-point fuel injection.

Base V-12 (S600, CL600): 60-degree, dual-overhead-cam, 12-cylinder (48-valve). Aluminum alloy block and heads. Displacement: 353.1 cid (5,786 cc). Bore & stroke: 3.31 x 3.43 in. (84.0 x 87.0 mm). Compression ratio: 10.0:1. Brake horsepower: 362 at 5,500 rpm. Torque: 391 lbs.-ft. at 4,100 rpm. Sequential fuel injection.

CHASSIS

Wheelbase: (C-Class) 106.9 in.; (CLK) 105.9 in.; (E-Class) 111.5 in.; (S-Class) 123.6 in.; (CL) 113.6 in.; (SLK) 94.5 in.; (SL) 99.0 in. Overall length: (C-Class) 178.3 in.; (CLK) 180.2

2001 E320 wagon

2001 SL320

in.; (E-Class) 189.4 in.; (S-Class) 205.2 in.; (CL) 196.6 in.; (SLK) 157.3 in.; (SL) 176.0 in. Height: (C-Class) 55.2 in.; (CLK coupe) 53.0 in.; (CLK Conv) 54.3 in.; (E-Class) 56.2 in.; (S-Class) 58.3 in.; (CL) 55 in.; 56.3 in.; (SLK) 50.7 in.; (SL500) 51.3 in. Width: (C-Class) 68.0 in.; (CLK) 67.8 in.; (E-Class) 70.8 in.; (S-Class) 74.3 in.; (CL) 73.1 in.; (SLK) 67.5 in.; (SL) 71.3 in. Front tread: (C-Class) 58.8 in.; (CLK) 59.3 in.; (E-Class) 60.2 in.; (S-Class) 63.2 in.; (CL) 62 in.; (SLK) 58.6 in.; (SL) 60.4 in. Rear tread: (C-Class) 57.6 in.; (CLK) 58.0 in.; (CLK55) 58.6 in.; (E-Class) 59.9 in.; (E320 wagon) 58.7 in.; (S-Class) 62.2 in.; (CL) 62 in.; (SLK) 58.1 in.; (SL) 60.0 in.

TECHNICAL

Layout: front-engine, rear-drive; (4Matic) four-wheel drive. Transmission: driver-adaptive five-speed automatic transmission; (SLK and C240) six-speed manual standard. Steering: power recirculating ball; (S-Class, E-Class, CL-

Class, and C-Class) rack and pinion. Brakes: front/rear disc. Body construction: steel unibody.

PERFORMANCE

Acceleration (0-60 mph): (C320) 7.1 sec.; (CLK430) 6.5 sec.; (SLK320) 6.6 sec.; (E430 Sport) 6.1 sec.; (E55) 6.1 sec.; (S500) 6.2 sec.; (CL500) 5.8 sec. Acceleration (quarter mile): (C320) 15.4 sec.; (C280) 15.8 sec.; (CLK 430) 14.8 sec.; (SLK320) 14.9 sec.; (E430 Sport) 14.5 sec.; (E55) 14.8 sec.; (S500) 14.6 sec.; (CL500) 14.2 sec. EPA Fuel economy city/highway miles per gallon: (E320) 19/26. Performance Figures by *Motor Trend*.

Manufacturer: DaimlerChrysler AG, Stuttgart, Germany.

Distributor: Mercedes-Benz USA, Montvale, New Jersey

2001 SL600 Silver Arrow Limited Edition interior

2001 SL600 Silver Arrow Limited Edition

2001 SLK230

2001 SLK320 engine bay

2002

C-CLASS: Three new models expanded the C-Class into a comprehensive model family of its own. All C-Class models featured industry-leading dual-stage/dual threshold front airbags, head protection curtain airbags and side airbags.

· **C230 sport coupe:** 192 hp supercharged engine; six-speed standard; five-speed Touch Shift automatic optional; dual-zone climate control standard.

· **C320 wagon:** 215 hp V-6; five-speed Touch Shift automatic standard.

· **C32 AMG sedan:** 349 hp supercharged and intercooled hand-built V-6 engine, AMG SpeedShift transmission, AMG suspension, racing-derived brakes, twin-spoke alloy wheels.

CL-CLASS, S-CLASS: Air conditioning refinements, including MAX COOL setting; new third memory position. Two new paint colors: Alabaster White and Everest Green.

CLK-CLASS: New CLK55 AMG Cabriolet model expanded the line to three coupes and three Cabriolets:

· **CLK55 AMG Cabriolet:** with 349 hp hand-built V-8 engine, standard Charcoal designo Edition Nappa leather interior, unique multi-piece alloy wheels, AMG suspension, racing derived brakes.

· **CLK320** was now available with sport package.

· **CLK430** coupe and cabriolet models received new five-spoke alloys wheels.

E-CLASS: New standard alloy wheel design for E320 model. Two new paint colors: Alabaster White and Everest Green.

G-CLASS: A rugged, no-compromise off-road sport utility with supreme luxury. The G500 was handcrafted in Graz, Austria and powered by 5.0-liter V-8. The G500 used a sophisticated four-wheel drive system employing three locking differentials and four-wheel traction control for go-anywhere capabilities. Also, the G500 came standard with the following: GPS Navigation system, nine-speaker audio system with CD changer, heated seats in front and back, full leather upholstery, plus ESP stability control, ABS, and Brake Assist.

M-CLASS: Revised for 2002 with new bodywork and interior design. New ML500 model, with a 5.0-liter V-8, replaced the ML430. Redesigned climate controls with automatic setting functions, new-design 17-inch alloy wheels for ML320 and for ML500, second-row ventilation fan and vents, larger fuel tank, redesigned center console with large cup holder.

SL-CLASS: Both SL500 and SL600 continued through the 2002 model year without changes, including a limited production run of 1,500 Silver Arrow Editions.

SLK-CLASS: New SLK32 AMG model expanded the line to three models.

· **SLK32 AMG:** with 349 hp handbuilt supercharged and intercooled V-6 engine, racing derived brakes, AMG SpeedShift transmission programming, AMG suspension calibration, twin-spoke alloy wheels.

· **For SLK230 and SLK320,** a redesigned optional sport package featured new side sills, front air dam, and rear fascia, plus new 5-spoke AMG Monoblock alloy wheels and projector beam fog lamps.

Model	Body Type	Engine Type	MSRP	Notes
C-CLASS				
C230 Kompressor	Sport Coupe	4-cylinder	$25,615	New for 2002
C240	Sedan	V-6	$31,215	
C320	Sedan	V-6	$37,615	
C320	Wagon	V-6	$39,115	New for 2002
C32 AMG	Sedan	V-6	$50,615	New for 2002
CL-CLASS				
CL500	Coupe	V-8	$91,415	
CL55 AMG	Coupe	V-8	$104,165	
CL600	Coupe	V-12	$119,615	
CLK-CLASS				
CLK320	Coupe	V-6	$43,215	
CLK320	Cabriolet	V-6	$50,265	
CLK430	Coupe	V-8	$50,915	
CLK430	Cabriolet	V-8	$57,965	
CLK55 AMG	Coupe	V-8	$69,115	
CLK55 AMG	Cabriolet	V-8	$79,665	New for 2002
E-CLASS				
E320	Sedan	V-6	$49,115	
E320 4Matic	Sedan	V-6	$51,965	
E320	Station Wagon	V-6	$49,915	
E320 4Matic	Station Wagon	V-6	$52,765	
E430	Sedan	V-8	$54,515	
E430 4Matic	Sedan	V-8	$57,365	
E55 AMG	Sedan	V-8	$72,015	
G-CLASS				
G500	Sport Utility	V-8	$73,165	New for 2002
M-CLASS				
ML320	Sport Utility	V-6	$36,965	
ML500	Sport Utility	V-8	$45,615	New for 2002
ML55 AMG	Sport Utility	V-8	$66,565	
S-CLASS				
S430	Sedan	V-8	$72,815	
S500	Sedan	V-8	$80,865	
S55 AMG	Sedan	V-8	$100,165	
S600	Sedan	V-12	$115,865	
SL				
SL500	Coupe/Roadster	V-8	$84,465	
SL600	Coupe/Roadster	V-12	$129,615	
SLK				
SLK230 Kompressor	Roadster	4-cylinder	$40,065	
SLK320	Roadster	V-6	$45,465	
SLK32 AMG	Roadster	V-6	$55,565	New for 2002

2002 CL500-2

2002 ML500

2002 S500 Guard

ENGINES

Most 2002 Mercedes-Benz models were powered by V-6, V-8, and V-12 engines with a twin-spark/three-valve-per-cylinder arrangement boasting up to 40-percent lower emissions, 13-percent better fuel efficiency, 25-percent lower weight, and a broader torque range than their previous inline-6, V-8, and V-12 counterparts.

A 2.6-liter V-6 engine powered the C240 sedan with 168 horsepower and 177 lbs.-ft. of torque. This engine was available with either a five-speed automatic transmission with Touch Shift manual gear selection capabilities, or a new six-speed manual transmission.

A 3.2-liter V-6 engine powered the E320 sedan and wagon (221 horsepower), the C320 sedan and wagon, the CLK320 coupe and cabriolet models, the SLK320 coupe/roadster, and the ML320 sport utility vehicle (all 215 horsepower).

A 4.3-liter V-8 powered the E430 sedan, CLK430 coupe and cabriolet, and S430 sedan (275 horsepower).

A 5.0-liter V-8 was used in the SL500 roadster, CL500 coupe, S500 sedan (302 horsepower), the ML500 sport utility (288 horsepower), and the G500 Sport Utility (292 horsepower).

Engine Note: These Mercedes-Benz engines all featured innovative three-valve-per-cylinder technology, which could reduce exhaust emissions dramatically — over 40-percent — during the critical warm-up stage. Catalysts must heat up to work effectively, and this takes nearly two minutes with most modern engines. Increasingly strict emissions limits meant converter light-off time must be reduced to about one minute, and the new Mercedes-Benz engines met that criteria.

Manufacturer: Daimler-Chrysler AG, Stuttgart, Germany.

Distributor: Mercedes-Benz USA, Montvale, New Jersey

CHASSIS

Model	Wheelbase	Length	Weight
C-Class Sedan, Wagon, Sport Coupe	106.9 in.	178.3 in.	3,360-3,439 lbs.
CL-Class Coupe	113.6 in.	196.6 in.	4,115 — 4,312 lbs.
CLK-Class Coupe and Cabriolet	105.9 in.	180.2 in.	3,213-3,665 lbs.
E-Class Sedan and Wagon	111.5 in.	189.4 in.	3,491-3,926 lbs.
G-Class Sport Utility	112.0 in.	183.5 in.	5,423 lbs.
M-Class Sport Utility	111.0 in.	180.6 in.	4,586-4,861 lbs.
S-Class Sedan	121.5 in.	203.1 in.	4,133-4,488 lbs.
SL-Class Coupe/Roadster	99.0 in.	177.1 in.	4,125-4,455 lbs.
SLK-Class Coupe/Roadster	94.5 in.	157.9 in.	3,055-3,099 lbs.

2002 E430 sedan

2002 E Class interior

2002 S500

2002 G500

2002 G500 interior

PERFORMANCE

Model	EPA Fuel Mileage Estimates	0-60 Acceleration	Top Speed
C240 Sedan (manual)	17/26 City/Hwy	8.2 seconds	130 mph
C240 Sedan (automatic)	19/26 City/Hwy	8.7 seconds	130 mph
C320 Sedan & Wagon	19/25 City/Hwy	6.9 seconds	130 mph
C230 Sport Coupe (manual)	19/29 City/Hwy	7.2 seconds	130 mph
C230 Sport Coupe (automatic)	21/28 City/Hwy	7.5 seconds	130 mph
C32 AMG Sedan	17/22 City/Hwy	4.9 seconds	155 mph
CL500 Coupe	16/23 City/Hwy	6.1 seconds	155 mph
CL55 AMG	16/22 City/Hwy	5.7 seconds	155 mph
CL600	15/22 City/Hwy	5.9 seconds	155 mph
CLK320 Coupe	20/27 City/Hwy	6.9 seconds	130 mph
CLK320 Cabriolet	19/26 City/Hwy	7.7 seconds	130 mph
CLK430 Coupe	18/24 City/Hwy	6.1 seconds	130 mph
CLK430 Cabriolet	17/24 City/Hwy	6.9 seconds	130 mph
CLK55 AMG	17/24 City/Hwy	4.9 seconds	155 mph
CLK55 AMG Cabriolet	16/22 City/Hwy	4.9 seconds	155 mph
E320 Sedan	20/28 City/Hwy	7.1 seconds	130 mph
E320 4Matic Sedan	20/27 City/Hwy	7.5 seconds	130 mph
E320 Wagon	20/27 City/Hwy	7.8 seconds	130 mph
E320 4Matic Wagon	19/26 City/Hwy	8.2 seconds	130 mph
E430 Sedan	17/24 City/Hwy	6.2 seconds	130 mph
E430 4Matic Sedan	17/23 City/Hwy	6.6 seconds	130 mph
E55 AMG Sedan	17/24 City/Hwy	5.4 seconds	155 mph
G500 Sport Utility	13/15 City/Hwy*	10.2 seconds	118 mph
ML320 Sport Utility	17/21 City/Hwy	9.0 seconds	121 mph
ML500 Sport Utility	14/17 City/Hwy	7.7 seconds	121 mph
ML55 AMG Sport Utility	14/17 City/Hwy	6.4 seconds	149 mph
S430 Sedan	17/24 City/Hwy	6.9 seconds	130 mph
S500 Sedan	16/23 City/Hwy	6.1 seconds	130 mph
S500 (Guard)	N/A	7.3 seconds	130 mph
S55 AMG	16/22 City/Hwy	5.7 seconds	130 mph
S600	15/22 City/Hwy	5.9 seconds	130 mph
SL500 Coupe/Roadster	16/23 City/Hwy	6.1 seconds	155 mph
SL600 Coupe/Roadster	13/19 City/Hwy	5.9 seconds	155 mph
SLK230 Kompressor (automatic)	23/30 City/Hwy	7.0 seconds	130 mph
SLK230 Kompressor (manual)	20/30 City/Hwy	6.9 seconds	130 mph
SLK320 (automatic)	20/26 City/Hwy	6.6 seconds	130 mph
SLK320 (manual)	17/26 City/Hwy	6.6 seconds	130 mph
SLK32 AMG	18/24 City/Hwy	4.8 seconds	155 mph

* preliminary

2002 CL500

2003

C-CLASS: New models: C320 sport coupe, C230 sport sedan, and C320 sport sedan. Also 4Matic all-wheel-drive variants of the C240 and C320 sedans and wagons were introduced. A new C240 wagon (2.6-liter V-6) joined the C320 wagon; a six-speed manual was standard on both models. New 1.8-liter, 189 hp supercharged four-cylinder engine replaced the previous four-cylinder engine in the sports coupe. Bi-Xenon headlamps were a new option on all models.

CL-CLASS: All models (CL500, CL55 AMG, CL600) received new front fascia, headlight and taillight glass, and interior updates. A new bi-turbo V-12 engine for CL600 model with 493 hp/590 lbs.-ft. of torque debuted. The CL55 AMG got a new supercharged V-8 for with 493 hp, redundant SpeedShift buttons on the steering wheel, a new racing-derived braking system, and a redesigned AMG interior.

CLK-CLASS: Two new-generation coupes with dynamic pillarless design: CLK320 (3.2-liter 215 hp V-6) and CLK500 (5.0-liter 302 hp V-8). Available features included Distronic adaptive cruise control, Keyless Go, and Bi-Xenon headlights. Existing cabriolet models continued production, CLK55

AMG models ceased production.

E-CLASS: Two new-generation sedans: the E320 (3.2-liter, 221 hp V-6) and E500 (5.0-liter 302 hp V-8). Both featured the award-winning electronic braking system and smart front airbags. A new four-link front suspension was joined by new Airmatic Dual Control suspension with adaptive damping and two different spring rates (two air chambers) and a rollover sensor.

G-CLASS: The G500 model was joined by a new G55 AMG (with a hand assembled 5.5-liter, 347 hp V-8). Both the G500 and G55 AMG used a sophisticated four-wheel drive system employing three locking differentials and four-wheel traction control. A heated steering wheel was now standard. Multi-contour seats, harman/kardon premium audio and rear parking assist were new options.

M-CLASS: ML320, ML500, ML55 AMG models continued. A DVD-based navigation system debuted and was retrofittable for M-Class vehicles back to 2000 model year— an industry first.

2003 SL500 sport

2003 C240 wagon

Model	Body Type	Engine Type	MSRP	Notes
C-CLASS				
C230 Kompressor	Sports Coupe	4-cylinder	$25,615	
C230 Kompressor	Sport Sedan	4-cylinder	$28,655	New for 2003
C240	Sedan	V-6	$30,565	
C240	Wagon	V-6	$32,065	New for 2003
C320	Sports Coupe	V-6	$27,965	New for 2003
C320	Sport Sedan	V-6	$35,865	New for 2003
C320	Sedan	V-6	$35,865	
C320	Wagon	V-6	$37,365	
C32 AMG	Sedan	V-6	$51,065	
CL-CLASS				
CL500	Coupe	V-8	$92,315	
CL55 AMG	Coupe	V-8	$115,265	
CL600	Coupe	V-12	$125,565	
CLK-CLASS				
CLK320	Coupe	V-6	$44,565	
CLK320	Cabriolet	V-6	$50,615	
CLK500	Coupe	V-8	$52,865	New for 2003
CLK430	Cabriolet	N/A	$58,315	
CLK55 AMG	Coupe	N/A	$69,115	
E-CLASS				
E320	Sedan	V-6	$47,615	
E320	Wagon	V-6	$49,915	
E500	Sedan	V-8	$55,515	New for 2003
G-CLASS				
G500	Sport Utility	V-8	$74,265	
G55 AMG	Sport Utility	V-8	$90,565	New for 2003
M-CLASS				
ML350	Sport Utility	V-6	$37,615	New for 2003
ML500	Sport Utility	V-8	$46,015	
ML55 AMG	Sport Utility	V-8	$66,565	
S-CLASS				
S430	Sedan	V-8	$73,265	
S500	Sedan	V-8	$81,665	
S55 AMG	Sedan	V-8	$107,165	
S600	Sedan	V-12	$121,205	
SL-CLASS				
SL500	Coupe/Roadster	V-8	$86,655	
SL55 AMG	Coupe/Roadster	V-8	$113,915	New for 2003
SLK-CLASS				
SLK230 Kompressor	Coupe/Roadster	4-cylinder	$40,265	
SLK320	Coupe/Roadster	V-6	$46,715	
SLK32 AMG	Coupe/Roadster	V-6	$56,115	

Note: The 4Matic option was available on the C240 and C320 models ($3,125), on the E320 Wagon ($2,850), and on the S430 and S500 ($2,900).

S-CLASS: Award-winning PRE-SAFE concept debuted on the 2003 S-Class models. Prior to impact, additional electric seat belt tensioners were activated and seats are adjusted to an optimum safety position: backrest raised and seat bottom moved rearwards. If skidding occurred, the sunroof closed. All models (S430, S500, S55 AMG, S600) received a new front fascia, headlight and taillight glass, and interior updates. Additionally:

- New 4Matic all-wheel-drive S430 and S500 models (40/60 torque split front/rear).

- A new bi-turbo V-12 engine for the S600 model with 493 hp/590 lbs.-ft. of torque.

- S55 AMG received a new supercharged V-8 for with 493 hp, redundant SpeedShift buttons on the steering wheel, new racing-derived braking system, and a redesigned AMG interior.

SL-CLASS: An all-new SL500 two-seater (from March 2002) featured an award-winning, industry-first electronic braking system, ABC active suspension, automatic retractable hardtop, and on-board navigation (all standard equipment). Additionally, new SL55 AMG model (August 2002) with a supercharged, 493 hp V-8 (0-60 mph in just 4.5 seconds), handling dynamics to match with reprogrammed active suspension, and racing-derived brakes was introduced. Special interior trim was also standard.

SLK-CLASS: SLK230 Kompressor, SLK320, and SLK32 AMG models continued.

ENGINES

Most 2003 Mercedes-Benz models were powered by V-6, V-8, or V-12 engines with a twin-spark/three-valve-per-cylinder arrangement. This cutting-edge technology boasted up to 40-percent lower emissions, 13-percent better fuel efficiency, and

2003 SL500 interior

2003 SL500

25-percent lower weight, not to mention a broader torque range than their previous designs.

A 2.6-liter V-6 engine powered the C240 sedan and wagon with 168 horsepower and 177 lbs.-ft. of torque. This engine was available with either a five-speed automatic transmission with TouchShift manual gear selection capabilities, or a new 6-speed manual transmission.

A 3.2-liter V-6 engine powered the E320 sedan and wagon (221 horsepower), the C320 sedan and wagon, the CLK320 coupe and cabriolet models, the SLK320 coupe/roadster and the ML320 sport utility vehicle (all 215 horsepower).

A 4.3-liter V-8 powered the S430 sedan (275 horsepower), while a 5.0-liter V-8 was used in the E500 sedan, SL500 roadster, CL500, and CLK500 coupes, S500 sedan (all 302 horsepower), the ML500 sport utility (288 horsepower) and the G500 sport utility (292 horsepower).

Both the S600 sedan and CL600 coupe were powered by a new V-12 engine that set an even higher refinement standard than the previous V-12, which itself, was a remarkable Power plant. Generating 493 horsepower and an overwhelming 590 lbs.-ft. of torque, the new turbocharged V-12 came clothed in luxury, convenience, and refinement that defined the segment.

2003 ML500

CHASSIS

Model	Wheelbase	Length	Weight
C-Class Sedan, Wagon, Sports Coupe	106.9 in.	178.3 in.	3,250-3,540 lbs.
CL-Class Coupe	113.6 in.	196.6 in.	N/A
CLK-Class Coupe	106.9 in.	182.6 in.	3,515-3,665 lbs.
CLK-Class Cabriolet	105.9 in.	180.2 in	3,515-3,665 lbs.
E-Class Sedan and Wagon	112.4 in.	190.3 in.	3,635-3,815 lbs.
G-Class Sport Utility	112.0 in.	183.5 in.	5,423 lbs.
M-Class Sport Utility	111.0 in.	180.6 in.	4,586-4,861 lbs.
S-Class Sedan	121.5 in.	203.1 in.	4,160-4,610 lbs.
SL-Class Coupe/Roadster	100.8 in.	178.5 in.	4,045-4,280 lbs.
SLK-Class Coupe/Roadster	94.5 in.	157.9 in.	3,055-3,099 lbs.

PERFORMANCE

Model	EPA Fuel Mileage Estimates	0-60 Acceleration	Top Speed
C-CLASS			
C230 Kompressor Sports Coupe (automatic)	23/32 City/Hwy	7.5 seconds	130 mph
C230 Kompressor Sports Coupe (manual)	21/31 City/Hwy	7.2 seconds	130 mph
C230 Kompressor Sport Sedan (automatic)*	19/25 City/Hwy	N/A	130 mph
C230 Kompressor Sport Sedan (manual)*	17/25 City/Hwy	N/A	130 mph
C240 Sedan (automatic)	19/25 City/Hwy	8.7 seconds	130 mph
C240 Sedan (manual)	17/26 City/Hwy	8.2 seconds	130 mph
C240 Wagon (automatic)	19/25 City/Hwy	N/A	130 mph
C240 Wagon (manual)	17/25 City/Hwy	N/A	130 mph
C240 4Matic Wagon (automatic)	19/25 City/Hwy	N/A	130 mph
C320 Sedan/Sport Sedan (automatic)	20/26 City/Hwy	6.9 seconds	130 mph
C320 Sedan/Sport Sedan (manual)*	17/25 City/Hwy	N/A	130 mph
C320 Sports Coupe (automatic)*	20/26 City/Hwy	N/A	130 mph
C320 Sports Coupe (manual)*	17/25 City/Hwy	N/A	130 mph
C320 Wagon (automatic)	20/26 City/Hwy	7.0 seconds	130 mph
C320 4Matic Wagon (automatic)	19/25 City/Hwy	N/A	130 mph
C32 AMG Sedan	17/21 City/Hwy	4.9 seconds	155 mph
CL-CLASS			
CL500 Coupe	16/22 City/Hwy	6.1 seconds	155 mph
CL55 AMG	14/22 City/Hwy	4.6 seconds	155 mph
CL600	13/19 City/Hwy	4.6 seconds	155 mph
CLK-CLASS			
CLK320 Coupe	19/27 City/Hwy	7.4 seconds	130 mph
CLK320 Cabriolet	20/27 City/Hwy	7.4 seconds	130 mph
CLK430 Cabriolet	18/24 City/Hwy	N/A	130 mph
CLK500 Coupe	16/23 City/Hwy	5.7 seconds	130 mph
CLK55 AMG Coupe	16/22 City/Hwy	N/A	155 mph

E-CLASS

E320 Sedan	19/27 City/Hwy	7.1 seconds	130 mph
E320 Wagon	20/27 City/Hwy	7.1 seconds	130 mph
E320 4Matic Wagon	19/26 City/Hwy	7.1 seconds	130 mph
E500 Sedan	16/23 City/Hwy	5.8 seconds	130 mph

G-CLASS

G500	12/14 City/Hwy	10.2 seconds	118 mph
G55 AMG	14/15 City/Hwy	7.2 seconds	118 mph

ML-CLASS

ML350	15/18 City/Hwy	N/A	121 mph
ML500	14/17 City/Hwy	7.7 seconds	121 mph
ML55 AMG	14/18 City/Hwy	6.4 seconds	144 mph

S-CLASS

S430 Sedan	17/24 City/Hwy	6.9 seconds	130 mph
S430 4Matic Sedan	16/22 City/Hwy	6.9 seconds	130 mph
S500 Sedan	16/22 City/Hwy	6.1 seconds	130 mph
S500 4Matic Sedan	16/21 City/Hwy	6.1 seconds	130 mph
S500 (Guard)	16/22 City/Hwy	N/A	N/A
S55 AMG	14/22 City/Hwy	4.6 seconds	155 mph
S600 Sedan	13/19 City/Hwy	4.6 seconds	155 mph

SL-CLASS

SL500	15/22 City/Hwy	6.1 seconds	155 mph
SL55 AMG	14/20 City/Hwy	4.5 seconds	155 mph

SLK-CLASS

SLK230 Kompressor (automatic)	22/28 City/Hwy	7.0 seconds	130 mph
SLK230 Kompressor (manual)	19/28 City/Hwy	6.9 seconds	130 mph
SLK320 (automatic)	20/26 City/Hwy	6.6 seconds	130 mph
SLK320 (manual)	17/26 City/Hwy	6.6 seconds	130 mph
SLK32 AMG	17/22 City/Hwy	4.8 seconds	155 mph

(*Preliminary value)

2003 E500

The new V-12 engine provided effortless thrust with turbine-like smoothness. The high-technology V-12 had a vast torque band with 590 lbs.-ft. of torque at just 1,800 rpm. With its high-tech engine, smart TouchShift transmission, and the state-of-the art aerodynamics of the S600 Sedan and CL600 Coupe, the new V-12 enabled both cars to reach 60 miles per hour in less than 4.5 seconds, quicker than many out-and-out sports cars.

Manufacturer: DaimlerChrysler AG, Stuttgart, Germany.

Distributor: Mercedes-Benz USA, Montvale, New Jersey.

2004

C-CLASS: C-Class sedans and wagons were offered with 4Matic and heated seats for $1,250 less than the 2003 models. All sport coupes came with standard 17-inch, seven-spoke, alloy wheels and high-performance tires, three-spoke sport steering wheel, leather-covered sport shift knob, rubber-studded aluminum pedals, enlarged chrome exhaust tip, body-colored door handles, and patterned aluminum door sill.

All sport sedans came with standard 17-inch five-spoke, alloy wheels and high-performance tires, four-piston fixed caliper front brakes with drilled rotors, sport shift manual transmission, lowered sport suspension, three-spoke sport steering wheel, rubber-studded stainless steel pedals, stainless steel exhaust tip and a modified exhaust for sportier sound.

CL-CLASS: New standard DVD navigation, MP3 play capability and optional 18-inch wheels.

- The CL500 was equipped with the all-new seven-speed automatic transmission.

CLK-CLASS: Three new-generation cabriolets: CLK320, CLK500, and CLK55 AMG. New optional features include electronic trunk closer, Distronic adaptive cruise control, Keyless Go, and Bi-Xenon headlights. (Three new generation coupe models were launched in 2003.)

- Active ventilated, multi-contour seating and interior and exterior appearance options.

- A special edition CLK500 was built exclusively for the Saks Fifth Avenue's Key for the Cure.

E-CLASS: C-Class sedans and wagons were offered with 4Matic and heated seats for $1,250 less than the 2003 models. New E320 wagon and E500 4Matic wagon models: Two-wheel-drive E320 wagon standard; optional four-wheel-drive. V-8 and sport versions of the wagon were optional for first time. The next generation E55 AMG continued. (Launched in mid-2003.) The E500 sedan and wagon were now equipped with new seven-speed automatic transmission.

- 4Matic four-wheel-drive was available on sedans and wagons.

- New Bi-Xenon active lights were available on sedans and wagons.

Model	Body Type	Engine Type	MSRP	Notes
C-CLASS				
C230 Kompressor	Sport Coupe	4-cylinder	$26,020	
C230 Kompressor	Sport Sedan	4-cylinder	$28,710	
C240	Sedan	V-6	$32,280	
C240	Station Wagon	V-6	$33,780	
C320	Sport Coupe	V-6	$28,370	
C320	Sport Sedan	V-6	$35,920	
C320	Sedan	V-6	$37,630	
C320	Station Wagon	V-6	$39,130	
C32 AMG	Sedan	V-6	$51,120	
CL-CLASS				
CL500	Coupe	V-8	N/A	
CL55 AMG	Coupe	V-8	N/A	
CL600	Coupe	V-12	N/A	
CLK-CLASS				
CLK320	Coupe	V-6	$44,350	
CLK320	Cabriolet	V-6	$51,400	
CLK500	Coupe	V-8	$52,800	
CLK500	Cabriolet	V-8	$59,850	New For 2004
CLK55 AMG	Coupe	V-8	$70,620	
CLK55 AMG	Cabriolet	V-8	$80,220	New For 2004
E-CLASS				
E320	Sedan	V-6	N/A	
E320	Station Wagon	V-6	N/A	
E500	Sedan	V-8	N/A	
E500 (4Matic only)	Station Wagon	V-8	N/A	New For 2004
E55 AMG	Sedan	V-8	N/A	
G-CLASS				
G500	Sport Utility	V-8	$76,870	
G55 AMG	Sport Utility	V-8	N/A	
M-CLASS				
ML350	Sport Utility	V-6	$38,020	
ML500	Sport Utility	V-8	$46,070	
S-CLASS				
S430	Sedan	V-8	N/A	
S500	Sedan	V-8	N/A	
S55 AMG	Sedan	V-8	N/A	
S600	Sedan	V-12	N/A	
SL				
SL500	Coupe/Roadster	V-8	N/A	
SL55 AMG	Coupe/Roadster	V-8	N/A	
SL600	Coupe/Roadster	V-12	N/A	New Model
SLK				
SLK230 Kompressor	Coupe/Roadster	4-cylinder	$40,320	
SLK320	Coupe/Roadster	V-6	$45,770	
SLK32 AMG	Coupe/Roadster	V-6	$56,170	

Note: The 4Matic option was available on the C240 and C320 models ($1,200), on the E320 and E500 Sedans and wagons, and on the S430 and S500.

2004 S55 AMG

CHASSIS

Model	Wheelbase	Length	Weight
C-Class Sedan, Wagon, Sport Coupe	106.9 in.	178.9 in.	3,250-3,495 lbs.
CL-Class Coupe	113.6 in.	196.4in.	4,085-4,473 lbs.
CLK-Class Coupe/Cabriolet	106.9 in.	182.6 in.	3,515-3,960 lbs.
E-Class Sedan and Wagon	112.4 in.	190.3 in.	3,635-3,990 lbs.
G-Class Sport Utility	112.2 in.	185.6 in.	5,423-5,540 lbs.
M-Class Sport Utility	111.0 in.	182.6 in.	4,819-4,874 lbs.
S-Class Sedan	121.5 in.	203.1 in.	4,160-4,610 lbs.
SL-Class Coupe/Roadster	100.8 in.	178.5 in.	4,065-4,429 lbs.
SLK-Class Coupe/Roadster	94.5 in.	157.9 in.	3,055-3,220 lbs.

2004 C230 sport coupe

If you don't put it in your garage, it might wind up in a museum.

The vintage Mercedes-Benz vehicles offered for sale by the Classic Center in Fellbach, Germany are among the finest you'll find anywhere. They range from lovingly maintained daily drivers to frame-off restorations done by factory-trained craftsmen using authentic build sheets and genuine Mercedes-Benz parts. And while it's true that many of these cars are worthy of being displayed in museums, they'd be much happier if they found new homes in the garages of individual enthusiasts. We have a hunch you feel the same way. To review the superb vehicles currently available, and to find out how you can purchase one, please call us at 866-MBCLASSIC (622-5277). **Passion. Unlike any other.**

Mercedes-Benz

2004 300S ad

2004 SLK320 sport

2004 SL55 AMG

G-CLASS: Multi-contour seats, harman/kardon premium audio and rear park assist, were now standard.

M-CLASS: The ML350 replaced the ML320, mid-model year 2003. Inspiration Edition continued ML500 model continued. ML55 AMG was discontinued for 2004. DVD navigation was now a factory option for the ML350 (standard on ML500). In an industry first the DVD navigation was available for under $1,000. Model year 2000 and later M-Class vehicles were retrofittable.

S-CLASS: The S430 and S500 were equipped with an all-new seven-speed automatic transmission system.

- New standard DVD navigation, MP3 play capability, and optional 18-inch wheels.

- Award-winning PRE-SAFE technology continued on 2004 S-Class models.

SL-CLASS: The SL500 was equipped with an all-new, seven-speed automatic transmission. A new SL600 model, with a 5.5-liter intercooled twin turbocharged engine (493 hp), was introduced. New feature: a heated steering wheel.

SLK-CLASS: A special edition included 17-inch wheels, Nappa leather sport seats and roll bar, exterior chrome accents, and a painted front grill and spoiler. SLK230 Kompressor, SLK320, and SLK32 AMG models continued.

2004 E500 wagon

2004 E500 sedan

ENGINES

Most 2004 Mercedes-Benz models were powered by V-6, V-8, or V-12 engines with a twin-spark, three-valve-per-cylinder arrangement. This cutting-edge technology boasted up to 40-percent lower emissions, 13-percent better fuel efficiency, and 25-percent lower weight, not to mention a broader torque range, than their previous designs.

A 2.6-liter V-6 engine powered the C240 sedan and wagon with 168 horsepower and 177 lbs.-ft. of torque. This engine was also available with either a five-speed automatic transmission with TouchShift manual gear selection capabilities or a six-speed manual transmission.

A 3.2-liter V-6 engine powered the E320 sedan and wagon (221 horsepower), the C320 sedan and wagon, the CLK320 coupe and cabriolet models, and the SLK320 coupe/roadster (all 215 horsepower).

A 4.3-liter V-8 powered the S430 sedan (275 horsepower), while a 5.0-liter V-8 was used in the E500 sedan, SL500 roadster, CL500 and CLK500 coupes, S500 sedan (all 302 horsepower), the ML500 Sport Utility (288 horsepower), and the G500 sport utility (292 horsepower).

Engine Note: These Mercedes-Benz engines all featured innovative three-valve-per-cylinder technology, which could reduce exhaust emissions dramatically — over 40-percent — during the critical warm-up stage. Catalysts must heat up to work effectively, and this takes nearly two minutes with most modern engines. Increasingly strict emissions limits meant converter light-off time must be reduced to about one minute and the new Mercedes-Benz engines met that criteria.

Manufacturer: DaimlerChrysler AG, Stuttgart, Germany.

Distributor: Mercedes-Benz USA, Montvale, New Jersey

PERFORMANCE

MODEL	EPA FUEL MILEAGE ESTIMATES	0-60 ACCELERATION	TOP SPEED
C-CLASS			
C230 Kompressor Sport Coupe (automatic)	23/30 City/Hwy	7.5 seconds	130 mph
C230 Kompressor Sport Coupe (manual)	22/30 City/Hwy	7.2 seconds	130 mph
C230 Kompressor Sport Sedan (automatic)	23/30 City/Hwy	7.8 seconds	130 mph
C230 Kompressor Sport Sedan (manual)	22/30 City/Hwy	7.6 seconds	130 mph
C240 Sedan (automatic)	20/25 City/Hwy	8.7 seconds	130 mph
C240 4Matic Sedan (automatic)	19/25 City/Hwy	N/A	130 mph
C240 Wagon (automatic)	20/25 City/Hwy	8.7 seconds	130 mph
C240 4Matic Wagon (automatic)	19/25 City/Hwy	N/A	130 mph
C320 Sport Coupe (automatic)	20/26 City/Hwy	6.9 seconds	130 mph
C320 Sport Coupe (manual)	19/26 City/Hwy	6.8 seconds	130 mph
C320 Sport Sedan (automatic)	20/26 City/Hwy	6.9 seconds	130 mph
C320 Sport Sedan (manual)	19/26 City/Hwy	6.8 seconds	130 mph
C320 Sedan (automatic)	20/26 City/Hwy	6.9 seconds	130 mph
C320 4Matic Sedan (automatic)	19/27 City/Hwy	N/A	130 mph
C320 Wagon (automatic)	20/26 City/Hwy	7.0 seconds	130 mph
C320 4Matic Wagon (automatic)	19/27 City/Hwy	N/A	130 mph
C32 AMG Sedan (automatic)	16/21 City/Hwy	4.9 seconds	155 mph
CL-CLASS			
CL500 Coupe	N/A	N/A	155 mph
CL55 AMG	N/A	4.6 seconds	155 mph
CL600	N/A	4.6 seconds	155 mph
CLK-CLASS			
CLK320 Coupe	20/26 City/Hwy	7.4 seconds	130 mph
CLK320 Cabriolet	20/26 City/Hwy	8.0 seconds	130 mph
CLK500 Coupe	17/22 City/Hwy	5.7 seconds	130 mph
CLK500 Cabriolet	17/22 City/Hwy	6.0 seconds	130 mph
CLK55 AMG Coupe	15/22 City/Hwy	5.0 seconds	155 mph
CLK55 AMG Cabriolet	15/22 City/Hwy	5.2 seconds	155 mph

E-CLASS

E320 Sedan	19/27 City/Hwy	7.1 seconds	130 mph
E320 Wagon	19/27 City/Hwy	7.1 seconds	130 mph
E320 4Matic Wagon	N/A	7.1 seconds	130 mph
E500 Sedan	N/A	5.8 seconds	130 mph
E500 Wagon	N/A	5.8 seconds	130 mph
E500 4Matic Wagon	N/A	5.8 seconds	130 mph
E55 AMG	N/A	4.5 seconds	155 mph

G-CLASS

G500 Sport Utility	13/14 City/Hwy	10.2 seconds	118 mph
G55 AMG Sport Utility	14/15 City/Hwy	7.2 seconds	118 mph

ML-CLASS

ML350 Sport Utility	15/18 City/Hwy	8.5 seconds	121 mph
ML500 Sport Utility	14/17 City/Hwy	7.7 seconds	121 mph

S-CLASS

S430 Sedan	N/A	6.9 seconds	130 mph
S430 4Matic Sedan	N/A	6.9 seconds	130 mph
S500 Sedan	N/A	6.1 seconds	130 mph
S500 4Matic Sedan	N/A	6.1 seconds	130 mph
S600 Sedan	N/A	4.6 seconds	155 mph
S55 AMG Sedan	N/A	4.6 seconds	155 mph

SL-CLASS

SL500 Coupe/Roadster	N/A	6.1 seconds	155 mph
SL55 AMG Coupe/Roadster	N/A	4.5 seconds	155 mph
SL600 Coupe/Roadster	N/A	4.5 seconds	155 mph

SLK-CLASS

SLK230 Kompressor (automatic) Coupe/Roadster	22/28 City/Hwy	7 seconds	130 mph
SLK230 Kompressor (manual) Coupe/Roadster	21/29 City/Hwy	6.9 seconds	130 mph
SLK320 (automatic) Coupe/Roadster	20/26 City/Hwy	6.6 seconds	130 mph
SLK320 (manual) Coupe/Roadster	19/26 City/Hwy	6.6 seconds	130 mph
SLK32 AMG (automatic) Coupe/Roadster	17/22 City/Hwy	4.8 seconds	155 mph

2004 CLK320 coupe

2005 C230 sport

2005

In 2005, Mercedes-Benz marked the 100th anniversary of becoming the first import car maker to set up automobile manufacturing in the United States. Mercedes became the first import automobile to be made in the U.S.A. when its cars were built in Long Island City, New York from 1905 to 1907.

C-CLASS: Newly redesigned C-Class models were introduced: sport sedan, sport coupe, luxury sedan, and luxury wagon. All-new exterior and interior updates including body styling, headlamps and taillamps, radiator grilles, wheels, dashboard, instrument cluster, steering wheel, and improved seats. A new C55 AMG, with a hand-built, normally aspirated AMG V-8 engine producing 362 hp and 376 lbs.-ft. of torque, replaced the C32 AMG.

CL-CLASS: New CL65 AMG model: 6.0-liter twin-turbo V-12 producing 604 hp and 738 lbs.-ft. of torque and a newly developed AMG compound braking system with two-piece rotor and hub assembly.

CLK-CLASS: The CLK500 received a new AMG five-spoke wheel, rear spoiler, gearshift buttons, 7-speed automatic transmission, all standard. CLK320 received appearance package as standard: sport shift knob with chrome trim, enlarged chrome exhaust finisher, rubber-studded brushed aluminum pedals, 17-inch five-spoke alloy wheels with high-performance tires. All models received a redesigned center console with new buttons and shift knob.

E-CLASS: New E320 CDI: Highly fuel-efficient diesel version of the E-Class with innovative fully electronic fuel injection (CDI stands for Common-rail Direct Injection).

G-CLASS: New G55 AMG with an AMG 5.5-liter 24-valve supercharged and intercooled V-8 producing 469 hp and 16s lbs.-ft. of torque.

M-CLASS: M-Class Special Edition replaced the Inspiration Edition. It included unique 17-inch wheels, power dome hood, silver grille, aluminum roof rails, matte birch burl or dark burl walnut interior finish, and metallic paint.

S-CLASS: Award-winning Pre-Safe technology continued for the 2005 S-Class. 4Matic full-time all-wheel-drive system no-cost option on S430 and S500.

2005 CLK320

2005 CLS500

Model	Body Type	Engine Type	MSRP	Notes
C-CLASS				
C230 Kompressor	Sport Coupe	4-cylinder	$26,570	
C230 Kompressor	Sport Sedan	4-cylinder	$29,970	
C240	Sedan	V-6	$33,370	
C240	Wagon	V-6	$34,870	
C320	Sport Coupe	V-6	$28,970	
C320	Sport Sedan	V-6	$38,070	
C320	Sedan	V-6	$38,670	
C55 AMG	Sedan	V-8	$54,620	
CL-CLASS				
CL500	Coupe	V-8	$94,620	
CL55 AMG	Coupe	V-8	$119,620	
CL600	Coupe	V-8	$128,620	
CL65 AMG	Coupe	V-12	$178,220	New for 2005
CLK-CLASS				
CLK320	Coupe	V-6	$45,970	
CLK320	Cabriolet	V-6	$53,420	
CLK500	Coupe	V-8	$54,470	
CLK500	Cabriolet	V-8	$61,920	
CLK55 AMG	Coupe	V-8	$70,620	
CLK55 AMG	Cabriolet	V-8	$81,570	
E-CLASS				
E320	Sedan	V-6	$49,220	
E320	Wagon	V-6	$51,470	
E320 CDI	Sedan	Inline-6	$49,795	New for 2005
E500	Sedan	V-8	$57,620	
E500 (4Matic only)	Wagon	V-8	$61,220	
E55 AMG	Sedan	V-8	$80,220	
G-CLASS				
G500	Sport Utility	V-8	$78,420	
G55 AMG	Sport Utility	V-8	$100,620	
M-CLASS				
ML350	Sport Utility	V-6	$38,670	
ML500	Sport Utility	V-8	$47,120	
S-CLASS				
S430	Sedan	V-8	$76,020	
S500	Sedan	V-8	$84,620	
S55 AMG	Sedan	V-8	$112,620	
S600	Sedan	V-12	$125,470	
SL-CLASS				
SL500	Coupe/Roadster	V-8	$90,620	
SL55 AMG	Coupe/Roadster	V-8	$122,220	
SL600	Coupe/Roadster	V-12	$128,220	
SL65 AMG	Coupe/Roadster	V-12	$179,720	New Model
SLK				
SLK350	Coupe/Roadster	V-6	$46,220	
SLK55 AMG	Coupe/Roadster	V-8	N/A	

Note: The 4Matic option was available on the C240 and C320 models ($1,200), on the E320 and E500 sedans and wagons ($2,500), and on the S430 and S500 (at no cost).

SL-CLASS: New SL65 AMG. A 6.0-liter twin-turbo V-12 producing 604 hp and 738 lb-ft of torque and a newly developed AMG compound braking system with two-piece rotor and hub assembly.

An updated COMAND head unit with DVD navigation and a new center console was introduced.

SLK-CLASS: New SLK350. All-new platform and body design. Features included a new-generation engine with four-valve technology and variable valve timing; a more precise six-speed manual transmission; 17-inch, 10-spoke alloy wheels; and an available sport suspension. A new V-8-powered SLK55 AMG replaced the SLK32 AMG

Another technological first from Mercedes: AIRSCARF was an extra heating system built into the driver and passenger seats. At the touch of a button, warm air flowed from special vents in the head restraints, acting as an invisible scarf around the head and neck! For the new-generation SLK Roadster, Mercedes-Benz engineers wanted to extend the open-air driving season into the cooler months and AIRSCARF made that a reality.

ENGINES

A new high-tech Mercedes-Benz engine made its debut with the arrival of the new-generation 2005 SLK coupe/roadster. The first of an entirely new engine family, the V-6 powerplant featured four valves per cylinder and variable valve timing for

2005 E320 CDI

2005 CL55 AMG

2005 5600

2005 SL65 AMG

CHASSIS

Model	Wheelbase	Length	Weight
C-Class Sedan, Sport Sedan, Wagon, Sport Coupe	106.9 in.	171.2-179.0 in.	3,240-3,540 lbs.
CL-Class Coupe	113.6 in.	196.4in.	4,085-4,654 lbs.
CLK-Class Coupe and Cabriolet	106.9 in.	182.6 in.	3,515-3,960 lbs.
E-Class Sedan and Wagon	112.4 in.	189.7-191.7 in.	3,835-4,087 lbs.
G-Class Sport Utility	112.2 in.	185.6 in.	5,545-5,590 lbs.
M-Class Sport Utility	111.0 in.	182.6 in.	4,819-4,874 lbs.
S-Class Sedan	121.5 in.	203.1 in.	4,160-4,610 lbs.
SL-Class Coupe/Roadster	100.8 in.	178.5 in.	4,065-4,429 lbs.
SLK-Class Coupe/Roadster	95.7 in.	160.7-160.9 in.	3,231-3,397 lbs.
M-Class Sport Utility	111.0 in.	182.6 in.	4,819-4,874 lbs.

both the intake and exhaust valves, which required separate camshafts for the intake and exhaust valves. This represented the first time Mercedes-Benz had used double-overhead camshaft technology on their V-6 engines.

One of the most powerful engines for its size, the 3.5-liter all-aluminum V-6 produced 268 horsepower and 258 lbs.-ft. or torque, with maximum torque available from 2,500 rpm all the way up to 5,000 rpm. Beginning at 1,500 rpm the new V-6 developed 87 percent of its maximum torque.

Mercedes-Benz also debuted the world's first diesel engine with CDI, which stands for Common-rail Direct Injection. The first fully electronic fuel injection system for diesels, the CDI system instantly created a new paradigm for the diesel industry. CDI electronic injection provides much more precise control of injection quantity, simultaneously making more power while producing lower exhaust emissions with quieter operation.

Most electronic fuel injection systems, including those on gasoline engines, use a "common rail" or "ring main" fuel loop to supply the same pressurized fuel to all injector valves. However, the CDI system marked the first common-rail system for diesel engines and the 2005-model E320 CDI represented the first electronically injected Mercedes-Benz diesel to be marketed in the U.S.

Manufacturer: DaimlerChrysler AG, Stuttgart, Germany.

Distributor: Mercedes-Benz USA, Montvale, New Jersey

2005 S500

PERFORMANCE

Model	EPA Fuel Mileage Estimates	0-60 Acceleration	Top Speed
C-CLASS			
C230 Kompressor Sport Coupe (automatic)	23/32 City/Hwy	7.5 seconds	130 mph
C230 Kompressor Sport Coupe (manual)	23/31 City/Hwy	7.2 seconds	130 mph
C230 Kompressor Sport Sedan (automatic)	24/32 City/Hwy	7.8 seconds	130 mph
C230 Kompressor Sport Sedan (manual)	23/32 City/Hwy	7.6 seconds	130 mph
C240 Luxury Sedan (automatic)	20/25 City/Hwy	8.7 seconds	130 mph
C240 4Matic Luxury Sedan (automatic)	19/25 City/Hwy	N/A	130 mph
C240 4Matic Luxury Wagon (automatic)	20/25 City/Hwy	8.7 seconds	130 mph
C240 Luxury Wagon (automatic)	19/24 City/Hwy	N/A	130 mph
C320 Sport Coupe (automatic)	19/24 City/Hwy	6.9 seconds	130 mph

Model	EPA Fuel Mileage Estimates	0-60 Acceleration	Top Speed
C320 Sport Coupe (manual)	17/24 City/Hwy	6.8 seconds	130 mph
C320 Sport Sedan (automatic)	20/26 City/Hwy	6.9 seconds	130 mph
C320 Sport Sedan (manual)	19/26 City/Hwy	6.8 seconds	130 mph
C320 Luxury Sedan (automatic)	20/26 City/Hwy	6.9 seconds	130 mph
C320 4Matic Luxury Sedan (automatic)	19/26 City/Hwy	N/A	130 mph
C55 AMG Sedan	16/22 City/Hwy	4.9 seconds	155 mph

CL-CLASS

CL500 Coupe	16/24 City/Hwy	6.1 seconds	130 mph
CL55 AMG Coupe	14/22 City/Hwy	4.6 seconds	155 mph
CL600 Coupe	13/19 City/Hwy	4.6 seconds	155 mph
CL65 AMG Coupe	12/19 City/Hwy	4.2 seconds	155 mph

CLK-CLASS

CLK320 Coupe	20/28 City/Hwy	7.4 seconds	130 mph
CLK320 Cabriolet	20/26 City/Hwy	8.0 seconds	130 mph
CLK500 Coupe	17/25 City/Hwy	5.6 seconds	130 mph
CLK500 Cabriolet	17/25 City/Hwy	5.9 seconds	130 mph
CLK55 AMG Coupe	16/22 City/Hwy	5.0 seconds	155 mph
CLK55 AMG Cabriolet	16/22 City/Hwy	5.2 seconds	155 mph

E-CLASS

E320 Sedan	20/28 City/Hwy	7.1 seconds	130 mph
E320 4Matic Sedan	19/25 City/Hwy	N/A	130 mph
E320 Wagon	20/28 City/Hwy	7.5 seconds	130 mph
E320 4Matic Wagon	18/24 City/Hwy	N/A	130 mph
E320 CDI	27/37 City/Hwy	6.6 seconds	130 mph
E500 Sedan	17/25 City/Hwy	5.9 seconds	130 mph
E500 4Matic Sedan	16/20 City/Hwy	N/A	130 mph
E500 4Matic Wagon	16/20 City/Hwy	N/A	130 mph
E55 AMG	14/21 City/Hwy	4.5 seconds	155 mph

G-CLASS

G500	13/14 City/Hwy	N/A	125 mph
G55 AMG	12/14 City/Hwy	5.5 seconds	130 mph

M-CLASS

ML350	15/18 City/Hwy	8.5 seconds	130 mph
ML500	14/17 City/Hwy	7.3 seconds	130 mph

S-CLASS

S430 Sedan	17/26 City/Hwy	6.9 seconds	130 mph
S430 4Matic Sedan	17/22 City/Hwy	N/A	130 mph
S500 Sedan	16/24 City/Hwy	6.1 seconds	130 mph
S500 4Matic Sedan	16/22 City/Hwy	N/A	130 mph
S55 AMG Sedan	14/22 City/Hwy	4.6 seconds	155 mph
S600 Sedan	12/19 City/Hwy	4.6 seconds	155 mph

SL-CLASS

SL500 Coupe/Roadster	16/23 City/Hwy	6.1 seconds	155 mph
SL55 AMG Coupe/Roadster	14/20 City/Hwy	4.5 seconds	155 mph
SL600 Coupe/Roadster	13/19 City/Hwy	4.5 seconds	155 mph
SL65 AMG Coupe/Roadster	12/19 City/Hwy	4.2 seconds	155 mph

SLK-CLASS

SLK350 Kompressor (automatic) Cpe/Roadster	19/25 City/Hwy	5.5 seconds	155 mph
SLK350 Kompressor (manual) Coupe/Roadster	18/25 City/Hwy	5.4 seconds	155 mph
SLK55 AMG (automatic) Coupe/Roadster	N/A	4.9 seconds	155 mph

2005 SLK350

2005 CLS55

2006

C-CLASS: An all-sedan lineup featured a range of new four-valve, twin-cam V-6 engines: 201 hp 2.5-liter V-6 in the C230, 228 hp 3.0-liter for the C280, and a 268 hp 3.5-liter C350.

New active front head restraints were standard on the entire C-Class line.

CL-CLASS: AMG Sport Package was standard on the CL500 and CL600. Keyless Go, heated steering wheel, and an electronic truck closer were also now standard on the CL600.

CLK-CLASS: A facelift for the CLK Coupes and Cabriolets included a new grill and redesigned taillights. New active front head restraints standard on entire CLK line. The CLK320 was replaced by the CLK350 with a 3.5-liter, 268 hp four-valve V-6 and seven-speed automatic CLK350 also gets new wheels and front apron. The CLK500 received a sportier interior and AMG exhaust.

CLS-CLASS: The first-ever four-door coupe — another totally new class. Two models — the 302 hp CLS500 and the 469 hp CLS55 AMG were introduced. New active front head restraints were standard on both CLS models.

E-CLASS: The E320 was replaced by the E350 model (3.5-liter, twin-cam, four-valve per-cylinder V-6 engine). New active front head restraints were standard on the entire E-Class line with new 17-inch wheels for the E350 and E500 models.

G-CLASS: The Grand Edition G-Class model debuted in the summer of 2005. It was a special badged, numbered edition offered throughout the year.

M-CLASS: An all-new second-generation M-Class re-established the benchmark among luxury Sport Utilitys. Two-models were offered, a 268 hp 3.5-liter V-6-powered ML350 and the 302 hp 5.0-liter V-8 ML500. A seven-speed automatic transmission with Direct Select column-mounted shifter was standard.

R-CLASS: An entirely new class of Mercedes-Benz vehicles was introduced. It was a new way for six adults to travel. It combined the all-weather traction of a Sport Utility with station wagon versatility and sports sedan performance. Two models, a 268 hp 3.5-liter V-6-powered R350 and a 302 hp 5.0-liter V-8 R500 were offered.

S-CLASS: A new S65 AMG model with 604 hp V-12. It was the world's quickest four-door: 0-60 mph in 4.2 seconds. The AMG Sport Package was a no-cost option on the S430 and S500 rear-wheel-drive models. 4Matic all-wheel drive was a no-cost option for S430 and S500. Keyless Go, heated

steering wheel, electronic truck closer, and rear side blinds were standard on the S600.

SL-CLASS: Run-flat tires were a new option for the flagship roadster. Also, new 18-inch double-spoke wheels for the AMG Sport Package. Keyless Go, heated steering wheel, and corner illuminating fog lights were now standard on SL600.

SLK-CLASS: A new SLK280 model joined the SLK55 AMG and SLK350 Roadsters. The SLK280 featured a 3.0-liter, 228 hp version of the new twin-cam V-6 engine.

MODEL	BODY TYPE	ENGINE TYPE	MSRP	NOTES
C-CLASS				
C230	Sport Sedan	V-6	$29,975	
C280	Sedan	V-6	$33,725	
C350	Sport Sedan	V-6	$38,325	
C350	Sedan	V-6	$38,925	
C55 AMG	Sedan	V-8	$55,225	
CL-CLASS				
CL500	Coupe	V-8	$96,275	
CL55 AMG	Coupe	V-8	$121,275	
CL600	Coupe	V-12	$130,275	
CL65 AMG	Coupe	V-12	$180,375	
CLK-CLASS				
CLK350	Coupe	V-6	$46,525	
CLK350	Cabriolet	V-6	$54,475	
CLK500	Coupe	V-8	$55,125	
CLK500	Cabriolet	V-8	$63,075	
CLK55 AMG	Cabriolet	V-8	$83,275	
CLS-CLASS				
CLS500	Coupe	V-8	$65,675	New for 2006
CLS55 AMG	Coupe	V-8	$87,375	New for 2006
E-CLASS				
E350	Sedan	V-6	$50,825	
E350	Wagon	V-6	$53,075	
E320 CDI	Sedan	Inline-6	$51,825	
E500	Sedan	V-8	$59,175	
E500 4Matic	Wagon	V-8	$62,775	
E55 AMG	Sedan	V-8	$82,575	
E55 AMG	Wagon	V-8	$83,375	New for 2006
G-CLASS				
G500 Grand Edition	Sport Utility	V-8	$ 81,675	
G55 AMG Grand Edition	Sport Utility	V-8	$105,275	
ML-CLASS				
ML350	Sport Utility	V-6	$40,525	
ML500	Sport Utility	V-8	$49,275	
R-CLASS				
R350	Sports Tourer	V-6	$48,775	New for 2006
R500	Sports Tourer	V-8	$56,275	New for 2006
S-CLASS				
S350	Sedan	V-6	$65,675	New model
S430	Sedan	V-8	$78,025	
S500	Sedan	V-8	$86,825	
S55 AMG	Sedan	V-8	$114,925	
S600	Sedan	V-12	$128,725	
S65 AMG	Sedan	V-12	$169,775	New model
SL500	Coupe/Roadster	V-8	$93,675	
SL55 AMG	Coupe/Roadster	V-8	$ 125,775	
SL600	Coupe/Roadster	V-12	$131,675	
SL65 AMG	Coupe/Roadster	V-12	$185,775	
SLK-CLASS				
SLK280	Coupe/Roadster	V-6	$43,675	New for 2006
SLK350	Coupe/Roadster	V-6	$47,725	
SLK55 AMG	Coupe/Roadster	V-8	$62,275	

Note: The 4Matic option was available on the C280 and C350 models for $1,800, on the E350 sedan/wagon and E500 sedan for $2,500, and on the S430 and S500 sedans at no cost.

2006 CLS55 AMG

2006 CLK350 cabriolet

2006 CLK350 cabriolet

ENGINES

The high-tech engine that made its debut on the new-generation SLK coupe/roadster now powered many 2006 Mercedes-Benz models. Available this year in three different displacements, the latest V-6 engine featured four valves per cylinder and variable valve timing for both the intake and exhaust valves. This engine family represented the first time Mercedes-Benz had used double-overhead camshaft technology on their V-6 powerplants.

During the 1990s one of the most advanced engine technologies in the auto industry featured three valves per cylinder, in which a single exhaust valve kept exhaust temperature high and emissions low. In the ensuing years, Mercedes engineers developed new ways to minimize emissions, allowing them to utilize higher-flow four-valve architecture for the new engine family.

One of the most powerful engines for its size, the 3.5-liter

2006 S55 AMG

2006 ML500

aluminum block and heads V-6 produced 268 horsepower and 258 lbs.-ft. of torque with maximum torque available from 2,500 rpm all the way up to 5,000 rpm. Already from 1,500 rpm, the new V-6 developed 87 percent of its maximum torque. In addition to the SLK coupe/roadster, the 3.5-liter engine powered the C350 and E350 sedans, the new R350 Sports Tourer, the ML350 sport utility, and the CLK350 coupe and cabriolet models.

Also a 228 hp 3.0-liter version of the new-technology V-6 powered the C280 sedan, and the C230 sedan now came with a 201 hp, 2.5-liter version of the same basic engine.

Manufacturer: DaimlerChrysler AG, Stuttgart, Germany.

Distributor: Mercedes-Benz USA, Montvale, New Jersey

PERFORMANCE

MODEL	DRIVETRAIN	EPA FUEL MILEAGE ESTIMATES	0-60 ACCELERATION	TOP SPEED
C-CLASS				
C230 Sport Sedan	7-speed Automatic	21/30 City/Hwy	8.3 seconds	130 mph
C230 Sport Sedan	6-speed Manual	21/29 City/Hwy	8.1 seconds	130 mph
C280 Sedan	7-speed Automatic	21/28 City/Hwy	7.0 seconds	130 mph
C280 4Matic Sedan	5-speed Automatic	19/26 City/Hwy	7.4 seconds	130 mph
C350 Sport Sedan	6-speed Manual	20/28 City/Hwy	6.2 seconds	130 mph
C350 Sedan	7-speed Automatic	20/29 City/Hwy	6.2 seconds	130 mph
C350 4Matic Sedan	5-speed Automatic	19/24 City/Hwy	6.7 seconds	130 mph
C55 AMG Sedan	5-speed Automatic	17/22 City/Hwy	4.9 seconds	155 mph
CL-CLASS				
CL500 Coupe	7-speed Automatic	16/24 City/Hwy	6.1 seconds	130 mph
CL55 AMG Coupe	5-speed Automatic	15/22 City/Hwy	4.6 seconds	155 mph
CL600 Coupe	5-speed Automatic	13/19 City/Hwy	4.6 seconds	155 mph
CL65 AMG Coupe	5-speed Automatic	13/20 City/Hwy	4.2 seconds	155 mph
CLK-CLASS				
CLK350 Coupe	7-speed Automatic	19/28 City/Hwy	6.4 seconds	130 mph
CLK350 Cabriolet	7-speed Automatic	18/27 City/Hwy	6.7 seconds	130 mph
CLK500 Coupe	7-speed Automatic	17/25 City/Hwy	5.7 seconds	130 mph
CLK500 Cabriolet	7-speed Automatic	17/25 City/Hwy	6.0 seconds	130 mph
CLK55 AMG Cabriolet	5-speed Automatic	16/22 City/Hwy	5.2 seconds	155 mph
CLS-CLASS				
CLS500 Coupe	7-speed Automatic	16/22 City/Hwy	5.9 seconds	155 mph
CLS55 AMG Coupe	5-speed Automatic	14/20 City/Hwy	4.5 seconds	155 mph
E-CLASS				
E350 Sedan	7-speed Automatic	19/27 City/Hwy	6.5 seconds	130 mph
E350 4Matic Sedan	5-speed Automatic	18/24 City/Hwy	N/A	130 mph
E350 Wagon	7-speed Automatic	18/26 City/Hwy	6.9 seconds	130 mph
E350 4Matic Wagon	5-speed Automatic	18/24 City/Hwy	N/A	130 mph
E320 CDI Sedan	5-speed Automatic	27/37 City/Hwy	6.6 seconds	130 mph
E500 Sedan	7-speed Automatic	17/25 City/Hwy	5.9 seconds	130 mph
E500 4Matic Sedan	5-speed Automatic	16/20 City/Hwy	N/A	130 mph
E500 4Matic Wagon	5-speed Automatic	16/20 City/Hwy	N/A	130 mph
E55 AMG Sedan	5-speed Automatic	15/21 City/Hwy	4.5 seconds	155 mph
E55 AMG Wagon	5-speed Automatic	15/21 City/Hwy	4.5 seconds	155 mph
G-CLASS				
G500 Sport Utility	5-speed Automatic	13/14 City/Hwy	N/A	125 mph
G55 AMG Sport Utility	5-speed Automatic	12/14 City/Hwy	N/A	130 mph
ML-CLASS				
ML350 Sport Utility	7-speed Automatic	16/20 City/Hwy	8.2 seconds	131 mph
ML500 Sport Utility	7-speed Automatic	14/19 City/Hwy	6.7 seconds	131 mph

R-CLASS

R350 4Matic Sports Tourer	7-speed Automatic	16/21 City/Hwy	7.8 seconds	130 mph
R500 4Matic Sports Tourer	7-speed Automatic	13/18 City/Hwy	6.5 seconds	130 mph

S-CLASS

S350 Sedan	7-speed Automatic	17/25 City/Hwy	7.6 seconds	130 mph
S430 Sedan	7-speed Automatic	17/26 City/Hwy	6.9 seconds	130 mph
S430 4Matic Sedan	5-speed Automatic	17/22 City/Hwy	6.1 seconds	130 mph
S500 Sedan	7-speed Automatic	16/24 City/Hwy	6.1 seconds	130 mph
S500 4Matic Sedan	5-speed Automatic	16/22 City/Hwy	N/A	130 mph
S55 AMG Sedan	5-speed Automatic	15/22 City/Hwy	4.6 seconds	155 mph
S600 Sedan	5-speed Automatic	12/19 City/Hwy	4.6 seconds	155 mph
S65 AMG Sedan	5-speed Automatic	13/20 City/Hwy	4.2 seconds	155 mph

SL-CLASS

SL500 Coupe/Roadster	7-speed Automatic	16/24 City/Hwy	6.1 seconds	155 mph
SL55 AMG Coupe/Roadster	5-speed Automatic	14/20 City/Hwy	4.5 seconds	155 mph
SL600 Coupe/Roadster	7-speed Automatic	13/19 City/Hwy	4.5 seconds	155 mph
SL65 AMG Coupe/Roadster	5-speed Automatic	13/19 City/Hwy	4.2 seconds	155 mph

SLK-CLASS

SLK280 Coupe/Roadster	6-speed Manual	19/27 City/Hwy	6.1 seconds	155 mph
SLK280 Coupe/Roadster	7-speed Automatic	20/27 City/Hwy	6.1 seconds	155 mph
SLK350 Coupe/Roadster	6-speed Manual	18/25 City/Hwy	5.4 seconds	155 mph
SLK350 Coupe/Roadster	7-speed Automatic	19/24 City/Hwy	5.5 seconds	155 mph
SLK55 AMG Coupe/Roadster	7-speed Automatic	16/22 City/Hwy	4.8 seconds	155 mph

Note: Most models are rear-wheel-drive; 4Matic models were all-wheel-drive.

2006 R500

2006 SLK350

2006 SL500

2007

The Mercedes-Benz product family featured the most diverse model offerings in the luxury segment consisting of the mid-size C-Class sport sedans, the full-size E-Class line of sedans and wagons in gasoline and diesel configurations; the popular SLK roadster; the stylish CLK coupes and cabriolets, the unique four-door CLS-Class coupes, the flagship S-Class sedans and CL coupes, and the renowned SL coupes/roadsters. Four light trucks rounded out the model offering: the American-made ML-Class, the iconic, no compromise off-road G-Class, the refined R-Class Sports Tourer, and the full-sized, seven-passenger GL-Class.

C-CLASS Sedan: New exclusive wheel designs for sport and luxury models. Sport sedans now had an AMG rear spoiler, AMG dual tip exhaust, and black birds-eye maple interior trim. The C280 luxury sedan now came standard with dual power front seats and steering column with memory. A flexible-fuel vehicle, the C230, now could use E85 ethanol as well as gasoline. The C55 AMG was discontinued — the 2007 line included the C230, C280, and C350 models.

CL-CLASS Coupe: A new-generation V-8-powered CL550 coupe (382 hp, 391 lbs.-ft.) had debuted in late 2006. A V-12-powered CL600 model (510 hp, 612 lbs.-ft.) followed shortly thereafter.

CLK-CLASS Coupe and Cabriolet: A high-performance CLK63 AMG Cabriolet (475 hp, 465 lbs.-ft.) replaced the 362 hp CLK55 AMG while the CLK550 (382 hp, 391 lbs.-ft.) replaced the 302 hp CLK500, joining the CLK350. An all-new Sports Appearance Package was introduced for the CLK350.

CLS-CLASS Four-Door Coupe: The first-ever four-door coupes, all CLS-Class models were equipped with PRE-SAFE anticipatory safety system (from S-Class). Enhancements to the standard equipment included a 6-CD changer and harman/kardon sound system. The CLS550 (382 hp, 391 lbs.-ft) replaced the 302 hp CLS500, and the high-performance CLS63 AMG (507 hp, 465 lbs.-ft.) replaced the 469 hp CLS55 AMG.

E-CLASS Sedan and Wagon: A redesign featured a new front bumper, lower air dam, grille, headlights, and taillights. Enhancements to the standard equipment included a sunroof, 6-CD changer and harman/kardon sound system. A sport model included 18-inch wheels, lowered sport suspension, dual-chrome exhaust outlets, and birds-eye maple trim. All E-Class models received PRE-SAFE anticipatory safety system (from the S-Class). The E550 (382 hp, 391 lbs.-ft.) replaced the 302 hp E500, joining the E350 and new AMG and diesel models. A high-performance E63 AMG (507 hp, 465 lbs.-

Model	Body Type	Engine Type	MSRP
C-CLASS			
C230	Sport Sedan	V-6	$29,975
C280	Luxury Sedan	V-6	$33,725
C350	Sport Sedan	V-6	$37,325
CL-CLASS			
CL550	Coupe	V-8	$103,925
CL600	Coupe	V-12	$147,725
CL63 AMG	Coupe	V-8	$137,825
CL65 AMG	Coupe	V-12	$197,825
CLK-CLASS			
CLK350	Coupe	V-6	$47,025
CLK350	Cabriolet	V-6	$55,025
CLK550	Coupe	V-6	$55,725
CLK550	Cabriolet	V-6	$63,725
CLK63 AMG	Cabriolet	V-8	$90,025
CLK63 Black Series	Coupe	V-8	$135,825
CLS-CLASS			
CLS550	Coupe	V-8	$68,425
CLS63 AMG	Coupe	V-8	$94,025
E-CLASS			
E350	Sedan	V-6	$51,725
E350 4Matic	Sedan	V-6	$53,225
E320 BlueTEC	Sedan	V-6	$52,725
E350 4Matic	Wagon	V-6	$56,525
E550	Sedan	V-8	$60,225
E550 4Matic	Sedan	V-8	$61,725
E63 AMG	Sedan	V-8	$85,825
E63 AMG	Wagon	V-8	$86,625
G-CLASS			
G500	Sport Utility	V-8	$87,025
G55 AMG	Sport Utility	V-8	$110,725
GL-CLASS			
GL320 CDI	Sport Utility	V-6	$53,825
GL450	Sport Utility	V-8	$56,325
GL550	Sport Utility	V-8	$77,800
ML-CLASS			
ML320 CDI	Sport Utility	V-6	$45,475
ML350	Sport Utility	V-6	$44,475
ML550	Sport Utility	V-8	$53,225
ML63 AMG	Sport Utility	V-8	$87,475
R-CLASS			
R320 CDI 4WD	Sports Tourer	V-6	$46,225
R350 2WD	Sports Tourer	V-6	$42,725
R350	Sports Tourer	V-6	$45,225
R500	Sports Tourer	V-8	N/A
R63 AMG	Sports Tourer	V-8	N/A
S-CLASS			
S550	Sedan	V-8	$87,525
S550 4Matic	Sedan	V-8	$90,525
S600	Sedan	V-12	$145,025
S63 AMG	Sedan	V-8	$127,825
S65 AMG	Sedan	V-12	$194,825
SL-CLASS			
SL550	Coupe/Roadster	V-8	$$96,075
SL55 AMG	Coupe/Roadster	V-8	$130,075
SL600	Coupe/Roadster	V-12	$133,975
SL65 AMG	Coupe/Roadster	V-12	$187,975
SLK-CLASS			
SLK280	Coupe/Roadster	V-6	$44,725
SLK350	Coupe/Roadster	V-6	$50,025
SLK55 AMG	Coupe/Roadster	V-8	$63,775

ft.) replaced the 469 hp E55 AMG. And a super-clean E320 BlueTEC (208 hp, 388 lbs.-ft.) replaced the 201 hp E320 CDI diesel.

G-CLASS Sport Utility: The G500 and G55 AMG models continued. DVD navigation, Bi-Xenon headlights and seven-speed transmission were now standard. Also redesigned fog lamps and center console controls, a leather door handle grip, and improved front seat cushioning.

GL-CLASS Sport Utility: A totally new vehicle class. The first full-size Sport Utility from Mercedes-Benz. A V-8-powered GL450 (335 hp, 339 lbs.-ft.) made its debut. It featured luxurious seating for up to seven adults, with standard power folding third row seats.

M-CLASS Sport Utility: The ML63 AMG (503 hp, 465 lbs.-ft.) joined 268 hp ML350 and the 302 hp ML500. An efficient ML320 CDI diesel (221 hp, 398 lbs.-ft.) had joined the M-Class line-up in the fall of 2006.

R-CLASS Sports Tourer: An entirely new way for six adults to travel. A high-performance R63 AMG (507 hp, 465 lbs.-ft.) joined the 268 hp R350 and the 302 hp V-8 R500. The powerful R320 CDI diesel (221 hp, 398 lbs.-ft.) had joined the R-Class line in the fall of 2006.

S-CLASS Sedan: The ninth-generation S-Class debuted with the S550 (382 hp, 391 lbs.-ft.) in 2006 and two V-12-powered models followed: the S600 (510 hp, 612 lbs.-ft.) in spring and S65 AMG (604 hp, 738 lbs.-ft.) in summer.

SL-CLASS Coupe/Roadster: A redesign included more direct steering, deeper front air dam, new wheel designs, new 3-bar grille, clear taillights, and new interior colors. The SL550 (382 hp, 391 lb.-ft) replaced the 302 hp SL500 and joined the SL55 AMG, SL600, and SL65 AMG. The SL55 AMG power increased to 510 hp, 531 lbs.-ft. of torque and SL600 to 510 hp, 612 lbs.-ft. A 50th Anniversary Edition SL550 Roadster was offered early in the year to honor the first 300SL Roadster.

SLK-CLASS Coupe/Roadster: The SLK280, SLK350, and SLK55 AMG models continued. An enhanced AMG Sport Package and a new Appearance Package for SLK280 andSLK350 were available.

Accessory Note: Mercedes-Benz USA offered a convenient, high-tech accessory that allowed most Apple iPods to be docked in the glove box and played through the car's audio system. Even more impressive, iPod menus, playlists, and artist/title information appeared in the car's multifunction dash display and the driver could scroll through and choose selections using multifunction buttons on the steering wheel. The iPod interface made use of the audio system speakers as well as features such as a speed-sensitive volume control and the iPod was also kept charged while it was docked in the glove box.

The optional iPod integration system provided room in the glove box for up to 15,000 songs – the equivalent of nearly 1,000 CDs, which would have otherwise filled at least five suitcases. iPod integration was available for most Mercedes-Benz models, including the 2007 GL-Class sport utility, the R-Class sports tourer, the M-Class sport utility, SLK roadsters (only with optional COMAND), CLS coupe, and CLK vehicles, as well as E- and C-Class sedans and wagons. In addition, an enhanced iPod integration kit was available for the new-generation 2007 S-Class Sedan, which took full advantage of the car's advanced on-board electronics. The iPod kit could be retrofitted on the 2004 E-Class as well as several models back to the 2005 model year.

2007 SLK top folding

2007 R320 CDI

2007 CLS550

2007 G55

CHASSIS

Model	Wheelbase	Length	Weight
C-Class Sedan	108.7 in.	182.1 in.	3,421-3,498 lbs.
CL-Class Coupe	116.3 in.	199.4 in.	4,486-4,599 lbs.
CLK-Class Coupe and Cabriolet	106.9 in.	183.2 in.	3,585-3,960 lbs.
CLS-Class Coupe	112.4 in.	193.0 in.	4,020-4,210 lbs.
E-Class Sedan and Wagon	112.4 in.	192.3 in.	3,860-4,035 lbs.
G-Class Sport Utility	112.2 in.	185.6 in.	5545-5590 lbs.
GL-Class Sport Utility	121.1 in.	200.3 in.	5249-5313 lbs.
M-Class Sport Utility	114.7 in.	189.8 in.	4706-5093 lbs.
R-Class Sports Tourer	126.6 in.	203.0 in.	4829-5236 lbs.
S-Class Sedan	124.6 in.	205.0 in.	4270-4985 lbs.
SL-Class Coupe/Roadster	100.8 in.	178.5 in.	4220-4555 lbs.
SLK-Class Coupe/Roadster	95.7 in.	160.9 in.	3215-3420 lbs.

ENGINES

The 2007 model year marked the debut of a new Mercedes-Benz family of all-aluminum V-8 engines featuring four-valve-per-cylinder technology and variable valve timing, First, a 5.5-liter delivered 382 horsepower and 391 lbs.-ft. of torque in the new-generation S-Class sedan, followed by a 4.6-liter, 335-horsepower version in the new GL-Class sport utility. Beginning in the fall of 2006, the new 5.5-liter powerplant also replaced the previous 5.0-liter V-8 in five other classes. The SL roadster, the CLS coupe, the E-class sedan and wagon, the CLK coupe and cabriolet, and late in 2006, the new-generation CL coupe.

In the 1990s one of the most advanced engine technologies in the auto industry featured three valves per cylinder. In it, a single exhaust valve kept exhaust temperature high and emissions low. In the ensuing years, Mercedes engineers have developed new ways to minimize emissions, allowing them to utilize higher-flow four-valve technology for the new engine family.

2007 S-Class interior

PERFORMANCE

MODEL	DRIVETRAIN	EPA FUEL MILEAGE ESTIMATES	0-60 ACCELERATION	TOP SPEED
C-CLASS				
C300 Sedan	6-speed Manual	N/A	7.2*	130 mph
C300 Sedan	7-speed Automatic	N/A	7.2*	130 mph
C300 4Matic Sedan	5-speed Automatic	19/24	N/A	130 mph
C350 Sport Sedan	6-speed Manual	20/28	6.3*	130 mph
C350 Luxury Sedan	7-speed Automatic	20/29	6.3*	130 mph
CL-CLASS				
CL550 Coupe	7-speed Automatic	15/22	5.3	130 mph
CL600 Coupe	5-speed Automatic	13/19	4.5	130 mph

CLK-CLASS

Model	Transmission	MPG	0-60	Top Speed
CLK350 Coupe	7-speed Automatic	19/28	6.4	130 mph
CLK350 Cabriolet	7-speed Automatic	19/28	6.7	130 mph
CLK550 Coupe	7-speed Automatic	16/23	5.7	130 mph
CLK550 Cabriolet	7-speed Automatic	16/24	6	130 mph
CLK63 AMG Cabriolet	5-speed Automatic	13/20	4.5	155 mph

CLS-CLASS

Model	Transmission	MPG	0-60	Top Speed
CLS550 Coupe	7-speed Automatic	15/22	5.4	155 mph
CLS63 AMG Coupe	5-speed Automatic	13/20	4.3	155 mph

E-CLASS

Model	Transmission	MPG	0-60	Top Speed
E320 BlueTEC Sedan	7-speed Automatic	26/35	6.6	130 mph
E350 Sedan	7-speed Automatic	19/26	6.5	130 mph
E350 4Matic Sedan	5-speed Automatic	18/24	N/A	130 mph
E350 Wagon	7-speed Automatic	18/26	6.9	130 mph
E350 4Matic Wagon	5-speed Automatic	18/24	N/A	130 mph
E550 Sedan	7-speed Automatic	15/23	5.4	130 mph
E550 4Matic Sedan	5-speed Automatic	15/22	N/A	130 mph
E63 AMG Sedan	5-speed Automatic	14/20	4.3	155 mph
E63 AMG Wagon	5-speed Automatic	14/20	4.3	155 mph

G-CLASS

Model	Transmission	MPG	0-60	Top Speed
G500 Sport Utility	5-speed Automatic	13/14	N/A	125 mph
G55 AMG Sport Utility	5-speed Automatic	12/14	N/A	130 mph

GL-CLASS

Model	Transmission	MPG	0-60	Top Speed
GL320 CDI Sport Utility	7-speed Automatic	20/25	N/A	130 mph
GL450 Sport Utility	7-speed Automatic	14/18	7.4	130 mph

ML-CLASS

Model	Transmission	MPG	0-60	Top Speed
ML320 CDI Sport Utility	7-speed Automatic	21/27	7.9	131 mph
ML350 Sport Utility	7-speed Automatic	17/21	7.9	131 mph
ML500 Sport Utility	7-speed Automatic	14/19	6.7	131 mph
ML63 AMG Sport Utility	7-speed Automatic	12/16	4.8	155 mph

R-CLASS

Model	Transmission	MPG	0-60	Top Speed
R320 CDI 4Matic Sports Tourer	7-speed Automatic	21/28	8.0	130 mph
R350 4Matic Sports Tourer	7-speed Automatic	16/21	7.8	130 mph
R500 4Matic Sports Tourer	7-speed Automatic	14/19	6.5	130 mph
R63 AMG Sports Tourer	7-speed Automatic	12/16	4.9	155 mph

S-CLASS

Model	Transmission	MPG	0-60	Top Speed
S550 Sedan	7-speed Automatic	16/24	5.4	130 mph
S550 4Matic Sedan	7-speed Automatic	15/22	N/A	130 mph
S600 Sedan	5-speed Automatic	12/19	4.5	130 mph
S65 AMG Sedan	5-speed Automatic	13/20	4.2	155 mph

SL-CLASS

Model	Transmission	MPG	0-60	Top Speed
SL550 Coupe/Roadster	7-speed Automatic	14/22	5.3	155 mph
SL55 AMG Coupe/Roadster	5-speed Automatic	14/19	4.4	155 mph
SL600 Coupe/Roadster	7-speed Automatic	13/19	4.4	155 mph
SL65 AMG Coupe/Roadster	5-speed Automatic	13/19	4.2	155 mph

SLK-CLASS

Model	Transmission	MPG	0-60	Top Speed
SLK280 Coupe/Roadster	6-speed Manual	20/27	6.1	155 mph
SLK280 Coupe/Roadster	7-speed Automatic	20/27	6.1	155 mph
SLK350 Coupe/Roadster	6-speed Manual	18/25	5.4	155 mph
SLK350 Coupe/Roadster	7-speed Automatic	19/25	5.5	155 mph
SLK55 AMG Coupe/Roadster	7-speed Automatic	16/22	4.8	155 mph

* Preliminary

Note: Most models were rear-wheel-drive; 4Matic models are all-wheel-drive

The latest four-valve architecture actually made its debut on the Mercedes-Benz V-6 that powered the new-generation SLK coupe/roadster and was now available in three different displacements. The 3.5-liter V-6 produced 268 horsepower and 258 lbs.-ft. of torque, with maximum torque available from 2,500 rpm all the way up to 5,000 rpm. In addition to the SLK Coupe/Roadster, the 3.5-liter engine powered the C350 and E350 sedans, the R350 sports Tourer, the ML350 sport utility, and the CLK350 coupe and cabriolet models. In addition, a 228 hp 3.0-liter version of the new-technology V-6 powered the C280 sedan, and the C230 sedan came with a 201 hp, 2.5-liter version of the same basic engine.

BlueTEC technology made Mercedes-Benz the pioneer of a new generation of clean and powerful high-tech vehicles with highly effective exhaust gas treatment systems that gave them the potential to fulfill the world's most stringent emission limits in the future. At the same time, the basic technology for turbocharging and common-rail direct injection used in Mercedes CDI diesel engines had already proved itself in millions of vehicles in Europe.

BlueTEC ensures that diesels will continue to offer outstanding driving pleasure in the future, especially in the U.S. What's more, in view of continually rising fuel prices, BlueTEC represented the best choice for today and tomorrow.

The Mercedes-Benz E320 BlueTEC offered outstanding driving dynamics, unprecedented efficiency, and impressive environmental compatibility. Its three-liter V-6 engine combined the powerful torque of a large V-8 engine with the low fuel consumption of a four-cylinder compact. The E320 BlueTEC accelerated from 0 to 60 mph in just 6.6 seconds, making it one of the sportiest luxury sedans on the market.

Its tremendous torque of 400 lbs.-ft. exceeds most V-8-powered models. At the same time, the Mercedes-Benz E320 BlueTEC achieves 35 miles per gallon (6.7 liters/100 km) in combined cycle driving: a level of fuel efficiency normally found only in a compact car. The full-size E-Class vehicle was also environmentally friendly as a result of its excellent fuel economy and extremely low emissions.

The BlueTEC concept utilizes state-of-the-art diesel engines featuring common-rail direct injection, thereby providing all the benefits this drive system has to offer. Fuel consumption in these diesel vehicles was 20 to 40 percent lower than in cars equipped with a comparable gasoline engine. Torque, the key indicator of engine power, was 30 to 50 percent higher.

Manufacturer: DaimlerChrysler AG, Stuttgart, Germany.

Distributor: Mercedes-Benz USA, Montvale, New Jersey.

2007 GL450

2008 C300 Luxury

2008

C-CLASS Sedan: New-generation V-6-powered sedan feat-ured three models: C300 Sport, C300 Luxury (228 hp, 221 lbs.-ft.), and C350 Sport (268 hp, 258 lbs.-ft.). Redesigned 4Matic all-wheel drive available on C300 Sport and Luxury models. C300 Sport automatic and C300 Luxury are flex-fuel capable: can use E85 ethanol as well as gasoline.

CL-CLASS Coupe: V-8-powered CL63 AMG model (518 hp, 465 lbs.-ft.) and V-12-powered CL65 AMG (604 hp, 738 lbs.-ft.) joined the CL550 (382 hp, 391 lbs.-ft.) and CL600 (510 hp, 612 lbs.-ft.).

Limited production CL65 AMG 40th Anniversary Edition was painted with exclusive "Liquid Metal" paint.

CLK-CLASS Coupe and Cabriolet: Race-inspired CLK63 AMG Black Series coupe (500 hp, 465 lbs.-ft.) joins CLK63 AMG cabriolet (475 hp, 465 lbs.-ft.), CLK550 (382 hp, 391 lbs.-ft.), and CLK350 (268 hp, 258 lbs.-ft.). CLK350 receives standard sport suspension and twin six-spoke 18-inch wheels.

CLS-CLASS Four-Door Coupe: Both models, CLS550 (382 hp, 391 lb.-ft.) and high-performance CLS63 AMG (507 hp, 465 lbs.-ft.), receive standard satellite radio and 18-inch seven-spoke wheels.

E-CLASS Sedan and Wagon: New AMG Sport package including AMG front and rear aprons, 18-inch five-spoke

MODEL	BODY TYPE	ENGINE TYPE	MSRP	NOTES
C-CLASS				
C300	Sport Sedan	V-6	$31,975	New for 2008
C300 4Matic	Sport Sedan	V-6	$35,215	New for 2008
C300	Luxury Sedan	V-6	$33,675	New for 2008
C300 4Matic	Luxury Sedan	V-6	$35,475	New for 2008
C350	Sport Sedan	V-6	$37,275	New for 2008
C63 AMG	Sedan	V-8	N/A	New for 2008
CL-CLASS				
CL550	Coupe	V-8	$103,875	
CL600	Coupe	V-12	$147,675	
CL63 AMG	Coupe	V-8	$137,775	New for 2008
CL65 AMG	Coupe	V-12	$197,775	New for 2008
CLK-CLASS				
CLK350	Coupe	V-6	$46,975	
CLK350	Cabriolet	V-6	$54,975	
CLK550	Coupe	V-8	$55,675	
CLK550	Cabriolet	V-8	$63,675	
CLK63 AMG	Cabriolet	V-8	$89,975	
CLK63 AMG Black Series	Coupe	V-8	$135,775	New for 2008
CLS-CLASS				
CLS550	Coupe	V-8	$68,375	
CLS63 AMG	Coupe	V-8	$93,975	
E-CLASS				
E320 BlueTEC	Sedan	V-6	$52,675	
E350	Sedan	V-6	$51,675	
E350 4Matic	Wagon	V-6	$56,475	
E550	Sedan	V-8	$60,175	
E550 4Matic	Sedan	V-8	$61,675	
E63 AMG	Sedan	V-8	$85,775	
E63 AMG	Wagon	V-8	$86,575	
G-CLASS				
G500	Sport Utility	V-8	$86,975	
G55 AMG	Sport Utility	V-8	$110,675	
GL-CLASS				
GL320 CDI	Sport Utility	V-6	$53,775	
GL450	Sport Utility	V-8	$56,275	
GL550	Sport Utility	V-8	$77,750	New for 2008
ML-CLASS				
ML320 CDI	Sport Utility	V-6	$45,425	
ML350	Sport Utility	V-6	$44,425	
ML550	Sport Utility	V-8	$53,175	New for 2008
ML63 AMG	Sport Utility	V-8	$87,425	
R-CLASS				
R320 CDI	Sports Tourer	V-6	$46,175	
R350 2WD	Sports Tourer	V-6	$42,675	New for 2008
R350 4Matic	Sports Tourer	V-6	$45,175	
S-CLASS				
S550	Sedan	V-8	$87,475	
S550 4Matic	Sedan	V-8	$90,475	
S600	Sedan	V-12	$144,975	
S63 AMG	Sedan	V-8	$127,775	New for 2008
S65 AMG	Sedan	V-12	$194,775	
SL-CLASS				
SL550	Coupe/Roadster	V-8	$96,075	
SL55 AMG	Coupe/Roadster	V-8	$130,075	
SL600	Coupe/Roadster	V-12	$133,975	
SL65 AMG	Coupe/Roadster	V-12	$187,975	
SLK-CLASS				
SLK280	Coupe/Roadster	V-6	$44,675	
SLK350	Coupe/Roadster	V-6	$49,975	
SLK55 AMG	Coupe/Roadster	V-8	$63,725	

2008 CL600

2008 C300 Sport

2008 CLS550

2008 CLK550

CHASSIS

Model	Wheelbase	Length	Weight
C-Class Sedan	108.7 in.	182.3 in.	3,560-3,737 lbs.
CL-Class Coupe	116.3 in.	200.2 in.	4,485-5,016 lbs.
CLK-Class Coupe and Cabriolet	106.9 in.	183.4 in.	3,585-3,948 lbs.
CLS-Class Coupe	112.4 in.	194.0 in.	4,020-4,210 lbs.
E-Class Sedan and Wagon	112.4 in.	191.0 in.	3,740-4,035 lbs.
G-Class Sport Utility	112.2 in.	185.6 in.	5,545-5,590 lbs.
GL-Class Sport Utility	121.1 in.	200.6 in.	5,280-5,434 lbs.
M-Class Sport Utility	114.7 in.	188.5 in.	4,706-5,093 lbs.
R-Class Sports Tourer	126.6 in.	203.7 in.	4,817-5,092 lbs.
S-Class Sedan	124.6 in.	205.0 in.	4,465-5,035 lbs.
SL-Class Coupe/Roadster	100.8 in.	178.5 in.	4,220-4,555 lbs.
SLK-Class Coupe/Roadster	95.7 in.	160.7 in.	3,215-3,420 lbs.

2008 E350

wheels, dual chrome exhaust tips, and AMG steering wheel with shift paddles available on E350, E550 Sedan. E320 BlueTEC (210 hp, 388 lbs.-ft.) E350 (268 hp, 258 lbs.-ft.), E550 (382 hp, 391 lbs.-ft.), and E63 AMG sedan and wagon (507 hp, 465 lbs.-ft.) models continue. 4Matic all-wheel drive available on the E350 and E550.

G-CLASS Sport Utility: G500 (292 hp, 336 lbs.-ft.) and G55 AMG (493 hp, 516 lbs.-ft.) models continue. Both models receive a new instrument cluster, steering wheel, rear-view camera, taillight design, and hands-free communication/telephone interface. G500 receives a 7-speed automatic transmission (G55 AMG continues with a 5-speed automatic transmission).

GL-CLASS Sport Utility: GL550 (382 hp, 391 lbs.-ft.) joins award-winning GL450 model (335 hp, 339 lbs.-ft.) and GL320 CDI (210 hp, 388 lbs.-ft.). The GL550 is differentiated with a new grill, fender flares, and 21-inch wheels. The seven-passenger, full-size sport utility was a totally new vehicle class for Mercedes-Benz.

M-CLASS Sport Utility: ML550 (382 hp, 391 lbs.-ft.) replaced the ML500. ML550 gets standard AMG body styling, 19-inch AMG wheels, running boards, and power sunroof. The ML350 (268 hp, 258 lbs.-ft.) and ML320 CDI (215 hp, 398 lbs.-ft.) receive standard 19-inch five-spoke wheels, chrome grill and trim, blue glass, and power glass sunroof. ML350 Edition 10 features unique trim parts and two-tone interior. This limited edition commemorated the M-Class' ten-year anniversary. ML63 AMG (503 hp, 465 lb.-ft) remained unchanged.

R-CLASS Sports Tourer: R350 was now available with two-wheel or all-wheel drive. Seven passenger seating now available (three-seat second row). R320 CDI diesel (221 hp, 398 lbs.-ft.) and R350 (268 hp, 258 lbs.-ft) continue. All models come with standard AMG body styling and 18" wheels. R500 and R63 AMG models discontinued.

S-CLASS Sedan: V-8-powered S63 AMG model (518 hp, 465 lbs.-ft.) joined the S550 (382 hp, 391 lbs.-ft.), S600 (510 hp, 612 lbs.-ft.) and V-12-powered S65 AMG (604 hp, 738 lbs.-ft.).

A redesigned 4Matic all-wheel drive (lighter, more fuel-efficient) was available on the S550.

SL-CLASS Coupe/Roadster: New 18-inch 5-twin-spoke wheels standard for SL550. Premium Nappa Leather was now available as part of the SL550 trim package. SL550 (382 hp, 391 lb.-ft), SL55 AMG (510 hp, 531 lbs.-ft.), SL600 (510 hp, 612 lbs.-ft.), and SL65 AMG (604 hp, 738 lbs.-ft.) models continued.

SLK-CLASS Coupe/Roadster: SLK280 (228 hp, 221 lbs.-ft.), SLK350 (268 hp, 258 lbs.-ft.), and SLK55 AMG (355 hp, 376 lbs.-ft.) models continue. Ten-Year Anniversary SLK350 included standard automatic transmission, 17-inch wheels, Edition 10 emblems, red stitching on seats, and red dash trim.

NOTE: Mercedes-Benz USA offered fully integrated satellite radio in more than 80-percent of its 2008 model line. Satellite radio was now standard equipment on the S-Class sedan and the CLS coupe, as well as on SL roadsters, CL coupes, and all AMG and V-12-powered models. Available in the contiguous United States, SIRIUS satellite radio offered multiple benefits over conventional AM and FM radio. Any satellite radio channel could be tuned in from coast to coast, enabling the listener to drive across the country without having to change the channel.

The equipment needed to receive satellite radio was specifically engineered for each Mercedes-Benz model and fully integrated into the Mercedes-Benz audio system. Along with the familiar mode buttons for CD, phone, and radio on the audio system head unit, one labeled "SAT" accessed the satellite radio. MBUSA continues to offer the first six months of SIRIUS service in any vehicle equipped with satellite radio.

PERFORMANCE

Model	Transmission	EPA Fuel Mileage Est.	0-60 Acceleration	Top Speed
C-CLASS				
C300 Sport Sedan	6-speed Manual	18/26 City/Hwy	7.2*	130 mph
C300 Luxury Sedan	7-speed Automatic	18/25 City/Hwy	7.2*	130 mph
C300 4Matic Luxury Sedan	5-speed Automatic	17/25 City/Hwy	N/A	130 mph
C350 Sport Sedan	7-speed Automatic	17/25 City/Hwy	6.3*	130 mph
CL-CLASS				
CL550 Coupe	7-speed Automatic	14/21 City/Hwy	5.3	130 mph
CL600 Coupe	5-speed Automatic	11/17 City/Hwy	4.5	130 mph
CL63 AMG Coupe	7-speed Automatic	11/18 City/Hwy	4.5	155 mph
CL65 AMG Coupe	5-speed Automatic	11/17 City/Hwy	4.2	155 mph
CLK-CLASS				
CLK350 Coupe	7-speed Automatic	17/25 City/Hwy	6.4	130 mph
CLK350 Cabriolet	7-speed Automatic	17/25 City/Hwy	6.7	130 mph
CLK550 Coupe	7-speed Automatic	15/22 City/Hwy	5.7	130 mph
CLK550 Cabriolet	7-speed Automatic	15/21 City/Hwy	6.0	130 mph
CLK63 AMG Cabriolet	5-speed Automatic	12/18 City/Hwy	4.5	155 mph
CLK63 AMG Black Series Coupe	7-speed Automatic	12/19 City/Hwy	4.1	186 mph

CLS-CLASS

CLS550 Coupe	7-speed Automatic	14/21 City/Hwy	5.4	155 mph
CLS63 AMG Coupe	5-speed Automatic	12/18 City/Hwy	4.3	155 mph

E-CLASS

E320 BlueTEC Sedan	7-speed Automatic	23/32 City/Hwy	6.6	130 mph
E350 Sedan	7-speed Automatic	17/24 City/Hwy	6.5	130 mph
E350 4Matic Sedan	5-speed Automatic	16/22 City/Hwy	N/A	130 mph
E350 4Matic Wagon	5-speed Automatic	16/22 City/Hwy	6.9	130 mph
E550 Sedan	7-speed Automatic	15/22 City/Hwy	5.4	130 mph
E550 4Matic Sedan	5-speed Automatic	13/19 City/Hwy	N/A	130 mph
E63 AMG Sedan	5-speed Automatic	12/19 City/Hwy	4.3	155 mph
E63 AMG Wagon	5-speed Automatic	12/18 City/Hwy	4.3	155 mph

G-CLASS

G500 Sport Utility	7-speed Automatic	13/16 City/Hwy	N/A	125 mph
G55 AMG Sport Utility	5-speed Automatic	12/14 City/Hwy	N/A	130 mph

GL-CLASS

GL320 CDI 4Matic Sport Utility	7-speed Automatic	18/24 City/Hwy	N/A	130 mph
GL450 4Matic Sport Utility	7-speed Automatic	13/18 City/Hwy	N/A	130 mph
GL550 4Matic Sport Utility	7-speed Automatic	13/17 City/Hwy	N/A	130 mph

ML-CLASS

ML320 CDI 4Matic Sport Utility	7-speed Automatic	18/24 City/Hwy	7.9	130 mph
ML350 4Matic Sport Utility	7-speed Automatic	15/20 City/Hwy	7.9	131 mph
ML550 4Matic Sport Utility	7-speed Automatic	13/18 City/Hwy	5.6	131 mph
ML63 AMG 4Matic Sport Utility	7-speed Automatic	11/14 City/Hwy	4.8	155 mph

R-CLASS

R320 CDI 4Matic Sports Tourer	7-speed Automatic	18/24 City/Hwy	8.6	130 mph
R350 Sports Tourer	7-speed Automatic	15/20 City/Hwy	7.9	130 mph
R350 4Matic Sports Tourer	7-speed Automatic	15/19 City/Hwy	8.0	130 mph

S-CLASS

S550 Sedan	7-speed Automatic	14/21 City/Hwy	5.4	130 mph
S550 4Matic Sedan	7-speed Automatic	14/20 City/Hwy	N/A	130 mph
S600 Sedan	5-speed Automatic	12/19 City/Hwy	4.5	130 mph
S63 AMG Sedan	7-speed Automatic	11/17 City/Hwy	4.5	155 mph
S65 AMG Sedan	5-speed Automatic	11/17 City/Hwy	4.2	155 mph

SL-CLASS

SL550 Coupe/Roadster	7-speed Automatic	14/21 City/Hwy	5.3	155 mph
SL55 AMG Coupe/Roadster	5-speed Automatic	12/17 City/Hwy	4.5	155 mph
SL600 Coupe/Roadster	7-speed Automatic	11/18 City/Hwy	4.4	155 mph
SL65 AMG Coupe/Roadster	5-speed Automatic	11/18 City/Hwy	4.2	155 mph

SLK-CLASS

SLK280 Coupe/Roadster	6-speed Manual	17/25 City/Hwy	6.1	155 mph
SLK280 Coupe/Roadster	7-speed Automatic	18/24 City/Hwy	6.1	155 mph
SLK350 Coupe/Roadster	6-speed Manual	16/23 City/Hwy	N/A	155 mph
SLK350 Coupe/Roadster	7-speed Automatic	17/23 City/Hwy	5.5	155 mph
SLK55 AMG Coupe/Roadster	7-speed Automatic	14/20 City/Hwy	4.8	155 mph

Note: Most models are rear-wheel-drive; 4Matic models are all-wheel-drive

ENGINES

The latest Mercedes-Benz family of all-aluminum engines featured four-valve-per-cylinder technology and variable valve timing. Its 5.5-liter V-8, which delivered 382 horsepower and 391 lbs.-ft. of torque, made its debut in the new-generation S-Class sedan, followed by a 4.6-liter, 335-horsepower version in the GL-Class, the first full-size, seven-passenger sport utility from Mercedes-Benz. The 5.5-liter V-8 was now available in seven other classes; the new-generation CL coupe, the SL roadster, the CLS coupe, the E-Class sedan and wagon, and the CLK coupe and cabriolet.

The current four-valve architecture actually made its debut on the Mercedes-Benz V-6 in the SLK coupe/roadster. The 3.5-liter V-6 produced 268 horsepower and 258 lbs.-ft. of torque, with maximum torque available from 2,500 rpm all the way up to 5,000 rpm. In addition to the SLK coupe/roadster, the 3.5-liter engine now powered the new C350 and E350 sedans, the R350 and ML350 sport utilities, and the CLK350 coupe and cabriolet models. In addition, a 228 hp 3.0-liter version of the high-technology V-6 powered the C300 sedan.

For 2008, Mercedes-Benz also offered the only diesel-powered passenger car that was clean enough to be sold in all 50 states: — the E320 BlueTEC. The company also announced that it intended to offer three new BlueTEC models — the R-, M- and GL-Class sport utility vehicles — in all 50 states later in 2008. While all four models met the stringent "BIN 5" exhaust emissions standard, BlueTEC vehicles were more than just the cleanest diesel models in the world. They also consumed 20- to 40-percent less fuel than comparable vehicles with gasoline engines. For example, the E320 BlueTEC got 32 miles per gallon on the highway, making it by far the most economical vehicle in its class.

2008 ML550

2008 G500

2008 GL550

2008 SLK350 seat airscarf

2008 S-Class Infrared Nightview

Engine Note: BlueTEC is a multi-module emission control system that makes the diesel engine as clean as the modern gasoline engine. BlueTEC does an especially good job of reducing nitrogen oxides – the only exhaust compound that, in recent years, remained higher in diesels than in gasoline engines.

Mercedes-Benz developed two versions of BlueTEC. In the E-Class, an oxidation catalytic converter and particulate filter were combined with a durable NOx storage catalytic converter and an additional SCR catalytic converter. The oxidation catalyst promotes downstream after-burning of any leftover hydrocarbons, while a particulate filter traps soot, even microscopic particles, and is automatically cleaned periodically via what approximates an oven-cleaning cycle. The NOx storage catalyst temporarily stores oxides of nitrogen, and regeneration pulses release a form of nitrogen oxide that reacts with exhaust gas to become harmless nitrogen.

The second BlueTEC version, AdBlue, was even more efficient. AdBlue, a solution of water and urea, is injected into the exhaust flow, a process that releases ammonia and converts up to 80-percent of the nitrogen oxides into harmless nitrogen and water in the downstream SCR unit. AdBlue is carried in its own small tank and metered into the exhaust in minute quantities, so small that the tank only needs to be refilled during routine scheduled maintenance.

Manufacturer: Daimler AG, Stuttgart, Germany.

Distributor: Mercedes-Benz USA, Montvale, New Jersey.

Mecedes-Benz Price Guide

Vehicle Condition Scale

6	5	4	3	2	1
Parts car: May or may not be running, but is weathered, wrecked and/or stripped to the point of being useful primarily for parts.	**Restorable:** Needs complete restoration of body, chassis and interior. May or may not be running, but isn't weathered, wrecked or stripped to the point of being useful only for parts.	**Good:** A driveable vehicle needing no or only minor work to be functional. Also, a deteriorated restoration or a very poor amateur restoration. All components may need restoration to be "excellent," but the car is mostly useable "as is."	**Very Good:** Complete operable original or older restoration. Also, a very good amateur restoration, all presentable and serviceable inside and out. Plus, a combination of well-done restoration and good operable components or a partially restored car with all parts necessary to compete and/or valuable NOS parts.	**Fine:** Well-restored or a combination of superior restoration and excellent original parts. Also, extremely well-maintained original vehicle showing minimal wear.	**Excellent:** Restored to current maximum professional standards of quality in every area, or perfect original with components operating and apearing as new. A 95-plus point show car that is not driven.

	6	5	4	3	2	1
1951-53 Model 170S						
4d Sed	1,240	3,720	6,200	13,950	21,700	31,000
NOTE: Deduct 8 percent for lesser Models. Deduct 10 percent for diesel.						
1951-53 Model 180						
4d Sed	1,200	3,600	6,000	13,500	21,000	30,000
1951-53 Model 220						
4d Sed	1,280	3,840	6,400	14,400	22,400	32,000
2d Conv	2,400	7,200	12,000	27,000	42,000	60,000
2d Cpe	1,600	4,800	8,000	18,000	28,000	40,000
1951-53 Model 300						
4d Sed	1,400	4,200	7,000	15,750	24,500	35,000
4d Conv Sed	3,200	9,600	16,000	36,000	56,000	80,000
2d Cpe	3,680	11,040	18,400	41,400	64,400	92,000
1951-53 Model 300S						
4d Conv Sed	5,600	16,800	28,000	63,000	98,000	140,000
2d Conv	8,000	24,000	40,000	90,000	140,000	200,000
2d Cpe	4,200	12,600	21,000	47,250	73,500	105,000
2d Rds	9,200	27,600	46,000	103,500	161,000	230,000
1954 Model 170						
4d Sed	1,000	3,000	5,000	11,250	17,500	25,000
NOTE: Deduct 10 percent for diesel.						
1954 Model 180						
4d Sed	1,050	3,100	5,200	11,700	18,200	26,000
NOTE: Deduct 10 percent for diesel.						

	6	5	4	3	2	1
1954 Model 220a						
4d Sed	1,320	3,960	6,600	14,850	23,100	33,000
2d Conv	2,360	7,080	11,800	26,550	41,300	59,000
2d Cpe	1,960	5,880	9,800	22,050	34,300	49,000
1954 Model 300						
4d Sed	1,400	4,200	7,000	15,750	24,500	35,000
4d Conv Sed	3,200	9,600	16,000	36,000	56,000	80,000
2d Cpe	3,680	11,040	18,400	41,400	64,400	92,000
1954 Model 300b						
4d Sed	1,600	4,800	8,000	18,000	28,000	40,000
4d Conv Sed	3,400	10,200	17,000	38,250	59,500	85,000
2d Cpe	3,600	10,800	18,000	40,500	63,000	90,000
1954 Model 300S						
4d Sed	1,960	5,880	9,800	22,050	34,300	49,000
2d Conv	7,400	22,200	37,000	83,250	129,500	185,000
2d Cpe	4,200	12,600	21,000	47,250	73,500	105,000
2d Rds	8,800	26,400	44,000	99,000	154,000	220,000
1954 Model 300SL						
2d GW Cpe	15,400	46,200	77,000	173,250	269,500	385,000
1955 Model 170						
4d Sed	1,040	3,120	5,200	11,700	18,200	26,000
NOTE: Deduct 10 percent for diesel.						
1955 Model 180						
4d Sed	1,100	3,250	5,400	12,150	18,900	27,000
NOTE: Deduct 10 percent for diesel.						

1959 220SE cabriolet (left), 1971 280SE 3.5 (top) and 1997 E320 cabriolet

	6	5	4	3	2	1
1955 Model 190						
2d Rds	2,400	7,200	12,000	27,000	42,000	60,000
1955 Model 220a						
4d Sed	1,320	3,960	6,600	14,850	23,100	33,000
2d Conv	2,360	7,080	11,800	26,550	41,300	59,000
2d Cpe	1,960	5,880	9,800	22,050	34,300	49,000
1955 Model 300B						
4d Sed	1,600	4,800	8,000	18,000	28,000	40,000
4d Conv Sed	3,400	10,200	17,000	38,250	59,500	85,000
2d Cpe	3,600	10,800	18,000	40,500	63,000	90,000
1955 Model 300S						
4d Sed	1,960	5,880	9,800	22,050	34,300	49,000
2d Conv	7,400	22,200	37,000	83,250	129,500	185,000
2d Cpe	4,200	12,600	21,000	47,250	73,500	105,000
2d Rds	8,800	26,400	44,000	99,000	154,000	220,000
1955 Model 300SL						
2d GW Cpe	15,400	46,200	77,000	173,250	269,500	385,000
1956-57 Model 180						
4d Sed	760	2,280	3,800	8,550	13,300	19,000

NOTE: Deduct 10 percent for diesel.

	6	5	4	3	2	1
1956-57 Model 190						
4d Sed	800	2,400	4,000	9,000	14,000	20,000
SL Rds	1,880	5,640	9,400	21,150	32,900	47,000

NOTE: Add 10 percent for removable hardtop.

	6	5	4	3	2	1
1956-57 Model 219						
4d Sed	880	2,640	4,400	9,900	15,400	22,000
1956-57 Model 220S						
4d Sed	920	2,760	4,600	10,350	16,100	23,000
Cpe	1,120	3,360	5,600	12,600	19,600	28,000
Cabr	2,280	6,840	11,400	25,650	39,900	57,000
1956-57 Model 300c						
4d Sed	1,560	4,680	7,800	17,550	27,300	39,000
4d Limo	1,920	5,760	9,600	21,600	33,600	48,000
4d Conv Sed	3,440	10,320	17,200	38,700	60,200	86,000
2d Cpe	4,040	12,120	20,200	45,450	70,700	101,000
1956-57 Model 300S						
4d Sed	1,920	5,760	9,600	21,600	33,600	48,000
2d Conv	7,200	21,600	36,000	81,000	126,000	180,000
2d Cpe	3,800	11,400	19,000	42,750	66,500	95,000
2d Rds	8,000	24,000	40,000	90,000	140,000	200,000
1956-57 Model 300Sc						
4d Sed	2,080	6,240	10,400	23,400	36,400	52,000
2d Conv	12,600	37,800	63,000	141,750	220,500	315,000
2d Rds	13,200	39,600	66,000	148,500	231,000	330,000
1956-57 Model 300SL						
2d GW Cpe	15,600	46,800	78,000	175,500	273,000	390,000
1958-60 Model 180a						
4d Sed	680	2,040	3,400	7,650	11,900	17,000

NOTE: Deduct 10 percent for diesel.

1958-60 Model 190

	6	5	4	3	2	1
4d Sed	720	2,160	3,600	8,100	12,600	18,000
SL Rds	1,840	5,520	9,200	20,700	32,200	46,000
SL Cpe	1,840	5,520	9,200	20,700	32,200	46,000

NOTE: Add 10 percent for removable hardtop. Deduct 10 percent for diesel.

1958-60 Model 219

	6	5	4	3	2	1
4d Sed	760	2,280	3,800	8,550	13,300	19,000

1958-60 Model 220S

	6	5	4	3	2	1
2d Cpe	1,040	3,120	5,200	11,700	18,200	26,000
4d Sed	840	2,520	4,200	9,450	14,700	21,000
2d Conv	2,200	6,600	11,000	24,750	38,500	55,000

1958-60 Model 220SE

	6	5	4	3	2	1
4d Sed	1,000	3,000	5,000	11,250	17,500	25,000
2d Cpe	1,200	3,600	6,000	13,500	21,000	30,000
2d Conv	3,000	9,000	15,000	33,750	52,500	75,000

1958-60 Model 300d

	6	5	4	3	2	1
4d HT	1,200	3,600	6,000	13,500	21,000	30,000
4d Conv	4,040	12,120	20,200	45,450	70,700	101,000

1958-60 Model 300SL

	6	5	4	3	2	1
2d Rds	12,000	36,000	60,000	135,000	210,000	300,000

NOTE: Add 5 percent for removable hardtop.

1961-62

	6	5	4	3	2	1
180 4d Sed	600	1,800	3,000	6,750	10,500	15,000
180D 4d Sed	640	1,920	3,200	7,200	11,200	16,000
190 4d Sed	620	1,860	3,100	6,980	10,850	15,500
190D 4d Sed	660	1,980	3,300	7,430	11,550	16,500
190SL Cpe/Rds	1,840	5,520	9,200	20,700	32,200	46,000
220 4d Sed	760	2,280	3,800	8,550	13,300	19,000
220S 4d Sed	800	2,400	4,000	9,000	14,000	20,000
220SE 4d Sed	840	2,520	4,200	9,450	14,700	21,000
220SE Cpe	1,120	3,360	5,600	12,600	19,600	28,000
220SE Cabr	2,000	6,000	10,000	22,500	35,000	50,000
220SEb Cpe	1,280	3,840	6,400	14,400	22,400	32,000
220SEb Cabr	1,880	5,640	9,400	21,150	32,900	47,000
220SEb 4d Sed	880	2,640	4,400	9,900	15,400	22,000
300 4d HT	2,000	6,000	10,000	22,500	35,000	50,000
300 4d Cabr	4,560	13,680	22,800	51,300	79,800	114,000
300SE 4d Sed	1,000	3,000	5,000	11,250	17,500	25,000
300SE 2d Cpe	1,480	4,440	7,400	16,650	25,900	37,000
300SE 2d Cabr	3,480	10,440	17,400	39,150	60,900	87,000
300SL Rds	11,200	33,600	56,000	126,000	196,000	280,000

NOTE: Add 5 percent for removable hardtop.

1963

	6	5	4	3	2	1
180Dc 4d Sed	550	1,700	2,800	6,300	9,800	14,000
190c 4d Sed	450	1,400	2,300	5,180	8,050	11,500
190Dc 4d Sed	600	1,750	2,900	6,530	10,200	14,500
190SL Rds	1,800	5,400	9,000	20,250	31,500	45,000

NOTE: Add 10 percent for removable hardtop.

	6	5	4	3	2	1
220 4d Sed	650	1,900	3,200	7,200	11,200	16,000
220S 4d Sed	700	2,050	3,400	7,650	11,900	17,000
220SE 4d Sed	700	2,150	3,600	8,100	12,600	18,000
220SEb Cpe	900	2,650	4,400	9,900	15,400	22,000
220SEb Cabr	1,600	4,800	8,000	18,000	28,000	40,000
300SE 4d Sed	1,050	3,100	5,200	11,700	18,200	26,000
300SE Cpe	1,250	3,700	6,200	13,950	21,700	31,000
300SE Cabr	3,100	9,250	15,400	34,650	53,900	77,000
300 4d HT	1,300	3,850	6,400	14,400	22,400	32,000
300SL Rds	11,200	33,600	56,000	126,000	196,000	280,000

NOTE: Add 5 percent for removable hardtop.

1964

	6	5	4	3	2	1
190c 4d Sed	450	1,300	2,200	4,950	7,700	11,000
190Dc 4d Sed	550	1,700	2,800	6,300	9,800	14,000
220 4d Sed	650	1,900	3,200	7,200	11,200	16,000
220S 4d Sed	700	2,050	3,400	7,650	11,900	17,000
220SE 4d Sed	700	2,150	3,600	8,100	12,600	18,000
220SEb Cpe	900	2,750	4,600	10,350	16,100	23,000
220SEb Cabr	1,550	4,700	7,800	17,550	27,300	39,000
230SL Cpe/Rds	1,050	3,100	5,200	11,700	18,200	26,000
300SE 4d Sed	900	2,650	4,400	9,900	15,400	22,000
300SE 4d Sed (112)	920	2,760	4,600	10,350	16,100	23,000
300SE Cpe	1,300	3,850	6,400	14,400	22,400	32,000
300SE Cabr	3,150	9,500	15,800	35,550	55,300	79,000

1965

	6	5	4	3	2	1
190c 4d Sed	450	1,300	2,200	4,950	7,700	11,000
190Dc 4d Sed	550	1,700	2,800	6,300	9,800	14,000
220b 4d Sed	650	1,900	3,200	7,200	11,200	16,000
220Sb 4d Sed	650	2,000	3,300	7,430	11,600	16,500
220SEb 4d Sed	700	2,050	3,400	7,650	11,900	17,000
220SEb Cpe	800	2,400	4,000	9,000	14,000	20,000
220SEb Cabr	1,500	4,550	7,600	17,100	26,600	38,000
230SL Cpe/Rds	1,100	3,250	5,400	12,150	18,900	27,000
250SE Cpe	900	2,650	4,400	9,900	15,400	22,000
250SE Cabr	1,550	4,700	7,800	17,550	27,300	39,000
300SE 4d Sed	750	2,300	3,800	8,550	13,300	19,000
300SEL 4d Sed	850	2,500	4,200	9,450	14,700	21,000
300SE Cpe	900	2,750	4,600	10,350	16,100	23,000
300SE Cabr	3,150	9,500	15,800	35,550	55,300	79,000
600 4d Sed	2,000	6,000	10,000	22,500	35,000	50,000
600 Limo	2,400	7,200	12,000	27,000	42,000	60,000

	6	5	4	3	2	1
1966						
200 4d Sed	450	1,300	2,200	4,950	7,700	11,000
200D 4d Sed	550	1,700	2,800	6,300	9,800	14,000
230 4d Sed	450	1,400	2,300	5,180	8,050	11,500
230S 4d Sed	450	1,400	2,350	5,270	8,200	11,700
230SL Cpe/Rds	1,200	3,600	6,000	13,500	21,000	30,000
250SE Cpe	900	2,650	4,400	9,900	15,400	22,000
250SE Cabr	1,550	4,700	7,800	17,550	27,300	39,000
250S 4d Sed	650	1,900	3,200	7,200	11,200	16,000
250SE 4d Sed	650	2,000	3,300	7,430	11,600	16,500
300SE Cpe	900	2,750	4,600	10,350	16,100	23,000
300SE Cabr	3,150	9,500	15,800	35,550	55,300	79,000
600 4d Sed	2,000	6,000	10,000	22,500	35,000	50,000
600 Limo	2,400	7,200	12,000	27,000	42,000	60,000
1967						
200 4d Sed	450	1,400	2,300	5,180	8,050	11,500
200D 4d Sed	600	1,750	2,900	6,530	10,200	14,500
230 4d Sed	550	1,700	2,800	6,300	9,800	14,000
230S 4d Sed	550	1,700	2,850	6,390	9,950	14,200
230SL Cpe/Rds	1,100	3,350	5,600	12,600	19,600	28,000
250S 4d Sed	650	1,900	3,200	7,200	11,200	16,000
250SE 4d Sed	650	2,000	3,300	7,430	11,600	16,500
250SE Cpe	900	2,650	4,400	9,900	15,400	22,000
250SE Cabr	1,200	3,600	6,000	13,500	21,000	30,000
250SL Cpe/Rds	1,150	3,500	5,800	13,050	20,300	29,000
280SE Cpe	900	2,750	4,600	10,350	16,100	23,000
280SE Cabr	1,750	5,300	8,800	19,800	30,800	44,000
300SE Cpe	1,050	3,100	5,200	11,700	18,200	26,000
300SE Cabr	3,150	9,500	15,800	35,550	55,300	79,000
300SE 4d Sed	950	2,900	4,800	10,800	16,800	24,000
300SEL 4d Sed	1,000	3,000	5,000	11,250	17,500	25,000
600 4d Sed	2,000	6,000	10,000	22,500	35,000	50,000
600 Limo	2,400	7,200	12,000	27,000	42,000	60,000
1968						
220 4d Sed	450	1,400	2,300	5,180	8,050	11,500
220D 4d Sed	600	1,750	2,900	6,530	10,200	14,500
230 4d Sed	560	1,680	2,800	6,300	9,800	14,000
250 4d Sed	600	1,750	2,900	6,570	10,200	14,600
280 4d Sed	600	1,800	2,950	6,660	10,400	14,800
280SE 4d Sed	650	1,900	3,200	7,200	11,200	16,000
280SEL 4d Sed	700	2,050	3,400	7,650	11,900	17,000
280SE Cpe	920	2,760	4,600	10,350	16,100	23,000
280SE Cabr	1,850	5,500	9,200	20,700	32,200	46,000
280SL Cpe/Rds	1,440	4,320	7,200	16,200	25,200	36,000
300SEL 4d Sed	1,000	3,000	5,000	11,250	17,500	25,000
600 4d Sed	2,000	6,000	10,000	22,500	35,000	50,000
600 Limo	2,400	7,200	12,000	27,000	42,000	60,000
1969						
220 4d Sed	600	1,850	3,100	6,980	10,900	15,500
220D 4d Sed	650	2,000	3,300	7,430	11,600	16,500
230 4d Sed	650	1,900	3,150	7,110	11,100	15,800
250 4d Sed	650	1,900	3,200	7,200	11,200	16,000
280S 4d Sed	650	1,950	3,200	7,250	11,300	16,100
280SE 4d Sed	650	1,900	3,200	7,200	11,200	16,000
280SEL 4d Sed	650	2,000	3,300	7,430	11,600	16,500
280SE Cpe	900	2,750	4,600	10,350	16,100	23,000
280SE Cabr	1,900	5,750	9,600	21,600	33,600	48,000
280SL Cpe/Rds	1,450	4,300	7,200	16,200	25,200	36,000
300SEL 4d Sed	950	2,900	4,800	10,800	16,800	24,000
300SEL 6.3 4d Sed	1,160	3,480	5,800	13,050	20,300	29,000
600 4d Sed	2,000	6,000	10,000	22,500	35,000	50,000
600 Limo	2,400	7,200	12,000	27,000	42,000	60,000
1970						
220 4d Sed	550	1,700	2,800	6,300	9,800	14,000
220D 4d Sed	600	1,750	2,900	6,530	10,200	14,500
250 4d Sed	550	1,700	2,850	6,390	9,950	14,200
250C Cpe	700	2,050	3,400	7,650	11,900	17,000
280S 4d Sed	600	1,850	3,100	6,980	10,900	15,500
280SE 4d Sed	650	1,900	3,200	7,200	11,200	16,000
280SEL 4d Sed	650	2,000	3,300	7,430	11,600	16,500
280SE Cpe	1,200	3,600	6,000	13,500	21,000	30,000
280SE Cpe 3.5	1,700	5,150	8,600	19,350	30,100	43,000
280SE Cabr	2,000	6,000	10,000	22,500	35,000	50,000
280SE Cabr 3.5	2,600	7,800	13,000	29,250	45,500	65,000
280SL Cpe/Rds	1,500	4,450	7,400	16,650	25,900	37,000
300SEL 4d Sed	900	2,750	4,600	10,350	16,100	23,000
300SEL 6.3 4d Sed	1,160	3,480	5,800	13,050	20,300	29,000
600 4d Sed	2,000	6,000	10,000	22,500	35,000	50,000
600 Limo	2,400	7,200	12,000	27,000	42,000	60,000
1971						
220 4d Sed	550	1,700	2,800	6,300	9,800	14,000
220D 4d Sed	600	1,750	2,900	6,530	10,200	14,500
250 4d Sed	550	1,700	2,800	6,300	9,800	14,000
250C Cpe	650	1,900	3,200	7,200	11,200	16,000
280S 4d Sed	600	1,850	3,100	6,980	10,900	15,500
280SE 4d Sed	650	1,900	3,200	7,200	11,200	16,000
280SE 4.5 4d Sed	800	2,400	4,000	9,000	14,000	20,000
280SEL 4d Sed	650	2,000	3,300	7,430	11,600	16,500
280SE 3.5 Cpe	1,200	3,600	6,000	13,500	21,000	30,000
280SE 3.5 Cabr	3,100	9,250	15,400	34,650	53,900	77,000
280SL Cpe/Rds	1,500	4,550	7,600	17,100	26,600	38,000
300SEL 4d Sed	950	2,900	4,800	10,800	16,800	24,000
300SEL 6.3 4d Sed	1,160	3,480	5,800	13,050	20,300	29,000
600 4d Sed	2,000	6,000	10,000	22,500	35,000	50,000
600 4d Limo	2,400	7,200	12,000	27,000	42,000	60,000

	6	5	4	3	2	1
1972						
220 4d Sed	550	1,700	2,800	6,300	9,800	14,000
220D 4d Sed	600	1,750	2,900	6,530	10,200	14,500
250 4d Sed	600	1,800	3,000	6,750	10,500	15,000
250C Cpe	700	2,050	3,400	7,650	11,900	17,000
280SE 4d Sed	650	1,900	3,200	7,200	11,200	16,000
280SE 4.5 4d Sed	800	2,400	4,000	9,000	14,000	20,000
280SE 3.5 Cpe	900	2,650	4,400	9,900	15,400	22,000
280SE 3.5 Cabr	1,550	4,700	7,800	17,550	27,300	39,000
280SEL 4d Sed	700	2,050	3,400	7,650	11,900	17,000
300SEL 4d Sed	900	2,750	4,600	10,350	16,100	23,000
350SL Cpe/Rds	1,450	4,300	7,200	16,200	25,200	36,000
600 4d Sed	2,000	6,000	10,000	22,500	35,000	50,000
600 Limo	2,400	7,200	12,000	27,000	42,000	60,000
1973						
220 4d Sed	550	1,700	2,800	6,300	9,800	14,000
220D 4d Sed	600	1,800	3,000	6,750	10,500	15,000
280 4d Sed	600	1,850	3,100	6,980	10,900	15,500
280C Cpe	700	2,150	3,600	8,100	12,600	18,000
280SE 4d Sed	700	2,050	3,400	7,650	11,900	17,000
280SE 4.5 4d Sed	850	2,500	4,200	9,450	14,700	21,000
280SEL 4d Sed	700	2,100	3,500	7,880	12,300	17,500
280SEL 4.5 4d Sed	880	2,640	4,400	9,900	15,400	22,000
300SEL 4d Sed	900	2,750	4,600	10,350	16,100	23,000
450SE 4d Sed	700	2,100	3,500	7,880	12,300	17,500
450SEL 4d Sed	750	2,200	3,700	8,330	13,000	18,500
450SL Cpe/Rds	1,350	4,100	6,800	15,300	23,800	34,000
450SLC Cpe	1,100	3,350	5,600	12,600	19,600	28,000
1974						
230 4d Sed	600	1,750	2,900	6,530	10,200	14,500
240D 4d Sed	600	1,800	3,000	6,750	10,500	15,000
280 4d Sed	650	1,900	3,200	7,200	11,200	16,000
280C Cpe	700	2,150	3,600	8,100	12,600	18,000
450SE 4d Sed	750	2,300	3,800	8,550	13,300	19,000
450SEL 4d Sed	850	2,500	4,200	9,450	14,700	21,000
450SL Cpe/Rds	1,300	3,950	6,600	14,850	23,100	33,000
450SLC Cpe	1,100	3,350	5,600	12,600	19,600	28,000
1975						
230 4d Sed	600	1,800	3,000	6,750	10,500	15,000
240D 4d Sed	650	1,900	3,200	7,200	11,200	16,000
300D 4d Sed	700	2,050	3,400	7,650	11,900	17,000
280 4d Sed	700	2,150	3,600	8,100	12,600	18,000
280C Cpe	750	2,300	3,800	8,550	13,300	19,000
280S 4d Sed	700	2,150	3,600	8,100	12,600	18,000
450SE 4d Sed	800	2,400	4,000	9,000	14,000	20,000
450SEL 4d Sed	850	2,500	4,200	9,450	14,700	21,000
450SL Cpe/Rds	1,400	4,200	7,000	15,750	24,500	35,000
450SLC Cpe	1,100	3,350	5,600	12,600	19,600	28,000

	6	5	4	3	2	1
1976						
230 4d Sed	700	2,050	3,400	7,650	11,900	17,000
240D 4d Sed	700	2,050	3,400	7,650	11,900	17,000
300D 4d Sed	700	2,100	3,500	7,880	12,300	17,500
280 4d Sed	700	2,150	3,600	8,100	12,600	18,000
280C Cpe	850	2,500	4,200	9,450	14,700	21,000
280S 4d Sed	750	2,200	3,700	8,330	13,000	18,500
450SE 4d Sed	900	2,650	4,400	9,900	15,400	22,000
450SEL 4d Sed	900	2,750	4,600	10,350	16,100	23,000
450SL Cpe/Rds	1,400	4,200	7,000	15,750	24,500	35,000
450SLC Cpe	1,100	3,250	5,400	12,150	18,900	27,000
1977						
230 4d Sed	650	1,900	3,200	7,200	11,200	16,000
240D 4d Sed	700	2,100	3,500	7,880	12,300	17,500
300D 4d Sed	700	2,150	3,600	8,100	12,600	18,000
280E 4d Sed	750	2,200	3,700	8,330	13,000	18,500
280SE 4d Sed	750	2,300	3,800	8,550	13,300	19,000
450SEL 4d Sed	900	2,750	4,600	10,350	16,100	23,000
450SL Cpe/Rds	1,400	4,200	7,000	15,750	24,500	35,000
450SLC Cpe	1,100	3,250	5,400	12,150	18,900	27,000
1978						
230 4d Sed	650	1,900	3,200	7,200	11,200	16,000
240D 4d Sed	650	2,000	3,300	7,430	11,600	16,500
300D 4d Sed	700	2,050	3,400	7,650	11,900	17,000
300CD Cpe	700	2,150	3,600	8,100	12,600	18,000
300SD 4d Sed	800	2,350	3,900	8,780	13,700	19,500
280E 4d Sed	700	2,100	3,500	7,880	12,300	17,500
280CE Cpe	800	2,350	3,900	8,780	13,700	19,500
280SE 4d Sed	800	2,400	4,000	9,000	14,000	20,000
450SEL 4d Sed	950	2,900	4,800	10,800	16,800	24,000
450SL Cpe/Rds	1,350	4,100	6,800	15,300	23,800	34,000
450SLC Cpe	1,150	3,500	5,800	13,050	20,300	29,000
6.9 4d Sed	1,100	3,350	5,600	12,600	19,600	28,000
1979						
240D 4d Sed	550	1,700	2,800	6,300	9,800	14,000
300D 4d Sed	600	1,800	3,000	6,750	10,500	15,000
300CD Cpe	700	2,050	3,400	7,650	11,900	17,000
300TD Sta Wag	900	2,750	4,600	10,350	16,100	23,000
300SD 4d Sed	750	2,300	3,800	8,550	13,300	19,000
280E 4d Sed	650	1,900	3,200	7,200	11,200	16,000
280CE Cpe	700	2,150	3,600	8,100	12,600	18,000
280SE 4d Sed	750	2,300	3,800	8,550	13,300	19,000
450SEL 4d Sed	900	2,650	4,400	9,900	15,400	22,000
450SL Cpe/Rds	1,300	3,850	6,400	14,400	22,400	32,000
450SLC Cpe	1,100	3,350	5,600	12,600	19,600	28,000
6.9 4d Sed	1,050	3,100	5,200	11,700	18,200	26,000

	6	5	4	3	2	1

1980

	6	5	4	3	2	1
240D 4d Sed	600	1,800	3,000	6,750	10,500	15,000
300D 4d Sed	650	1,900	3,200	7,200	11,200	16,000
300CD 2d Cpe	700	2,150	3,600	8,100	12,600	18,000
300TD 4d Sta Wag	900	2,750	4,600	10,350	16,100	23,000
300SD 4d Sed	800	2,400	4,000	9,000	14,000	20,000
280E 4d Sed	750	2,300	3,800	8,550	13,300	19,000
280CE 2d Cpe	800	2,400	4,000	9,000	14,000	20,000
280SE 4d Sed	750	2,300	3,800	8,550	13,300	19,000
450SEL 4d Sed	800	2,400	4,000	9,000	14,000	20,000
450SL 2d Conv	1,350	4,100	6,800	15,300	23,800	34,000
450SLC 2d Cpe	1,050	3,100	5,200	11,700	18,200	26,000

1981

	6	5	4	3	2	1
240D 4d Sed	600	1,800	3,000	6,750	10,500	15,000
300D 4d Sed	650	1,900	3,200	7,200	11,200	16,000
300CD 2d Cpe	700	2,150	3,600	8,100	12,600	18,000
300TD-T 4d Turbo Sta Wag	1,050	3,100	5,200	11,700	18,200	26,000
300SD 4d Sed	750	2,300	3,800	8,550	13,300	19,000
280E 4d Sed	700	2,150	3,600	8,100	12,600	18,000
280CE 2d Cpe	750	2,300	3,800	8,550	13,300	19,000
280SEL 4d Sed	950	2,900	4,800	10,800	16,800	24,000
380SL 2d Conv	1,450	4,300	7,200	16,200	25,200	36,000
380SLC 2d Cpe	1,100	3,250	5,400	12,150	18,900	27,000

1982

	6	5	4	3	2	1
240D 4d Sed	650	1,900	3,200	7,200	11,200	16,000
300D-T 4d Sed	700	2,050	3,400	7,650	11,900	17,000
300CD-T 2d Cpe	750	2,300	3,800	8,550	13,300	19,000
300TD-T 4d Turbo Sta Wag	1,050	3,100	5,200	11,700	18,200	26,000
300SD 4d Sed	800	2,400	4,000	9,000	14,000	20,000
380SEL 4d Sed	1,000	3,000	5,000	11,250	17,500	25,000
380SL 2d Conv	1,600	4,800	8,000	18,000	28,000	40,000
380SEC 2d Cpe	1,200	3,600	6,000	13,500	21,000	30,000

1983

	6	5	4	3	2	1
240D 4d Sed	650	1,900	3,200	7,200	11,200	16,000
300D-T 4d Sed	700	2,050	3,400	7,650	11,900	17,000
300CD-T 2d Cpe	750	2,300	3,800	8,550	13,300	19,000
300TD-T 4d Turbo Sta Wag	1,050	3,100	5,200	11,700	18,200	26,000
300SD 4d Sed	800	2,400	4,000	9,000	14,000	20,000
300SEL 4d Sed	1,000	3,000	5,000	11,250	17,500	25,000
380SL 2d Conv	1,600	4,800	8,000	18,000	28,000	40,000
380SEC 2d Cpe	1,200	3,600	6,000	13,500	21,000	30,000

1984

	6	5	4	3	2	1
190E 4d Sed	650	1,900	3,200	7,200	11,200	16,000
190D 4d Sed	600	1,800	3,000	6,750	10,500	15,000
300D-T 4d Sed	650	2,000	3,300	7,430	11,600	16,500
300CD-T 2d Cpe	700	2,050	3,400	7,650	11,900	17,000
300TD-T 4d Turbo Sta Wag	1,050	3,100	5,200	11,700	18,200	26,000
300SD 4d Sed	900	2,750	4,600	10,350	16,100	23,000
500SEL 4d Sed	1,100	3,250	5,400	12,150	18,900	27,000
500SEC 2d Cpe	1,200	3,600	6,000	13,500	21,000	30,000
380SE 4d Sed	900	2,750	4,600	10,350	16,100	23,000
380SL 2d Conv	1,500	4,450	7,400	16,650	25,900	37,000

1985

	6	5	4	3	2	1
190E 4d Sed	650	1,900	3,200	7,200	11,200	16,000
190D 4d Sed	600	1,850	3,100	6,980	10,900	15,500
300D-T 4d Sed	700	2,100	3,500	7,880	12,300	17,500
300CD-T 2d Cpe	700	2,150	3,600	8,100	12,600	18,000
300TD-T 4d Turbo Sta Wag	1,050	3,100	5,200	11,700	18,200	26,000
300SD 4d Sed	950	2,900	4,800	10,800	16,800	24,000
500SEL 4d Sed	1,100	3,350	5,600	12,600	19,600	28,000
500SEC 2d Cpe	1,250	3,700	6,200	13,950	21,700	31,000
380SE 4d Sed	950	2,900	4,800	10,800	16,800	24,000
380SL 2d Conv	1,450	4,300	7,200	16,200	25,200	36,000

1986

	6	5	4	3	2	1
190E 4d Sed	650	2,000	3,300	7,430	11,600	16,500
190D 4d Sed	650	1,900	3,200	7,200	11,200	16,000
190D 1.6 4d Sed	700	2,050	3,400	7,650	11,900	17,000
300E 4d Sed	750	2,200	3,700	8,330	13,000	18,500
300SDL 4d Sed	1,100	3,250	5,400	12,150	18,900	27,000
420SEL 4d Sed	1,150	3,500	5,800	13,050	20,300	29,000
560SEL 4d Sed	1,250	3,700	6,200	13,950	21,700	31,000
560SEC 2d Cpe	1,300	3,950	6,600	14,850	23,100	33,000
560SL 2d Conv	1,500	4,550	7,600	17,100	26,600	38,000

1987

	6	5	4	3	2	1
190D 4d Sed	700	2,150	3,600	8,100	12,600	18,000
190D-T 4d Sed	750	2,200	3,700	8,330	13,000	18,500
190E 4d Sed	800	2,350	3,900	8,780	13,700	19,500
190 2.6 4d Sed	800	2,450	4,100	9,230	14,300	20,500
190E-16V 4d Sed	1,000	3,050	5,100	11,480	17,900	25,500
260E 4d Sed	900	2,750	4,600	10,350	16,100	23,000
300E 4d Sed	1,000	3,000	5,000	11,250	17,500	25,000
300D 4d Sed	950	2,800	4,700	10,580	16,500	23,500
300TD-T 4d Sta Wag	1,020	3,060	5,100	11,480	17,850	25,500
300SDL-T 4d Sed	1,150	3,500	5,800	13,050	20,300	29,000
420SEL 4d Sed	1,200	3,550	5,900	13,280	20,700	29,500
560SEL 4d Sed	1,500	4,450	7,400	16,650	25,900	37,000
560SEC 2d Cpe	1,500	4,550	7,600	17,100	26,600	38,000
560SL 2d Conv	1,450	4,300	7,200	16,200	25,200	36,000

	6	5	4	3	2	1
1988						
190D 4d Sed	750	2,300	3,800	8,550	13,300	19,000
190E 4d Sed	850	2,500	4,200	9,450	14,700	21,000
190E 2.6 4d Sed	950	2,900	4,800	10,800	16,800	24,000
260E 4d Sed	1,000	3,000	5,000	11,250	17,500	25,000
300E 4d Sed	1,100	3,250	5,400	12,150	18,900	27,000
300CE 2d Cpe	1,300	3,950	6,600	14,850	23,100	33,000
300TE 4d Sta Wag	1,200	3,650	6,100	13,730	21,400	30,500
300SE 4d Sed	1,100	3,350	5,600	12,600	19,600	28,000
300SEL 4d Sed	1,200	3,600	6,000	13,500	21,000	30,000
420SEL 4d Sed	1,300	3,850	6,400	14,400	22,400	32,000
560SEL 4d Sed	1,500	4,450	7,400	16,650	25,900	37,000
560SEC 2d Cpe	1,550	4,700	7,800	17,550	27,300	39,000
560SL 2d Conv	1,650	4,900	8,200	18,450	28,700	41,000
1989						
190D 4d Sed	950	2,900	4,800	10,800	16,800	24,000
190E 2.6 4d Sed	900	2,750	4,600	10,350	16,100	23,000
260E 4d Sed	1,200	3,600	6,000	13,500	21,000	30,000
300E 4d Sed	1,300	3,850	6,400	14,400	22,400	32,000
300CE 2d Cpe	1,400	4,200	7,000	15,750	24,500	35,000
300TE 4d Sta Wag	1,300	3,850	6,400	14,400	22,400	32,000
300SE 4d Sed	1,200	3,600	6,000	13,500	21,000	30,000
300SEC 4d Sed	1,250	3,700	6,200	13,950	21,700	31,000
420SEL 4d Sed	1,400	4,200	7,000	15,750	24,500	35,000
560SEL 4d Sed	1,600	4,800	8,000	18,000	28,000	40,000
560SEC 2d Cpe	1,800	5,400	9,000	20,250	31,500	45,000
560SL 2d Conv	2,300	6,850	11,400	25,650	39,900	57,000
1990						
190E 2.6 4d Sed	900	2,650	4,400	9,900	15,400	22,000
300E 2.6 4d Sed	950	2,900	4,800	10,800	16,800	24,000
300D 2.5 4d Turbo Sed	1,000	3,000	5,000	11,250	17,500	25,000
300E 4d Sed	1,300	3,950	6,600	14,850	23,100	33,000
300E Matic 4d Sed	1,350	4,100	6,800	15,300	23,800	34,000
300CE 2d Cpe	1,450	4,300	7,200	16,200	25,200	36,000
300TE 4d Sta Wag	1,300	3,950	6,600	14,850	23,100	33,000
300TE Matic 4d Sta Wag	1,350	4,100	6,800	15,300	23,800	34,000
300SE 4d Sed	1,250	3,700	6,200	13,950	21,700	31,000
300SEL 4d Sed	1,300	3,950	6,600	14,850	23,100	33,000
350SDL 4d Turbo Sed	1,280	3,840	6,400	14,400	22,400	32,000
420SEL 4d Sed	1,500	4,550	7,600	17,100	26,600	38,000
560SEL 4d Sed	1,650	4,900	8,200	18,450	28,700	41,000
560SEC 2d Cpe	1,800	5,400	9,000	20,250	31,500	45,000
300SL 2d Conv	2,200	6,600	11,000	24,750	38,500	55,000
500SL 2d Conv	2,300	6,950	11,600	26,100	40,600	58,000

	6	5	4	3	2	1
1991						
2.3 4d Sed	700	2,050	3,400	7,650	11,900	17,000
2.6 4d Sed	750	2,300	3,800	8,550	13,300	19,000
300TD 4d Turbo Sed	880	2,640	4,400	9,900	15,400	22,000
300E 4d Sed	950	2,900	4,800	10,800	16,800	24,000
300E Matic 4x4 4d Sed	1,080	3,240	5,400	12,150	18,900	27,000
300CE 2d Cpe	1,200	3,600	6,000	13,500	21,000	30,000
300TE 4d Sta Wag	1,150	3,500	5,800	13,050	20,300	29,000
300TE Matic 4x4 4d Sta Wag	1,250	3,700	6,200	13,950	21,700	31,000
300SE 4d Sed	1,050	3,100	5,200	11,700	18,200	26,000
300SEL 4d Sed	1,100	3,350	5,600	12,600	19,600	28,000
350SD 4d Sed	1,300	3,850	6,400	14,400	22,400	32,000
350SDL 4d Turbo Sed	1,320	3,960	6,600	14,850	23,100	33,000
420SEL 4d Sed	1,550	4,700	7,800	17,550	27,300	39,000
560SEL 4d Sed	1,700	5,050	8,400	18,900	29,400	42,000
560SEC 2d Cpe	1,900	5,750	9,600	21,600	33,600	48,000
300SL 2d Conv	2,250	6,700	11,200	25,200	39,200	56,000
500SL 2d Conv	2,350	7,100	11,800	26,550	41,300	59,000
1992						
190 2.3 4d Sed	700	2,150	3,600	8,100	12,600	18,000
190 2.6 4d Sed	750	2,300	3,800	8,550	13,300	19,000
300E 2.6 4d Sed	800	2,400	4,000	9,000	14,000	20,000
300DT 2.5 4d Sed	900	2,700	4,500	10,130	15,700	22,500
300E 4d Sed	1,000	2,950	4,900	11,030	17,200	24,500
300E 4d Sed 4Matic	1,120	3,360	5,600	12,600	19,600	28,000
300CE 2d Cpe	1,250	3,700	6,200	13,950	21,700	31,000
300TE 4d Sta Wag	1,200	3,600	6,000	13,500	21,000	30,000
300TE 4d Sta Wag 4Matic	1,300	3,850	6,400	14,400	22,400	32,000
300SDT 4d Sed	1,050	3,100	5,200	11,700	18,200	26,000
300SE 4d Sed	1,100	3,350	5,600	12,600	19,600	28,000
400E 4d Sed	1,100	3,250	5,400	12,150	18,900	27,000
400SE 4d Sed	1,150	3,500	5,800	13,050	20,300	29,000
500E 4d Sed	1,250	3,700	6,200	13,950	21,700	31,000
500SEL 4d Sed	1,350	4,100	6,800	15,300	23,800	34,000
600SEL 4d Sed	1,450	4,300	7,200	16,200	25,200	36,000
300SL 2d Conv	2,300	6,850	11,400	25,650	39,900	57,000
500SL 2d Conv	2,400	7,200	12,000	27,000	42,000	60,000

	6	5	4	3	2	1
1993						
190E 2.3 4d Sed	700	2,150	3,600	8,100	12,600	18,000
190E 2.6 4d Sed	750	2,200	3,650	8,190	12,700	18,200
300E 2.8 4d Sed	750	2,300	3,800	8,550	13,300	19,000
300DT 2.5 4d Sed	950	2,900	4,850	10,890	16,900	24,200
300E 4d Sed	1,200	3,600	6,000	13,500	21,000	30,000
300E Matic 4d Sed	1,200	3,600	6,050	13,590	21,100	30,200
300CE 2d Cpe	1,250	3,700	6,200	13,950	21,700	31,000
300CE 2d Conv	2,300	6,850	11,400	25,650	39,900	57,000
300TE 4d Sta Wag	1,300	3,950	6,600	14,850	23,100	33,000
300TE Matic 4d Sta Wag	1,350	4,100	6,800	15,300	23,800	34,000
300SDT 4d Sed	1,150	3,500	5,800	13,050	20,300	29,000
300SE 4d Sed	1,200	3,550	5,900	13,280	20,700	29,500
400E 4d Sed	1,200	3,600	6,000	13,500	21,000	30,000
400SEL 4d Sed	1,250	3,700	6,200	13,950	21,700	31,000
500E 4d Sed	1,300	3,950	6,600	14,850	23,100	33,000
500SEL 4d Sed	1,350	4,100	6,800	15,300	23,800	34,000
500SEL 2d Cpe	1,450	4,300	7,200	16,200	25,200	36,000
600SEL 4d Sed	1,500	4,550	7,600	17,100	26,600	38,000
600SEL 2d Cpe	1,650	4,900	8,200	18,450	28,700	41,000
300SL 2d Rds	2,300	6,950	11,600	26,100	40,600	58,000
500SL 2d Rds	2,400	7,200	12,000	27,000	42,000	60,000
600SL 2d Rds	2,500	7,550	12,600	28,350	44,100	63,000
1994 C CLASS						
220C 4d Sed	750	2,300	3,800	8,550	13,300	19,000
280C 4d Sed	850	2,500	4,200	9,450	14,700	21,000
1994 E CLASS						
320C 2d Cpe	1,250	3,700	6,200	13,950	21,700	31,000
320E 2d Conv	1,850	5,500	9,200	20,700	32,200	46,000
320E 4d Sed	1,250	3,700	6,200	13,950	21,700	31,000
420E 4d Sed	1,600	4,800	8,000	18,000	28,000	40,000
500E 4d Sed	1,650	4,900	8,200	18,450	28,700	41,000
320E 4d Sta Wag	1,150	3,500	5,800	13,050	20,300	29,000
1994 S CLASS						
500S 2d Cpe	2,050	6,100	10,200	22,950	35,700	51,000
600S 2d Cpe	2,250	6,700	11,200	25,200	39,200	56,000
320S 4d Sed	1,250	3,700	6,200	13,950	21,700	31,000
350S 4d Sed Diesel Turbo	1,300	3,850	6,400	14,400	22,400	32,000
420S 4d Sed	1,450	4,300	7,200	16,200	25,200	36,000
500S 4d Sed	1,650	4,900	8,200	18,450	28,700	41,000
600S 4d Sed	2,100	6,350	10,600	23,850	37,100	53,000
1994 SL CLASS						
320SL 2d Rds	1,650	4,900	8,200	18,450	28,700	41,000
500SL 2d Rds	2,050	6,100	10,200	22,950	35,700	51,000
600SL 2d Rds	2,450	7,300	12,200	27,450	42,700	61,000

	6	5	4	3	2	1
1995 C CLASS						
220C 4d Sed	750	2,300	3,800	8,550	13,300	19,000
280C 4d Sed	850	2,500	4,200	9,450	14,700	21,000
36C 4d Sed	1,150	3,500	5,800	13,050	20,300	29,000
1995 E CLASS						
300E 4d Sed Diesel Turbo	700	2,150	3,600	8,100	12,600	18,000
320E 2d Cpe	1,250	3,700	6,200	13,950	21,700	31,000
320E 2d Conv	1,850	5,500	9,200	20,700	32,200	46,000
320E 4d Sed	1,100	3,350	5,600	12,600	19,600	28,000
320E 4d Sta Wag	1,150	3,500	5,800	13,050	20,300	29,000
420E 4d Sed	1,600	4,800	8,000	18,000	28,000	40,000
1995 S CLASS						
320SW 4d Sed	1,250	3,700	6,200	13,950	21,700	31,000
320SV 4d Sed	1,300	3,950	6,600	14,850	23,100	33,000
350S 4d Sed Diesel Turbo	1,300	3,850	6,400	14,400	22,400	32,000
420S 4d Sed	1,450	4,300	7,200	16,200	25,200	36,000
500S 2d Cpe	2,050	6,100	10,200	22,950	35,700	51,000
500S 4d Sed	1,650	4,900	8,200	18,450	28,700	41,000
600S 2d Cpe	2,250	6,700	11,200	25,200	39,200	56,000
600S 4d Sed	2,100	6,350	10,600	23,850	37,100	53,000
1995 SL CLASS						
320SL 2d Rds	1,650	4,900	8,200	18,450	28,700	41,000
500SL 2d Rds	2,050	6,100	10,200	22,950	35,700	51,000
600SL 2d Rds	2,450	7,300	12,200	27,450	42,700	61,000
1996 C CLASS						
C220 4d Sed	700	2,150	3,600	8,100	12,600	18,000
C280 4d Sed	800	2,400	4,000	9,000	14,000	20,000
C36 4d Sed	1,100	3,350	5,600	12,600	19,600	28,000
1996 E CLASS						
E300 4d Sed Diesel	760	2,280	3,800	8,550	13,300	19,000
E320 4d Sed	1,100	3,250	5,400	12,150	18,900	27,000
1996 S CLASS						
S320W 4d Sed	1,200	3,600	6,000	13,500	21,000	30,000
S320V 4d Sed	1,300	3,850	6,400	14,400	22,400	32,000
S420 4d Sed	1,400	4,200	7,000	15,750	24,500	35,000
S500 2d Cpe	2,000	6,000	10,000	22,500	35,000	50,000
S500 4d Sed	1,600	4,800	8,000	18,000	28,000	40,000
S600 2d Cpe	2,200	6,600	11,000	24,750	38,500	55,000
S600 4d Sed	2,100	6,250	10,400	23,400	36,400	52,000
1996 SL CLASS						
SL320 2d Rds	1,600	4,800	8,000	18,000	28,000	40,000
SL500 2d Rds	2,000	6,000	10,000	22,500	35,000	50,000
SL600 2d Rds	2,400	7,200	12,000	27,000	42,000	60,000

NOTE: Add 5 percent for Spt Pkg.

	6	5	4	3	2	1

1997 C CLASS

	6	5	4	3	2	1
C230 4d Sed	760	2,280	3,800	8,550	13,300	19,000
C280 4d Sed	800	2,400	4,000	9,000	14,000	20,000
C36 4d Sed	1,120	3,360	5,600	12,600	19,600	28,000

1997 E CLASS

	6	5	4	3	2	1
E300D 4d Sed Diesel	760	2,280	3,800	8,550	13,300	19,000
E320 4d Sed	1,080	3,240	5,400	12,150	18,900	27,000
E420 4d Sed	1,180	3,540	5,900	13,280	20,650	29,500

1997 S CLASS

	6	5	4	3	2	1
S320W 4d Sed	1,200	3,600	6,000	13,500	21,000	30,000
S320V 4d Sed	1,280	3,840	6,400	14,400	22,400	32,000
S420 4d Sed	1,400	4,200	7,000	15,750	24,500	35,000
S500 2d Cpe	1,920	5,760	9,600	21,600	33,600	48,000
S500 4d Sed	1,800	5,400	9,000	20,250	31,500	45,000
S600 2d Cpe	2,200	6,600	11,000	24,750	38,500	55,000
S600 4d Sed	2,080	6,240	10,400	23,400	36,400	52,000

1997 SL CLASS

	6	5	4	3	2	1
SL320 2d Rds	1,600	4,800	8,000	18,000	28,000	40,000
SL500 2d Rds	2,000	6,000	10,000	22,500	35,000	50,000
SL600 2d Rds	2,400	7,200	12,000	27,000	42,000	60,000

NOTE: Add 5 percent for Spt Pkg.

1998 C CLASS, 4-cyl. & V-6

	6	5	4	3	2	1
C230 4d Sed	760	2,280	3,800	8,550	13,300	19,000
C280 4d Sed	800	2,400	4,000	9,000	14,000	20,000

1998 CLK CLASS, V-6

	6	5	4	3	2	1
CLK320 2d Cpe	860	2,580	4,300	9,680	15,050	21,500

1998 E CLASS, 6-cyl. & V-6

	6	5	4	3	2	1
E300TD 4d Sed turbo diesel	760	2,280	3,800	8,550	13,300	19,000
E320 4d Sed	680	2,040	3,400	7,650	11,900	17,000
E320 4d Sed AWD	780	2,340	3,900	8,780	13,650	19,500
E320 4d Sta Wag	760	2,280	3,800	8,550	13,300	19,000
E320 4d Sta Wag AWD	800	2,400	4,000	9,000	14,000	20,000
E320 4d Sed (V-8 only)	780	2,340	3,900	8,780	13,650	19,500

1998 S CLASS, 6-cyl. & V-8

	6	5	4	3	2	1
S320W 4d Sed	1,200	3,600	6,000	13,500	21,000	30,000
S320V 4d Sed	1,280	3,840	6,400	14,400	22,400	32,000
S420 4d Sed	1,400	4,200	7,000	15,750	24,500	35,000
S500 4d Sed	1,800	5,400	9,000	20,250	31,500	45,000
S600 4d Sed (V-12 only)	2,080	6,240	10,400	23,400	36,400	52,000

1998 CL CLASS

	6	5	4	3	2	1
CL500 2d Cpe (V-8 only)	1,680	5,040	8,400	18,900	29,400	42,000
CL600 2d Cpe (V-12 only)	2,120	6,360	10,600	23,850	37,100	53,000

1998 SLK CLASS, Supercharged 4-cyl.

	6	5	4	3	2	1
SLK280 "Kompressor" 2d Rds	880	2,640	4,400	9,900	15,400	22,000

1998 SL CLASS

	6	5	4	3	2	1
SL500 2d Rds (V-8 only)	1,800	5,400	9,000	20,250	31,500	45,000
SL600 2d Rds (V-12 only)	2,200	6,600	11,000	24,750	38,500	55,000

NOTE: Add 5 percent for Spt Pkg.

1999 C CLASS

	6	5	4	3	2	1
C230K 4d Sed (supercharged 4-cyl.)	760	2,280	3,800	8,550	13,300	19,000
C280 4d Sed (V-6)	800	2,400	4,000	9,000	14,000	20,000
C43 4d Sed AMG V-8	880	2,640	4,400	9,900	15,400	22,000

1999 CLK CLASS

	6	5	4	3	2	1
CLK320 2d Cpe (V-6)	860	2,580	4,300	9,680	15,050	21,500
CLK320 2d Conv (6-cyl.)	1,000	3,000	5,000	11,250	17,500	25,000
CLK430 2d Cpe (V-8)	940	2,820	4,700	10,580	16,450	23,500

1999 E CLASS, 6-cyl. & V-8

	6	5	4	3	2	1
E300TD 4d Sed turbo diesel	760	2,280	3,800	8,550	13,300	19,000
E320 4d Sed	680	2,040	3,400	7,650	11,900	17,000
E320 4d Sed AWD	780	2,340	3,900	8,780	13,650	19,500
E320 4d Sta Wag	760	2,280	3,800	8,550	13,300	19,000
E320 4d Sta Wag AWD	800	2,400	4,000	9,000	14,000	20,000
E430 4d Sed (V-8 only)	780	2,340	3,900	8,780	13,650	19,500

1999 S CLASS, 6-cyl. & V-8

	6	5	4	3	2	1
S320W 4d Sed	1,200	3,600	6,000	13,500	21,000	30,000
S320V 4d Sed	1,280	3,840	6,400	14,400	22,400	32,000
S420 4d Sed	1,400	4,200	7,000	15,750	24,500	35,000
S500 4d Sed	1,800	5,400	9,000	20,250	31,500	45,000
S600 4d Sed (V-12 only)	2,080	6,240	10,400	23,400	36,400	52,000

1999 CL CLASS

	6	5	4	3	2	1
CL500 2d Cpe (V-8 only)	1,680	5,040	8,400	18,900	29,400	42,000
CL600 2d Cpe (V-12 only)	2,120	6,360	10,600	23,850	37,100	53,000

1999 SLK CLASS, Supercharged 4-cyl.

	6	5	4	3	2	1
SLK230 "Kompressor" 2d Rds	880	2,640	4,400	9,900	15,400	22,000

NOTE: Add 5 percent for Sport Pkg.

	6	5	4	3	2	1
1999 SL CLASS						
SL500 2d Rds (V-8 only)	1,800	5,400	9,000	20,250	31,500	45,000
SL600 2d Rds (V-12 only)	2,200	6,600	11,000	24,750	38,500	55,000

NOTE: Add 5 percent for Sport Pkg.

	6	5	4	3	2	1
2000 C CLASS						
C230K 4d Sed (supercharged 4-cyl.)	760	2,280	3,800	8,550	13,300	19,000
C280 4d Sed (V-6)	800	2,400	4,000	9,000	14,000	20,000
C43 4d Sed AMG V-8	880	2,640	4,400	9,900	15,400	22,000
2000 CLK CLASS						
CLK320 2d Cpe (V-6)	860	2,580	4,300	9,680	15,050	21,500
CLK320 2d Conv (6-cyl.)	1,000	3,000	5,000	11,250	17,500	25,000
CLK430 2d Cpe (V-8)	940	2,820	4,700	10,580	16,450	23,500
CLK430 2d Conv (V-8)	1,100	3,300	5,500	12,380	19,250	27,500
2000 E CLASS, 6-cyl. & V-8						
E320 4d Sed	680	2,040	3,400	7,650	11,900	17,000
E320 4d Sed AWD	780	2,340	3,900	8,780	13,650	19,500
E320 4d Sta Wag	760	2,280	3,800	8,550	13,300	19,000
E320 4d Sta Wag AWD	800	2,400	4,000	9,000	14,000	20,000
E430 4d Sed (V-8 only)	780	2,340	3,900	8,780	13,650	19,500
E430 4d Sed AWD (V-8 only)	820	2,460	4,100	9,230	14,350	20,500
E55 4d Sed (V-8 only)	1,140	3,420	5,700	12,830	19,950	28,500
2000 S CLASS, V-8						
S430 4d Sed	1,320	3,960	6,600	14,850	23,100	33,000
S500 4d Sed	1,720	5,160	8,600	19,350	30,100	43,000
2000 CL CLASS, V-8						
CL500 2d Cpe	1,800	5,400	9,000	20,250	31,500	45,000
2000 SLK CLASS, Supercharged 4-cyl.						
SLK230 "Kompressor" 2d Rds	880	2,640	4,400	9,900	15,400	22,000

NOTE: Add 5 percent for Sport pkg.

	6	5	4	3	2	1
2000 SL CLASS						
SL500 2d Rds (V-8 only)	1,800	5,400	9,000	20,250	31,500	45,000
SL600 2d Rds (V-12 only)	2,200	6,600	11,000	24,750	38,500	55,000

NOTE: Add 5 percent for Sport pkg.

	6	5	4	3	2	1
2001 C CLASS, V-6						
C240K 4d Sed	760	2,280	3,800	9,500	13,300	19,000
C320 4d Sed	800	2,400	4,000	10,000	14,000	20,000
2001 CLK CLASS, V-6 & V-8						
CLK320 2d Cpe (V-6)	860	2,580	4,300	10,750	15,050	21,500
CLK320 2d Conv (V-6)	1,000	3,000	5,000	12,500	17,500	25,000
CLK430 2d Cpe (V-8)	940	2,820	4,700	11,750	16,450	23,500
CLK430 2d Conv (V-8)	1,100	3,300	5,500	13,750	19,250	27,500
CLK55 AMG 2d Cpe (V-8)	1,040	3,120	5,200	13,000	18,200	26,000
2001 E CLASS, V-6 & V-8						
E320 4d Sed (V-6)	680	2,040	3,400	8,500	11,900	17,000
E320 4d Sed AWD (V-6)	780	2,340	3,900	9,750	13,650	19,500
E320 4d Sta Wag (V-6)	760	2,280	3,800	9,500	13,300	19,000
E320 4d Sta Wag AWD (V-6)	800	2,400	4,000	10,000	14,000	20,000
E430 4d Sed (V-8)	780	2,340	3,900	9,750	13,650	19,500
E430 4d Sed AWD (V-8)	820	2,460	4,100	10,250	14,350	20,500
E55 AMG 4d Sed (V-8)	1,140	3,420	5,700	14,250	19,950	28,500

NOTE: Add 5 percent for Sport pkg. (excluding E55 Sed).

	6	5	4	3	2	1
2001 S CLASS, V-8						
S430 4d Sed	1,320	3,960	6,600	16,500	23,100	33,000
S500 4d Sed	1,720	5,160	8,600	21,500	30,100	43,000
S55 AMG 4d Sed	1,800	5,400	9,000	22,500	31,500	45,000
S600 4d Sed (V-12)	1,980	5,940	9,900	24,750	34,650	49,500
2001 CL CLASS, V-8						
CL500 2d Cpe	1,800	5,400	9,000	22,500	31,500	45,000
CL55 AMG 2d Cpe	1,860	5,580	9,300	23,250	32,550	46,500
CL600 2d Cpe (V-12)	2,020	6,060	10,100	25,250	35,350	50,500
2001 SLK CLASS, Supercharged 4-cyl.						
SLK320 "Kompressor" 2d Rds	880	2,640	4,400	11,000	15,400	22,000
SLK230 2d Rds (V-6)	960	2,880	4,800	12,000	16,800	24,000

NOTE: Add 5 percent for detachable HT. Add 5 percent for Sport pkg.

	6	5	4	3	2	1
2001 SL CLASS, V-8, V-12s						
SL500 2d Rds	1,800	5,400	9,000	22,500	31,500	45,000
SL600 2d Rds (V-12)	2,200	6,600	11,000	27,500	38,500	55,000

NOTE: Add 5 percent for detachable HT. Add 5 percent for Sport pkg. AMG wheels on SL600 and body cladding on both Models are standard equipment.

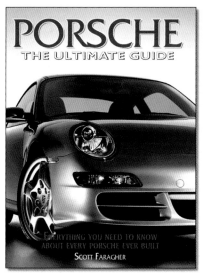

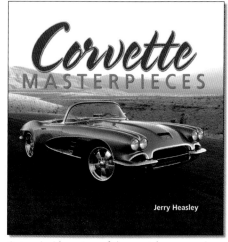
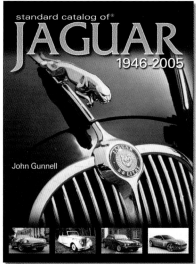
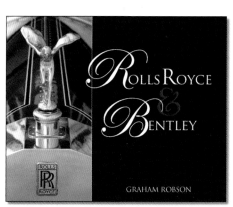
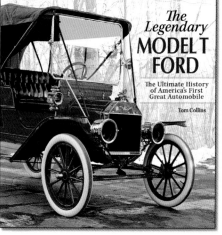